Transportation, Logistics, and Supply Chain Management in Home Healthcare:

Emerging Research and Opportunities

Jalel Euchi
LOGIQ Laboratory, Sfax University, Tunisia

A volume in the Advances in Logistics, Operations, and Management Science (ALOMS) Book Series

IGI Global
DISSEMINATOR OF KNOWLEDGE

Published in the United States of America by
IGI Global
Business Science Reference (an imprint of IGI Global)
701 E. Chocolate Avenue
Hershey PA, USA 17033
Tel: 717-533-8845
Fax: 717-533-8661
E-mail: cust@igi-global.com
Web site: http://www.igi-global.com

Library of Congress Cataloging-in-Publication Data

Names: Euchi, Jalel, 1980- editor.
Title: Transportation, logistics, and supply chain management in home healthcare: Emerging research and opportunities / Jalel Euchi, editor.
Description: Hershey : Business Science Reference, [2019] | Includes bibliographical references. | Summary: "This book examines applications of transportation, logistics, and supply chain management in home healthcare"-- Provided by publisher.
Identifiers: LCCN 2019019473 | ISBN 9781799802686 (h/c) | ISBN 9781799802693 (s/c) | ISBN 9781799802709 (ebook)
Subjects: LCSH: Home care services. | Transportation. | Business logistics.
Classification: LCC RA645.3 .E865 2019 | DDC 362.14068--dc23
LC record available at https://lccn.loc.gov/2019019473

This book is published in the IGI Global book series Advances in Logistics, Operations, and Management Science (ALOMS) (ISSN: 2327-350X; eISSN: 2327-3518)

British Cataloguing in Publication Data
A Cataloguing in Publication record for this book is available from the British Library.

For electronic access to this publication, please contact: eresources@igi-global.com.

Advances in Logistics, Operations, and Management Science (ALOMS) Book Series

John Wang
Montclair State University, USA

ISSN:2327-350X
EISSN:2327-3518

MISSION

Operations research and management science continue to influence business processes, administration, and management information systems, particularly in covering the application methods for decision-making processes. New case studies and applications on management science, operations management, social sciences, and other behavioral sciences have been incorporated into business and organizations real-world objectives.

The **Advances in Logistics, Operations, and Management Science** (ALOMS) Book Series provides a collection of reference publications on the current trends, applications, theories, and practices in the management science field. Providing relevant and current research, this series and its individual publications would be useful for academics, researchers, scholars, and practitioners interested in improving decision making models and business functions.

COVERAGE

- Computing and information technologies
- Marketing engineering
- Services management
- Production Management
- Operations Management
- Finance
- Decision analysis and decision support
- Organizational Behavior
- Risk Management
- Information Management

IGI Global is currently accepting manuscripts for publication within this series. To submit a proposal for a volume in this series, please contact our Acquisition Editors at Acquisitions@igi-global.com or visit: http://www.igi-global.com/publish/.

The Advances in Logistics, Operations, and Management Science (ALOMS) Book Series (ISSN 2327-350X) is published by IGI Global, 701 E. Chocolate Avenue, Hershey, PA 17033-1240, USA, www.igi-global.com. This series is composed of titles available for purchase individually; each title is edited to be contextually exclusive from any other title within the series. For pricing and ordering information please visit http://www.igi-global.com/book-series/advances-logistics-operations-management-science/37170. Postmaster: Send all address changes to above address.

Titles in this Series

For a list of additional titles in this series, please visit:
https://www.igi-global.com/book-series/advances-logistics-operations-management-science/37170

Business Management and Communication Perspectives in Industry 4.0
Ayşegül Özbebek Tunç (Istanbul University, Turkey) and Pınar Aslan (Bursa Technical University, Turkey)
Business Science Reference • © 2020 • 337pp • H/C (ISBN: 9781522594161) • US $215.00 (our price)

Handbook of Research on Urban and Humanitarian Logistics
Jesus Gonzalez-Feliu (Ecole Nationale Superieure des Mines de Saint-Étienne, France) Mario Chong (Universidad del Pacifico, Peru) Jorge Vargas Florez (Pontificia Universidad Católica del Perú, Peru) and Julio Padilla Solis (Universidad de Lima, Peru)
Information Science Reference • © 2019 • 497pp • H/C (ISBN: 9781522581604) • US $295.00 (our price)

Industry 4.0 and Hyper-Customized Smart Manufacturing Supply Chains
S.G. Ponnambalam (University Malaysia Pahang, Malaysia) Nachiappan Subramanian (University of Sussex, UK) Manoj Kumar Tiwari (Indian Institute of Technology Kharagpur, India) and Wan Azhar Wan Yusoff (University Malaysia Pahang, Malaysia)
Business Science Reference • © 2019 • 347pp • H/C (ISBN: 9781522590781) • US $225.00 (our price)

Additive Manufacturing Technologies From an Optimization Perspective
Kaushik Kumar (Birla Institute of Technology Mesra, India) Divya Zindani (National Institute of Technology Silchar, India) and J. Paulo Davim (University of Aveiro, Portugal)
Engineering Science Reference • © 2019 • 350pp • H/C (ISBN: 9781522591672) • US $205.00 (our price)

Handbook of Research on Women in Management and the Global Labor Market
Elisabeth T. Pereira (University of Aveiro, Portugal) and Paola Paoloni (Sapienza University of Rome, Italy)
Business Science Reference • © 2019 • 423pp • H/C (ISBN: 9781522591719) • US $285.00 (our price)

IGI Global
DISSEMINATOR OF KNOWLEDGE

701 East Chocolate Avenue, Hershey, PA 17033, USA
Tel: 717-533-8845 x100 • Fax: 717-533-8661
E-Mail: cust@igi-global.com • www.igi-global.com

Table of Contents

Preface

Violent competition in today's global market offers a powerful motivation for developing the ever more sophisticated supply chains and logistic systems. This book, written for the computer science manager and researcher, presents a survey of the modern theory and application of logistics, supply chain management and an application in the field of transportation and supply chain management in all domains, especially in-home healthcare. The goal of the book is to present the state of the art in the science of logistics management and their optimization in all areas in computer science, engineering, transport, public transport.

This edited book is intended to discuss application applications of Transportation, Logistics, and Supply Chain Management in Home Healthcare. The focus of this volume is to bring all the related areas in transportation and optimization in the field of health care and no limited. The book will present techniques, case studies, and methodologies that combine the use of intelligence approaches with optimization methods for facing problems in transport, logistics and supply chain problems.

The book will present detailed techniques and research studies that manage with common industrial and public problems in several fields, as transportation, logistics, and supply chain management in home healthcare. Home health care (HHC) companies are extensive in European countries and wish to serve patients at home to help them recover from complaint and injury in a personal environment. From the time when transportation costs are amid the biggest sources of disbursement in company activities, it is of great significance to optimize this in the HHC industry. From the perspective of optimizing the cost of transportation, this book studies the Vehicle Routing Scheduling problem as it applies to HHC companies. According to a review of the HHC corporations, during the process of distributing medication drugs, the quantity of drugs necessary for each patient is non-deterministic when the company creates planned tours.

The goal of the book is to provide theoretical and empirical research and application in the science of logistics management and transportation, scheduling routing and their applications in-home health care and logistics. This book provides a regular and rigorous presentation of the theory of transportation, logistics and supply management and of the main methodologies for its application in-home health care, engineering, management, transport economic, etc., also it provides empirical research findings in the area. The aim of this book is to helps researchers and practitioners to understand the optimization of the transportation model and a supply chain logistics to health care through IT logistics tools and the state-of-the-art in transportation, logistics and supply chain management. It provides a comprehensive discussion on supply chain planning models; logistics and transport; transportation and scheduling; metaheuristics to solve complex supply chain; logistics and transportation problems; algorithms and applications of transport in-home health care; real case applications; home health care logistics planning; management and social science; routing and scheduling optimization; quantitative methods and decision support systems; economics in logistics; technical logistics and logistics engineering; IT for logistics; the design, operation, and use of application systems or IT networks for logistical tasks.

The papers in this edited volume search for building on the legacy of published routing and scheduling problems (RSP) studies in three ways. They recapitulate the most significant results of the HHC routing and its variants. They present significant methodological developments or new methods for resolving current RSP. They present original problems that have risen in the routing area and highlight new challenges for the field.

This book is organized into two sections: review and directions in modeling and algorithms (3 papers), and practical applications (3 papers). We hope that the researchers ingoing the field and specialists in health care will find all papers in this volume fascinating, informative, and beneficial.

We thank all of the authors for their contribution to the excellent volume. We also thank IGI Global administration for their reinforcement and support.

Jalel Euchi
College of Business and Economics, Qassim University, Saudi Arabia
August 2019

Acknowledgment

We express our gratitude towards all the authors, who made the volume possible. We would also like to thank the publisher IGI Global and the editorial staff who invited us to publish this book and provided encouragement and support throughout the entire process.

Section 1

Chapter 1
Improvement of the Level Service on a Hospital Warehouse Using Forecast Techniques

Paloma María Teresa Martínez-Sánchez
https://orcid.org/0000-0003-3938-995X
Universidad El Bosque, Colombia

Carlos Hernán Hernán Fajardo-Toro
https://orcid.org/0000-0003-4596-9627
Universidad EAN, Colombia

Úrsula Gomes Rosa Maruyama
Federal Center for Technological Education of Rio de Janeiro, Brazil

Paola Andrea Sánchez Sánchez
https://orcid.org/0000-0002-3320-016X
Universidad Simón Bolivar, Colombia

ABSTRACT

This article presents a study case focused on the establishment and improvement of the service level in a central warehouse of a hospital organization in Colombia which provide the products of medical use, clothing, anesthetics, and supplies, to nineteen medical dependencies. The warehouse is managed by a person, developing planning processes, purchases, reception, and administration of products or inventories who depends on the administrative and financial sub-direction of the institution. Through the use of interviews and surveys conducted at different dependencies. As well as the collection of information in the field, there were problems with the availability of products due to problems related to planning purchases which are done empirically without data analysis. Taking into account the problematic previously raised, we took different models of predictions as well as the use of the Mean Squared Error (MSE) and the accuracy of predictions to determine the best model according to with the product analyzed.

DOI: 10.4018/978-1-7998-0268-6.ch001

INTRODUCTION

Health is considered as an own good and a fundamental right for people (Herazo, 2010; Jaberidoost, Nikfar, Abdollahiasl, & Dinarvand, 2013). However, it is notice that in some cases is undermined by the provision of an inadequate service by health entities. This translates into failures and complaints from users (Argas et al., 2010), primarily if the necessary elements such as medical and surgical supplies, which sometimes considered critical, are not available (Little and Coughlan, 2008), and as it is figured to have indicators or metrics such as the level of service (Narayana et al., 2014). Is fundamental in health services (Kelle et al., 2012), which in turn allows establishing the availability of products playing an essential role to save lives (Londoño, Morera, & Laverde, 2008).

The European commission defines the necessity of increase the sustainability of the public health services in 2007 (Azzi, Persona, Sgarbossa, & Bonin, 2013). To achieve that, the commission defines the next challenges to be face:

1. *Demographic changes.* The Statistical Office of the European communities estimates that, by 2060, 30% of the population of the EU countries will be over 65 years of age. This makes the ratio of productive individuals low, which mean means that healthcare expenses will increase exponentially as individuals grow older.
2. *Inefficient and redundant processes* (often "law-oriented"). The excess costs, within the healthcare supply chain, this result from inefficient and redundant processes.
3. *Patient safety needs to be improved through high quality and safe processes.* Is imperative guarantee the safety as well as the availability of the medicines and services required by the user of the system.

To facing these challenges, is necessary that all the institutions start to apply concepts of management practices that allows controlling all the operations, to achieve the efficiency and effectiveness required. Within these practices are the management of the supply chain and the operations.

The supply chain is conjunction of all processes involved, directly or indirectly, to give an adequate response to the necessities of the final consumers of a good or service. This includes all processes of provisioning, production, distribution, warehousing and replenishment, among others, where the main aim is the integration of all the steps of the chain from suppliers to final costumers.

In the case of Health services, its supply chain management refers to obtain all the resources, supplies, and delivering goods and services from providers (hospitals, doctors and health units) and their patients. To achieve this, physical goods and information about medical products and services go through manufacturers, insurance companies, hospitals, providers, and several agencies (Jarrett, 1998; Lee, Lee, & Schniederjans, 2011; Yadav, 2015).

One critical aspect for many organizations is the inventory management. The inventory is the mechanism through which the companies guarantee cover the necessities of the demand, products of services, whether with raw materials, supplies or finished goods. However, depending on the strategy used to respond to its demand, the companies will define the type of inventory and the way to manage it. To determine both capacity and inventory levels is necessary to have forecasting, and based, on that establish service levels and provisioning distribution strategies (Shah, 2004; Singh & Verma, 2018; Bowersox and Closs, 2002).

Forecasting Management in Health Services

As has been mentioned above, forecasting is important for planning and making decisions Ballou (2004) defines forecasting are the basic input needed to do good planning and implementation of policies in all the functional areas of the company allowing foresee the resource requirements in the future. The above refers to planning and define policies related to aspects like capacity required to provide a service or production level as well as the number of goods to be produced to cover a possible demand. The decision maker at the organizations in charge of obtaining the forecasts, have the basic task is to make decisions with future consequences, and therefore, they must prepare forecasts, which indicates what will happen in the future with the variables studied, establishing not only the value expected but also the variability associated. On the other hand, they must foresee scenarios that allow them to anticipate possible eventualities, being able to evaluate adequately the convenience or inconvenience of an alternative.

The forecast could be on qualitative, quantitative or computational Basis. The qualitative are based on expert criteria influenced by the experience or subjectivity of whom give the forecast. The quantitative are based on mathematical or statistical techniques, where there is Two large classes of models can be used to prepare forecasts, causal and the based-on time series (Abdollahzade et al., 2015; Gooijer and Hyndman, 2005). The models based on computational algorithms are adaptive nature, which is the artificial intelligence principle.

In other point of view, Pérez and Briceño (2013), affirms that forecasting can be classified as qualitative, quantitative and causal. The qualitative is used, especially in environments where the market conditions are dynamic. The second classification, presents an adequate cumulative data over time, time series data, and evidence that a past situation is expected to repeat in the future, and the causal forecasting, is based on the relationships that exist between 1 dependent variable and 1 or more independent variables.

Regarding the types of forecasts, these can be classified according to three criteria: (i) according to the time horizon, (ii) according to the economic environment covered and (iii) according to the procedure used (Hanke & Deitsch,1996):

- Depending on the time horizon. They can be long, medium or short term, and their usefulness ranges go from the preparation of plans at the strategic level to those at the operational level respectively.
- Depending on the economic environment. Can be micro or macro
- According to the procedure used. As have been mentioned above, they can be: (i) purely qualitative; in those cases, in which an open manipulation of data is not required and only the judgment or intuition of the expert who releases the forecasts; or (ii) purely quantitative, when using mathematical and statistical procedures that do not require subjective elements. Finally, (iii) Computational methods based on IA algorithms, which are the current tendency with the high volume of data as well as the needs of automation.

For all quantitative method, it is necessary a metric establish the efficiency and effectiveness of the model chosen. In the case of Causal models, where the decisions makers have to select de variables to be related, the correlation will be the first but after that, they have to analyze the collinearity and the heteroscedasticity. Once de model is accepted, has to establish the forecast and prediction intervals, based on the standard error of the model, that could be linear or not linear. On the other hand, the models developed based on time series has to be calculated four basic indexes. The MSE (mean square error) defines the accuracy of a model, and is the index that allows choosing the best model between the selected initially. The MAE (Mean Absolute Error), MPE (Mean Percentage error) and MAPE (Mean Absolute Percentage Error) allows seeing the effectiveness of the model chosen (Makridakis et al., 1982; Martínez, 2010).

With the improvements in computational techniques, emerge the artificial intelligence (AI) and machine learning techniques. Nowadays have a relevant spot to the development of forecast models. The principal advantage that employing AI techniques allows, is that they adapt easily to manage stochastic non-linear behavior, and to problems in which the collinearity is present, high variability and no stationarity (Behnamian & Fatemi Ghomi, 2010; Wang, Wang, & Zhang, 2013; Fajardo-Toro, Mula, & Poler, 2018).

The AI techniques used to obtain forecasts include neural networks (ANN) (Adhikari, 2015; Dunea, Pohoata, & Iordache, 2015; Egrioglu, Aladag, & Yolcu, 2013; Günay, 2016; Sánchez-Sánchez & García-González, 2017; Yu, Wang, & Lai, 2009). Support vector machines (Chen & Lee, 2015; de Oliveira & Ludermir, 2015; Gui, Wei, Shen, Qi, & Guo, 2015; Shafaei & Kisi, 2016), case-based reasoning (CBR)

(Chang, Liu, Lin, Fan, & Ng, 2009; Chun & Park, 2006; Corchado & Aiken, 2002; Fdez-Riverola & Corchado, 2003; Toro, Gómez Meire, Gálvez, & Fdez-Riverola, 2013) and fuzzy logic-based techniques and optimization heuristics, like genetic algorithms (Bajestani & Zare, 2011; P.-C. Chang, Liu, & Lai, 2008; Egrioglu et al., 2013; Li & Hu, 2012)

On the case of the health services context, there is the necessity to forecast a different kind of variables, both to define service levels (e. g. numbers of doctors, surgery rooms available or number of possible emergency services) as well as amount of medicines and supplies required (Biggerstaff et al., 2018; Jalalpour, Gel, & Levin, 2015; Khaldi, Afia, & Chiheb, 2019; Kroezen, Van Hoegaerden, & Batenburg, 2018; Park, Han, Kim, & Lee, 2016). Because of the estimation of all these variables, is possible to say that always that values will affect the provisioning required of medicine and supplies. This because e.g. if there is a pandemic, implies the preparation of a high number of beds available at the hospitals, doctors, and medicines. The same occurs when some catastrophic event is relatively predictable or in certain seasons the volume of accidents or violent events increase (Biggerstaff et al., 2018, Li, Li, Lu, & Panagiotelis, 2019).

On the other hand, there are the suppliers of the health systems, which could be from transportation services to pharmaceutical provisions comprised of medicines and medical supplies. At the pharmaceutical industry, the models used tries to estimate demand of the according to an estimation of the possible number of sick people as well as the demand based on time series methods (Merkuryeva, Valberga, & Smirnov, 2019; Nikolopoulos, Buxton, Khammash, & Stern, 2016). Concerning the hospitals or attention centers, they try to estimate the behavior or some sickness, like influenza or the flu, as well as the probable number of services required by emergencies associated to different causes like heart diseases or accidents (Bouckaert, Van den Heede, & Van de Voorde, 2018; Jalalpour et al., 2015).

For the work presented in this document, the forecasting methods based on time series analysis has been chosen. The models have to be selected according to the behavior of the series. The Methods selection for a specific series is based on the components or patterns of the time series, which are random variation, tendency, seasonality, and cyclicity (Makridakis et al., 1982; Hanke & Deitsch, 1996). The Models selected are Simple moving average, double moving average, single exponential smoothing; winter´s triple exponential smoothing, Browns, and Holt's double exponential smoothing.

Inventory Management in Health Services

Amaya, Beaulieu, Landry, Rebolledo and Velasco (2010) consider that "hospital logistics classify the activities of transformation and flow of resources and patients that support the provision of health services" (p. 85). Moons, Waeyenbergh and

Pintelon (2018), affirm that the internal functions associated to a hospital supply chain include the processes of purchases, inventories, distribution and consumption.

In regard to the inventory management, is known that is a daily problem in organizations. The inventory is a buildup of raw materials, supplies or finished goods that later will be used to satisfy future demand. Their objective is getting a balance between the quality of service offered to customers and the necessary economic investment by implementing a variety of models that must have parameters, such as demand, delivery time and associated costs. the main scope of inventory management refers the relationship between replenishment lead time, costs of inventory, asset management, the forecasting, valuation, visibility, and future price of the inventory, physical inventory control, the physical space available and required, the quality management, replenishment, returns, and defective goods (Singh & Verma, 2018).

The inventory is determined as the existence of a product or resource used in an organization that performs a double occupation affecting the cost of products and services, but also contributes to the order fulfillment. At present the organizations are dealing with the challenge of endure acceptable levels of inventory that supply to cover those differences between predicted demand and actual demand (Coyle, Langley, Novack, & Gibson, 2013). On the other hand, the inventory control includes a series of policies and mechanisms that verify inventory levels, the right time to stock up and how large the orders should be (Chase & Jacobs, 2014).

Concerning the inventory models, there are many aspects to taking into account. By one hand, there is all reference to a classification of the inventory. This could be according to its nature, raw materials, supplies, product in process, finished goods. According to its cost and volume required as it is with ABC classification, which is a method based on Pareto Analysis, and in the case of health services, according to the importance of the medicament or supply (Oztekin, Pajouh, Delen, & Swim, 2010).

On the other hand, there are models to define the policies of purchase, replenishment with lead times, reorder points and security stock. The models could deterministic, which is the case of the EOQ model, or probabilistic as well as with continuous or periodic revision. Normally the models are probabilistic due to the stochastic nature of the variables that intervene or affects the behavior of the phenomena, for this case the demand (De Vries, 2011).

A way to determine the inventory levels is to set up an objective level of service, which can be understood as the expected probability of not running out of inventory during a cycle (Krajewski, Ritzman, & Malhotra, 2016). This perspective involves the availability of the product and the costs of supplying a certain level of product convenience.

In the case of the health systems, the inventory of medicines and supplies is not only for the sustainability and for competitiveness of the business but also because the nefarious consequences that could have with humans lives, since a scarcity on the inventory can cause death or permanent injuries or diseases

Lapierre & Ruiz, (2007) propose that in the health institutions, there are two main approaches regarding logistics activities planning: inventory oriented and schedule oriented. In the inventory-oriented approach, the reorder point criteria are used. Aside from that implies the used of model based on EOQ concepts, also is needed a good forecast process as well as space for storage with the consequent labor, control system and cost associated. The scheduling-oriented approach focuses on the optimization of the supply chain and, based on that, handling purchasing operations. In this approach, replenishments, purchasing activities and supplier deliveries are well scheduled, helping to avoid stock-outs and used a periodic revision, while in the inventory approach normally is a continuous revision (Nicholson, Vakharia, & Selcuk Erenguc, 2004). As the care of patients is a sensitive issue due to unpredictable nature of services need from health institutions, especially those that give intensive care, a minimum stock that guarantees to adequately face situations like disease outbreak is important or emergencies caused by catastrophic events (Pan & Pokharel, 2007). The health sector is no unaware to this context. The Dinero magazine (2017) establish that aspects related to hospital logistics represent 15-18% of total administrative expenditure in hospitals in Colombia.

Respect to the Information technologies used to inventory management, there is many options, but one frequently used is the RFID. This technology helps to lace the exact position of materials or goods and specific space. In hospitals, this technology helps the medical personnel to locate medicines, medical equipment or supplies (van der Togt, Bakker, & Jaspers, 2011; Çakıcı, Groenevelt, & Seidmann, 2011; Fisher & Monahan, 2008; Oztekin et al., 2010). On the other hand, to improve the provisioning and replenishment problem, especially if the strategy is centered in a scheduled approach where the purchase could be more frequently, the e-procurement has become an option. This strategy allows integrating at a low cost the pharmaceutical distributors with the hospital o general pharmacies, making more efficient the control of inventory levels, especially under a periodic revision strategy (Mettler & Rohner, 2009).

In order to carry out the control of inventories, it is taking into account the criteria that allow the administrative and operational on the products that add most value to the business. The variables that are frequently used in regard to: cost, staff turnover, volume and importance (Vidal, 2017), but for the health services institutions providers (Instituciones Prestadores de Servicios de Salud - IPS) the cost and the analysis of profitability loses importance in front of the cost of a person's health or even their life.

An approach to classify the inventory is based on the criterion of medical criticality in which the inventory is classified by its importance in the medical method, according to Londoño, Morera and Laverde (2008). This are divided into basic, essential and complementary products, being the first two fundamental to safeguard the lives of patients. Due to the basic is considered as that element that can lead to serious problems for health and even death, and the essential is that who takes part in 95% of the patient's pathologies and not using them can lead to effects or disabilities.

CASE ANALYSIS

The present develops in a health service institution provider in Colombia, which has two warehouses that supply products for medical use: the first one is managed by means of Outsourcing, and the second, took place under the direct administration Hospital, supplying 19 dependencies doctors with a portfolio of 395 references.

The surgery rooms, within the dependencies represent 60% of the consumption, followed by the unit emergency with 8.5%, being the main customers of the warehouse regarding to the volume of products.

In meetings at the hospital, as well as visits made to the warehouse there were problems in the planning and control of inventory, just like failures in the collection and use of information, in such a way that the level of service and calculate the supply opportunity which is important in the improvement of medical procedures and patient's health.

METHODOLOGY

This study was developed in 3 phases, diagnosis, model design and evaluation of service levels. In the diagnosis, the problems were evident in the central warehouse. The warehouse is centered in an inventory-oriented approach, but they not have defined a security and service level based on statistical data. Because of that, the first step was to organize and collect the information necessary to construct a good model. to achieve that aim, it was decided collecting the information during a period of 3 years in order to establish the products with typical use and service levels.

Subsequently, the forecast models were applied. The time series models were chosen to elaborate on the forecasts.to done that, the first step was to analyze the behavior of the series, observing the patterns they had. Based on the observation of those patterns the initial models were applied, chosen the best one in each case based on the Mean Square Error - MSE - Criteria.

Finally, we proceeded to develop a model that supports the changes in which inventories are suppress contributing to the reliability in the service by the warehouse, and concludes with the evaluation of compliance for the model by monitoring the behavior of the products analyzed during a period of 3 months.

DATA ANALYSIS AND DISCUSSION

In order to delve into the problem of IPS, interviews are conducted with each of the dependencies of the central warehouse supplies, evidencing that 47% provide a negative, bad or regular rating of the service due to they have presented problems in relation to the availability and timeliness of product delivery, the pervious is generated by the lack of data analysis and metrics for decision making.

In the warehouse four processes are carried out: purchase planning, product purchase, product reception and inventory management, the planning being the focal point of this study.

The planning is carried out through each unit empirically without knowing the real value of what they require and / or the number of products they have, and afterwards, it is sent to the warehouse in order to consolidate and have an aggregate of product requests. Subsequently, the available inventory is review and quotations from suppliers are requested, including delivery times. The purchase plan is prepared by presenting it to the purchasing working group, which evaluates the quantities requested, if there are some adjustments to do, the quantities are lowered or raised in order to fulfill with the monthly budget assigned to the warehouse.

The products of the warehouse were classified taking into account the criteria of the medical specialists, as well as the division into products: Basic, essential and complementary, as proposed for Velasco, Barrera and Amaya (2012).

With the classification, it is analyzed that the warehouse has 180 products, 116 basic, 58 essential and 6 complementary. Basic and essential products are necessary in the IPS because they are used for medical procedures. However, 16 of these 180 products represents 95.7% of the consumption of the warehouse which is the purpose for the project.

The classification of the designated products with invented names for confidentiality of the information of the IPS, as well as their level of service illustrate under table 1:

To carry out the analysis and proposal of forecasting models we analyzed the simple, subjective, simple, double and triple exponential methods, without taking into account ARIMA, because there is not at least 72 monthly data to apply the model (Nahmias, 2007), through RMSE (Root Mean Squared Error), the 3 methods that best fit in the historical data are determined and the accuracy of the forecasting is analyzed.

Taking into account the set up, it is evident in Table 2, which results of the studies according to the selected method, the accuracy of the model and its variability.

The product identified as "P" has a very clear pattern of consumption for consume always 240 units every month except in June and December where the consumption is "0" in this class of behavior is not necessary a forecasting study because of we have the behavior pattern by itself.

Table 1. Products selected according to their classification and level of service

Product	Classification	Level of service
A	Basic	97%
B	Basic	93%
C	Basic	100%
D	Basic	99%
E	Basic	100%
F	Basic	100%
G	Basic	97%
H	Basic	94%
I	Essential	98%
J	Essential	98%
K	Essential	97%
L	Essential	99%
M	Essential	98%
N	Essential	86%
O	Essential	87%
P	Essential	95%

In view of the predictive methods are not 100% correct, safety inventories were established to minimize uncertainty, especially for those products whose precision is below 90% and the reorder point is calculated so as not to generate exhausted effects.

It is an Institution that Provides Health Services-IPS, the criteria for the establishment of inventory is structured according to the level of service that you want to offer, which is defined by the entity with 99%. Regarding with the this, security inventory controls and reorder points are performed. Table 3 show the summary of the data obtained from safety inventory, reorder point and maximum delivery time, according to the product.

Applying the conditions to demonstrate data runs and comparing these against the real ones, it is evident that the proposed of inventory models generated an increase in the service level of the products studied, since 11 of the 15 products obtained 99% of level of service and 4 remaining products presented values of 97% or greater, regard to a period of analysis of 3 months, which creates a better service to the patient, and decrease the rate of cancellations or postponement of surgery due to missing of product in storage.

Table 2. Method of application, precision and variability according to product

Results of forecasting studied			
Product	**Method of forecasting**	**Average accuracy**	**Variability**
A	Triple exponential smoothing	97.38%	0.64%
B	Simple exponential smoothing	85.49%	11.27%
C	Simple exponential smoothing	92.43%	2.68%
D	Simple exponential smoothing	92.73%	3.63%
E	Double exponential smoothing	86.83%	7.07%
F	Triple exponential smoothing	47.79%	10.84%
G	Double exponential smoothing	92.54%	4.33%
H	Triple exponential smoothing	89.09%	7.39%
I	Average weighted 3 periods	88.4%	8.35%
J	Double exponential smoothing	79,00%	5.4%
K	Triple exponential smoothing	79,10%	12,80%
L	Double exponential smoothing	86.3%	3.25%
M	moving average 3 periods	74.4%	26.4%
N	Double exponential smoothing	84.6%	6,00%
O	Simple exponential smoothing	81.3%	16.36%
P	N/A	-	-

CONCLUSION

The study to IPS analyze the problems that presents in relation to planning and control in the central warehouse, which affect not only the level of service expected in each of the products, but can also lead to the presentation of events that pressure the lives of patients, due to the absence of these.

An interesting discovery of the project refers to the low number of studies in the health sector in opposition to the specific analysis of individual products, based on consumption histories in order to establish predictions models that allow improving their service levels.

The classify of the prediction method, as well as the safety inventory and the reorder point for each of the essential and basic products, which represents 95.7% of the consumption of the warehouse, supply the IPS with the parameters and adequate information to prevent the scarcity of products.

Table 1. Inventory of security, reorder point and maximum delivery time according to the product analyzed.

Product	Forecasting	Average error	Error standard deviation	Safe inventory	Reorder point	Delivery time
A	84.349	2.62%	0.64%	3.476	8.162	3
B	10.854	14.51%	11.27%	4.424	1.050	3
C	7.651	7.57%	2.68%	1.056	740	3
D	5.609	7.27%	3.63%	882	724	4
E	6.115	13.17%	7.07%	1.813	592	4
F	841	52.21%	10.84%	651	109	4
G	456	7.46%	4.33%	80	44	3
H	641	10.91%	7.39%	180	62	3
I	3.292	11.60%	8.35%	1021	319	3
J	4.614	21%	5.4%	1549	744	5
K	2.286	28.06%	12.84%	1324	295	4
L	1.841	13.69%	3.25%	391	178	3
M	746	25.19%	26.43%	647	96	4
N	464	15.4%	6%	136	75	5
O	278	18.71%	16.36%	158	27	3
P	240	-	-	-	-	5

The models lead to obtain service levels between 97 - 99%, creating a positive impact on fulfillment of rates in the central warehouse in opposition to the dependencies it supplies.

Lower rate of surgical cancellations or postponement due to absent product in warehouse

Future studies should intensify the analysis of the behavior of products in other IPS produce advanced models of prediction of demand, based for example on the area of hospitals or clinics, or the category of these.

In the same way, the use of technology in the IPS such as barcodes, RFID, VMI, should be strengthened in order to have more consistent information along the value chain.

REFRENCES

Abdollahzade, M., Miranian, A., Hassani, H., & Iranmanesh, H. (2015). A new hybrid enhanced local linear neurofuzzy model based on the optimized singular spectrum analysis and its application for nonlinear and chaotic time series forecasting. *Inf Sci*, *295*, 107–125. doi:10.1016/j.ins.2014.09.002

Adhikari, R. (2015). A neural network based linear ensemble framework for time series forecasting. *Neurocomputing*, *157*, 231–242. doi:10.1016/j.neucom.2015.01.012

Amaya, C., Beaulieu, M., Landry, S., Rebolledo, C., & Velasco, N. (2010). Potenciando la contribución de la logística hospitalaria: Tres casos, tres trayectorias. *Revista Gestión Internacional.*, *14*(4), 85–98.

Argas, I., Vázquez, M., & Mogollon, A. (2010). Acceso a la atención en salud en Colombia. *Revista de Salud Publica (Bogota, Colombia)*, *12*(5), 701–712. doi:10.1590/S0124-00642010000500001 PubMed

Azzi, A., Persona, A., Sgarbossa, F., & Bonin, M. (2013). Drug inventory management and distribution: Outsourcing logistics to third-party providers. *Strategic Outsourcing*, *6*(1), 48–64. doi:10.1108/17538291311316063

Bajestani, N. S., & Zare, A. (2011). Forecasting TAIEX using improved type 2 fuzzy time series. *Expert Systems with Applications*, *38*(5), 5816–5821. doi:10.1016/j.eswa.2010.10.049

Behnamian, J., & Fatemi Ghomi, S. M. T. (2010). Development of a PSO-SA hybrid metaheuristic for a new comprehensive regression model to time-series forecasting. *Expert Systems with Applications*, *37*(2), 974–984. doi:10.1016/j.eswa.2009.05.079

Biggerstaff, M., Johansson, M., Alper, D., Brooks, L. C., Chakraborty, P., Farrow, D. C., ... Reed, C. (2018). Results from the second year of a collaborative effort to forecast influenza seasons in the United States. *Epidemics*, *24*(February), 26–33. doi:10.1016/j.epidem.2018.02.003 PubMed

Bouckaert, N., Van den Heede, K., & Van de Voorde, C. (2018). Improving the forecasting of hospital services: A comparison between projections and actual utilization of hospital services. *Health Policy (Amsterdam)*, *122*(7), 728–736. doi:10.1016/j.healthpol.2018.05.010 PubMed

Bowersox, D., & Closs, D. (2002). Supply chain logistics management (1st ed.). NY: McGraw Hill education.

Çakıcı, Ö. E., Groenevelt, H., & Seidmann, A. (2011). Using RFID for the management of pharmaceutical inventory — system optimization and shrinkage control. *Decision Support Systems*, *51*(4), 842–852. doi:10.1016/j.dss.2011.02.003

Castrellón, J., Torres, J., & Adarme, W. (2014). Modelo para la operación logística de distribución de medicamentos del programa de salud pública en Colombia. *Dyna (Bilbao)*, *81*(187), 257–266. doi:10.15446/dyna.v81n187.46107

Chang, P., Liu, C., Lin, J., Fan, C., & Ng, C. S. P. (2009). A neural network with a case based dynamic window for stock trading prediction. *Expert Systems with Applications*, *36*(3), 6889–6898. doi:10.1016/j.eswa.2008.08.077

Chang, P.-C., Liu, C.-H., & Lai, R. K. (2008). A fuzzy case-based reasoning model for sales forecasting in print circuit board industries. *Expert Systems with Applications*, *34*(3), 2049–2058. doi:10.1016/j.eswa.2007.02.011

Chase, R., & Jacobs, R. (2014). *Administración de operaciones: Producción y cadena de suministros. (13a* (J. Romo, P. Mascaró, & M. Mauri, Trans. & Eds.). México: McGraw Hill.

Chen, T.-T., & Lee, S.-J. (2015). A weighted LS-SVM based learning system for time series forecasting. *Information Sciences*, *299*, 99–116. doi:10.1016/j.ins.2014.12.031

Chun, S. H., & Park, Y. J. (2006). A new hybrid data mining technique using a regression case based reasoning: Application to financial forecasting. *Expert Systems with Applications*, *31*(2), 329–336. doi:10.1016/j.eswa.2005.09.053

Corchado, J. M., & Aiken, J. (2002). Hybrid artificial intelligence methods in oceanographic forecast models. *IEEE Transactions on Systems, Man and Cybernetics. Part C, Applications and Reviews*, *32*(4), 307–313. doi:10.1109/TSMCC.2002.806072

Coyle, J., Langley, J., Novack, R., & Gibson, B. (2013) Administración de la Cadena de Suministro. (9a ed.). (Jaso, E., Cervantes, Y., & Velásquez, J, Trad). Mexico: Cengage.

de Oliveira, J. F. L., & Ludermir, T. B. (2015). A hybrid evolutionary decomposition system for time series forecasting. *Neurocomputing*, *180*, 1–8. doi:10.1016/j.neucom.2015.07.113

De Vries, J. (2011). The shaping of inventory systems in health services: A stakeholder analysis. *International Journal of Production Economics*, *133*(1), 60–69. doi:10.1016/j.ijpe.2009.10.029

Dunea, D., Pohoata, A., & Iordache, S. (2015). Using wavelet–feedforward neural networks to improve air pollution forecasting in urban environments. *Environmental Monitoring and Assessment, 187*(7), 477. doi:10.1007/s10661-015-4697-x PubMed

Egrioglu, E., Aladag, C. H., & Yolcu, U. (2013). Fuzzy time series forecasting with a novel hybrid approach combining fuzzy c-means and neural networks. *Expert Systems with Applications, 40*(3), 854–857. doi:10.1016/j.eswa.2012.05.040

Escalona, M., Ávila, G., Pérez, D., & Ávila, T. (2011). Calidad de la atención y su Satisfacción. Servicio de Urgencias Médicas. *Ciencias Holguín, XVII*(1), 1–11.

Fajardo-Toro, C. H., Mula, J., & Poler, R. (2018). Adaptive and Hybrid Forecasting Models—A Review. In *Engineering Digital Transformation - Lecture Notes in Management and Industrial Engineering* (pp. 315–322). Cham: Springer; doi:10.1007/978-3-319-96005-0_38

Fdez-Riverola, F., & Corchado, J. M. (2003). CBR based system for forecasting red tides. *Knowledge-Based Systems, 16*(5–6), 321–328. doi:10.1016/S0950-7051(03)00034-0

Figueroa, L., Wilches, M., Romero, D., & Aguirre, S. (2016). Análisis de la Logística Hospitalaria aplicada en las Entidades de Salud de Nivel 3 y 4 en la ciudad de Barranquilla. *Sciences et Techniques (Paris), 21*(4), 307–317. doi:10.22517/23447214.11391

Fisher, J., & Monahan, T. (2008). Tracking the social dimensions of RFID systems in hospitals. *International Journal of Medical Informatics, 77*(3), 176–183. doi:10.1016/j.ijmedinf.2007.04.010 PubMed

Gooijier, J. G., & Hyndman, R. J. (2006). 25 years of time series forecasting. *International Journal of Forecasting, 22*(3), 443–473. doi:10.1016/j.ijforecast.2006.01.001

Gui, B., Wei, X., Shen, Q., Qi, J., & Guo, L. (2015). Financial time series forecasting using support vector machine. Proceedings - 2014 10th International Conference on Computational Intelligence and Security, CIS 2014 (Vol. 55, pp. 39–43). Academic Press. doi:10.1109/CIS.2014.22

Günay, M. E. (2016). Forecasting annual gross electricity demand by artificial neural networks using predicted values of socio-economic indicators and climatic conditions: Case of Turkey. *Energy Policy, 90*, 92–101. doi:10.1016/j.enpol.2015.12.019

Hanke, J., & Reitsch, A. G. (1996). *Pronósticos en los Negocios*. México: Prentice Hall.

Herazo, B. (2010). Algunos problemas de la salud en Colombia. *Universitas Odontologica : Revista Cientifica de la Facultad de Odontologica, 29*(63), 37–39.

Jaberidoost, M., Nikfar, S., Abdollahiasl, A., & Dinarvand, R. (2013). Pharmaceutical supply chain risks: A systematic review. *Daru : Journal of Faculty of Pharmacy, Tehran University of Medical Sciences, 21*(1), 69. doi:10.1186/2008-2231-21-69 PubMed

Jalalpour, M., Gel, Y., & Levin, S. (2015). Forecasting demand for health services: Development of a publicly available toolbox. *Operations Research for Health Care, 5*, 1–9. doi:10.1016/j.orhc.2015.03.001

Jarrett, P. (1998). Logistics in the health care industry. *International Journal of Physical Distribution & Logistics Management, 28*(9–10), 741–742. doi:10.1108/09600039810248154

Kelle, P., Woosley, J., & Schneider, H. (2012). Pharmaceutical supply chain specifics and inventory solutions for a hospital case. Operations Research for Health Care, 1(2,3), 54-63. doi:. doi:10.1016/j.orhc.2012.07.001

Khaldi, R., El Afia, A., & Chiheb, R. (2019). Forecasting of weekly patient visits to emergency department: Real case study. *Procedia Computer Science, 148*, 532–541. doi:10.1016/j.procs.2019.01.026

Krajewski, L. J., Ritzman, L. P., & Malhotra, M. K. (2016). *Operations management: Processes and supply chains* (11th ed.). Upper Saddle River, NJ: Pearson/Prentice Hall.

Kroezen, M., Van Hoegaerden, M., & Batenburg, R. (2018). The Joint Action on Health Workforce Planning and Forecasting: Results of a European programme to improve health workforce policies. *Health Policy (Amsterdam), 122*(2), 87–93. doi:10.1016/j.healthpol.2017.12.002 PubMed

Lapierre, S. D., & Ruiz, A. B. (2007). Scheduling logistic activities to improve hospital supply systems. *Computers & Operations Research, 34*(3), 624–641. doi:10.1016/j.cor.2005.03.017

Lee, S. M., Lee, D. H., & Schniederjans, M. J. (2011). Supply chain innovation and organizational performance in the healthcare industry. *International Journal of Operations & Production Management, 31*(11), 1193–1214. doi:10.1108/01443571111178493

Li, C., & Hu, J. W. (2012). A new ARIMA-based neuro-fuzzy approach and swarm intelligence for time series forecasting. *Engineering Applications of Artificial Intelligence, 25*(2), 295–308. doi:10.1016/j.engappai.2011.10.005

Li, H., Li, H., Lu, Y., & Panagiotelis, A. (2019). A forecast reconciliation approach to cause-of-death mortality modeling. *Insurance, Mathematics & Economics, 86*, 122–133. doi:10.1016/j.insmatheco.2019.02.011

Little, J., & Coughlan, B. (2008). Optimal inventory policy within hospital space constraints. *Health Care Management Science, 11*(2), 177–183. doi:10.1007/s10729-008-9066-7 PubMed

Londoño, G., Morera, R., & Laverde, G. (2008). *Administración Hospitalaria* (3rd ed.). Bogotá, Colombia.

Makridakis, S., Wheelwright, S. C., & McGee, V. E. (1978). *Forecasting: Methods and Applications*. New York, NY: John Wiley & Sons.

Malagón, G., Pontón, G., Galán, R., & Laverde, G. P. (2008). *Administración Hospitalaria*. Bogotá, Colombia: Editorial Panamericana.

Martínez, T. G. (2010). ¿Cómo medir la precisión de los pronósticos? Retrieved from https://www.slideshare.net/tomgalvez/e-book-cmo-medir-la-precisin-de-los-pronsticos

Merkuryeva, G., Valberga, A., & Smirnov, A. (2019). Demand forecasting in pharmaceutical supply chains: A case study. *Procedia Computer Science, 149*, 3–10. doi:10.1016/j.procs.2019.01.100

Mettler, T., & Rohner, P. (2009). E-Procurement in Hospital Pharmacies. *An Exploratory Multi-Case Study from Switzerland, 4*(1), 23–38. doi:10.4067/S0718-18762009000100004

Moons, K., Waeyenbergh, G., & Pintelon, L. (2019). Measuring the logistics performance of internal hospital supply chains – A literature study. *Omega, 82*, 205–217. doi:10.1016/j.omega.2018.01.007

Nahamias, S., & Lennon, T. (2015). *Production and Operations Analysis* (7th ed.). IL: Waveland Press.

Nicholson, L., Vakharia, A. J., & Selcuk Erenguc, S. (2004). Outsourcing inventory management decisions in healthcare: Models and application. *European Journal of Operational Research, 154*(1), 271–290. doi:10.1016/S0377-2217(02)00700-2

Nikolopoulos, K., Buxton, S., Khammash, M., & Stern, P. (2016). Forecasting branded and generic pharmaceuticals. *International Journal of Forecasting*, *32*(2), 344–357. doi:10.1016/j.ijforecast.2015.08.001

Oztekin, A., Pajouh, F. M., Delen, D., & Swim, L. K. (2010). An RFID network design methodology for asset tracking in healthcare. *Decision Support Systems*, *49*(1), 100–109. doi:10.1016/j.dss.2010.01.007

Pan, Z. X., & Pokharel, S. (2007). Logistics in hospitals: A case study of some Singapore hospitals. *Leadership in Health Services*, *20*(3), 195–207. doi:10.1108/17511870710764041 PubMed

Park, S. Y., Han, E., Kim, J., & Lee, E. K. (2016). Factors influencing the difference between forecasted and actual drug sales volumes under the price–volume agreement in South Korea. *Health Policy (Amsterdam)*, *120*(8), 867–874. doi:10.1016/j.healthpol.2016.06.004 PubMed

Perez, A., & Briceño, S. (2013). *Modelo de Gestión y Control de Inventarios para la Empresa DIMATIC*. Bogota: Universidad El Bosque.

Sánchez-Sánchez, P. A., & García-González, J. R. (2017). A new methodology for neural network training ensures error reduction in time series forecasting. Journal of Computer Science, 13(7), 211.217. doi:10.3844/jcssp.2017.211.217

Shafaei, M., & Kisi, O. (2016). Lake Level Forecasting Using Wavelet-SVR, Wavelet-ANFIS and Wavelet-ARMA Conjunction Models. *Water Resources Management*, *30*(1), 79–97. doi:10.1007/s11269-015-1147-z

Shah, N. (2004). Pharmaceutical supply chains: Key issues and strategies for optimisation. *Computers & Chemical Engineering*, *28*(6–7), 929–941. doi:10.1016/j.compchemeng.2003.09.022

Singh, D., & Verma, A. (2018). Inventory Management in Supply Chain. *Materials Today: Proceedings*, *5*(2), 3867–3872. doi:10.1016/j.matpr.2017.11.641

Toro, C. H. F., Gómez Meire, S., Gálvez, J. F., & Fdez-Riverola, F. (2013). A hybrid artificial intelligence model for river flow forecasting. *Applied Soft Computing*, *13*(8), 3449–3458. doi:10.1016/j.asoc.2013.04.014

van der Togt, R., Bakker, P. J. M., & Jaspers, M. W. M. (2011). A framework for performance and data quality assessment of Radio Frequency IDentification (RFID) systems in health care settings. *Journal of Biomedical Informatics*, *44*(2), 372–383. doi:10.1016/j.jbi.2010.12.004 PubMed

Velasco, N., Barrera, D., & Amaya, C. (2012). Logística hospitalaria: lecciones y retos para Colombia. In O. Bernal & C. Gutiérrez (Eds.), *La salud en Colombia* (pp. 309–343). Bogotá, Colombia: Ediciones Uniandes.

Vidal, C. (2017). *Fundamentos de gestión de inventarios*. Cali, Colombia: Universidad del Valle.

Wang, Y., Wang, S., & Zhang, N. (2013). A novel wind speed forecasting method based on ensemble empirical mode decomposition and GA-BP neural network. IEEE Power and Energy Society General Meeting, 94, 629–636. doi:10.1109/PESMG.2013.6672195

Yadav, P. (2015). Health Product Supply Chains in Developing Countries: Diagnosis of the Root Causes of Underperformance and an Agenda for Reform. Health Systems & Reform, 1(2), 142–154. doi:10.4161/23288604.2014.968005

Yu, L., Wang, S., & Lai, K. K. (2009). A neural-network-based nonlinear metamodeling approach to financial time series forecasting. *Applied Soft Computing*, *9*(2), 563–574. doi:10.1016/j.asoc.2008.08.001

Chapter 2
Solving Nurse Scheduling Problem via Genetic Algorithm in Home Healthcare

Şahin İnanç
Bursa Uludağ University, Turkey

Arzu Eren Şenaras
https://orcid.org/0000-0002-3862-4551
Uludag University, Turkey

ABSTRACT

The nurse scheduling problem (NSP) is the problem involving allocating the monthly shifts (day and night shifts, holidays, and so on) for nurses under various constraints. Generally, the NSP has a lot of constraints. As a result, it needs a lot of knowledge and experience to make the scheduling table with its constraints, and it has been made by the head nurse or the authority in the hospitals. This allocation of the shifts gives a lot of burden (time and efforts) to them, and it has been growing the demand for the automatic nurse scheduling system. This chapter aims to develop a genetic algorithm application for the Nurse Scheduling Problem (NSP). The application will be developed using Microsoft Visual Studio in C# programming language.

INTRODUCTION

Nurse scheduling problem deals with the jobs, vacations, and shifts arrangement for the nursing staffs in hospital's daily operation. Many factors need to be considered while the nurse chiefs arrange the nurse scheduling activities, for instance, the hospital management policies, the government regulations, and the fairness among nurses (Tsai and Li, 2009).

DOI: 10.4018/978-1-7998-0268-6.ch002

Home health care is growing in the French medical sector since demands increase. Organizations providing home care services are willing to optimize their activities in order to meet the increasing demand for home care. Consequently, research on this problem has appeared by the end of the 20th century. Most of the work being application-based, the number of publications rises to cover the different variants of the problem. The problem is complicated by factors such as caregivers qualification, various patients demand, multiple home care offices, caregivers workload limitation, shared visits, patients availability and workload fairness among caregivers (Decerle et.al., 2017, Bertrand, 2010).

Home Health Care is a wide range of health care services that can be given in one's home for an illness or injury. In recent years, the health care industry has become one of the largest sectors of the economy in developed countries such as France, Germany, Australia, etc. Since the transportation cost is one of the most important spendings in the company activities, it is of great significance to optimize the vehicle routing problem in home health care company. According to a survey (Mankowska et al., 2014; Harris, 2015; Liu et al., 2013) of the home health care companies, each day, an HHC company carries out various logistics activities including the delivery of drugs or medical instruments from the pharmacy to patients, and pickup of the biological samples and waste from patients' home to the laboratory. A large number of patients are located in a town or village, and the task of a home health care company is to provide health care services to the patients at ones' homes one by one. The main operational process of the HHC can be summarized as three steps (Shi et.al., 2017: 13987):

1. The HHC company collects information from the patients, this information may include: name, address, sex, type of the illness, symptom and other related information;
2. The HHC company plan to arrange the visited routes and assign nurses according to the information collected;
3. The nurses are scheduled to visit the patients. Each nurse is assigned to a planned route, and he/she has to carry out all of the service-related activities for the route. This nurse will drive the vehicle to visit the patients one by one according to the designed route.

Among the first papers about home health care, Begur et al. (1997) described a decision support system not taking into account time window and shared visits in opposite to Cheng and Rich (1998) who considered patients and care givers time window as well as multiple home care offices. They solved small instances with exact and heuristic approaches. Shared visits have been lately studied in the literature. Eveborn et al. (2006) developed a decision support system for an application in Sweden including shared visits who have also been studied by Rasmussen et al. (2012) using a branch-and-price algorithm or by Mankowska et al. (2014) using an adaptive variable neighborhood search algorithm as solving approaches (Decerle, 2017: 14662).

A SHORT LITERATURE REWIEV

Aickelin and Dowsland (2004) studied Genetic Algorithms (GAs) approach to a manpower-scheduling problem arising at a major UK hospital. An alternative algorithm for solving a nurse-scheduling problem in the form of a GA coupled with a decoding routine. In comparison to the previous 'direct' GA approach described in Aickelin and Dowsland this has two advantages: Firstly, the GA solves an unconstrained problem leaving the constraint handling to the decoder that uses them to directly bias the search rather than in penalty functions alone. Secondly, all problem speci6c knowledge is held in the decoder routine, thus the algorithm can be quickly adapted to changes in problem specification. The overall results are better than those found by previous evolutionary approaches with a more flexible implementation than Tabu Search.

Tsai and Li (2009) developed a two-stage mathematical modeling for a nurse scheduling system wherein hospital management requirements, government regulations, and nursing staffs' shift preferences are incorporated. In the first stage, the nurse work and vacation schedules are arranged and genetic algorithm (GA) is used to solve for the optimal schedules and to check for any violation of government regulations, hospital management requirements, and the scheduling fairness. In the second stage, the nurse roster schedule is arranged and GA is further adopted to solve the optimal schedule. An empirical case study is performed and the results show that GA can be an efficient tool for solving the nurse scheduling problem. In addition, it can also be easily modified to suit different cases encountered in hospitals.

Cai and Li (2000) proposed a new genetic algorithm (GA) to solve the problem. The proposed GA differs from traditional GAs in the following components: (1) it performs its parent se-lection by using a ranking scheme that considers successively the three criteria; (2) it uses a multi-point cross over operator based on the hamming distance between schedules; and (3) it adopts a heuristic to resolve the problem of infeasibility created by crossover operations. Computational results are reported, which show the effectiveness of the proposed approach in finding desirable solutions.

Frifita et al. (2017) proposed a General Variable Neighbourhood Search approach to deal with HHC problem with time windows and synchronized visits. Experimental results demonstrate the efficiency of their approach. Experiments conducted on benchmark instances from the literature clearly show that their method is fast and outperforms the existing approaches on half of the instances.

GENETIC ALGORITHMS

The Genetic Algorithm (GA), often referred to as genetic algorithms, was invented by John Holland at the University of Michigan in the 1970s.22 It is similar to the (μ, l) Evolution Strategy in many respects: it iterates through fitness assessment, selection and breeding, and population reassembly. The primary difference is in how selection and breeding take place: whereas Evolution Strategies select all the parents and then create all the children, the Genetic Algorithm little-by-little selects a few parents and generates a few children until enough children have been created (Luke, 2015: 36).

To breed, we begin with an empty population of children. We then select two parents from the original population, copy them, cross them over with one another, and mutate the results. This forms two children, which we then add to the child population. We repeat this process until the child population is entirely filled (Luke, 2015, p. 36).

GAs are generally attributed to Holland and his students in the 1970s, although evolutionary computation dates back further (refer to Fogel for an extensive review of early approaches). GAs are stochastic meta-heuristics that mimic some features of natural evolution. Canonical GAs were not intended for function optimization, as discussed by De Jong. However, slightly modi6edversions proved very successful. For an introduction to GAs for function optimization, see Deb. Many examples of successful implementations can be found in Back, Chaiyaratana and Zalzala and others (Aickelin and Dowsland, 2004).

GENETIC ALGORITHM VIA C# FOR NURSE SCHEDULING

With the increasing population, the number of personnel in hospitals increases. These hospitals arc in hospitals to providc a quality service to the working staff. This is the increase in service quality and the analysis problem based on one.

The constraints of the problem are shown as below:

The problem aims to find the solution of nurse scheduling for a period of 1 week (7 day)
There are 3 shifts in a day.
In morning and evening shift there must be at least 2 nurses in charge.
In night shift there must be only one nurse in charge.
Each nurse will have one night shift per week
Each nurse should take 2 days off, 1 day on weekends and 1 day on weekdays
Must be an off day after the night shift

Morning (09:00 - 17:00)
Evening (17:00 - 01:00)
Night (01:00 - 09:00)

n: nurse number
d: off day in weekday
e: off day in weekend
a: off day after night shift

One of the most important steps in genetic algorithm is adjusting chromosome. In other words; chromosome contains the definition of the problem. In this problem, the chromosome is defined as follows;

Chromosome: [n1], [d], [e], [a] –
[n2], [d], [e], [a] –
[n3], [d], [e], [a] –
[n4], [d], [e], [a] –
[n5], [d], [e], [a] –
[n6], [d], [e], [a] –
[n7], [d], [e], [a]

The numerical view of one of the chromosomes can be like these;

Chromosome: [n1], [1], [6], [1] –
[n2], [4], [6], [3] –
[n3], [3], [7], [2] –
[n4], [5], [6], [7] –
[n5], [2], [7], [6] –
[n6], [1], [6], [5] –
[n7], [2], [6], [4]

The chromosome has 7 pieces for each nurse. Each pieces contains the possible solution for each nurses.

The value of parameter d can be one of the (1- 2 - 3 - 4 – 5)
The value of parameter e can be one of the (6 – 7)
The value of parameter a can be one of the (1 - 2 - 3 - 4 - 5 - 6 - 7)

Firstly for each piece of the chromosome, 20 points should be added to the solution point. If the value of d and a or d and e are the same, then -10 point should be added to the solution point. If d or e is not 1 point higher than a, then -10 point should be added to the solution point. The chromosome that has the worst point removes from the gen population and the chromosome that has the best solution re-added to gen population.

The chromosome that gives the best solution after some iteration is chosen as the solution of the problem.

Algorithm of Genetic Algorithm is shown as below:

1. Start
2. Define variables
3. Create initial population
4. Calculate fitness values
5. Is the maximum number of iterations reached go to step 9
6. Selection
7. Crossover
8. Mutation
9. Show results
10. End

As a result, each nurse works 5 days a week, rests for 2 days, and each nurse has a night shift and 1 day rest after night shift. The solution is described on Table 1.

Table 1. Solution of NSP

Nurses	Monday	Tuesday	Wednesday	Thursday	Friday	Saturday	Sunday
n1	x	x	x	o	x	n	o
n2	x	x	o	x	n	o	x
n3	n	o	x	x	o	x	x
n4	o	o	x	x	x	x	n
n5	o	n	o	x	x	x	x
n6	x	x	n	o	x	o	x
n7	x	x	x	n	o	x	o

x: Morning and evening shift
n: Night shift
o: Off day

Figure 1. Flowchart of Scheduling Nurses Via Genetic Algorithm

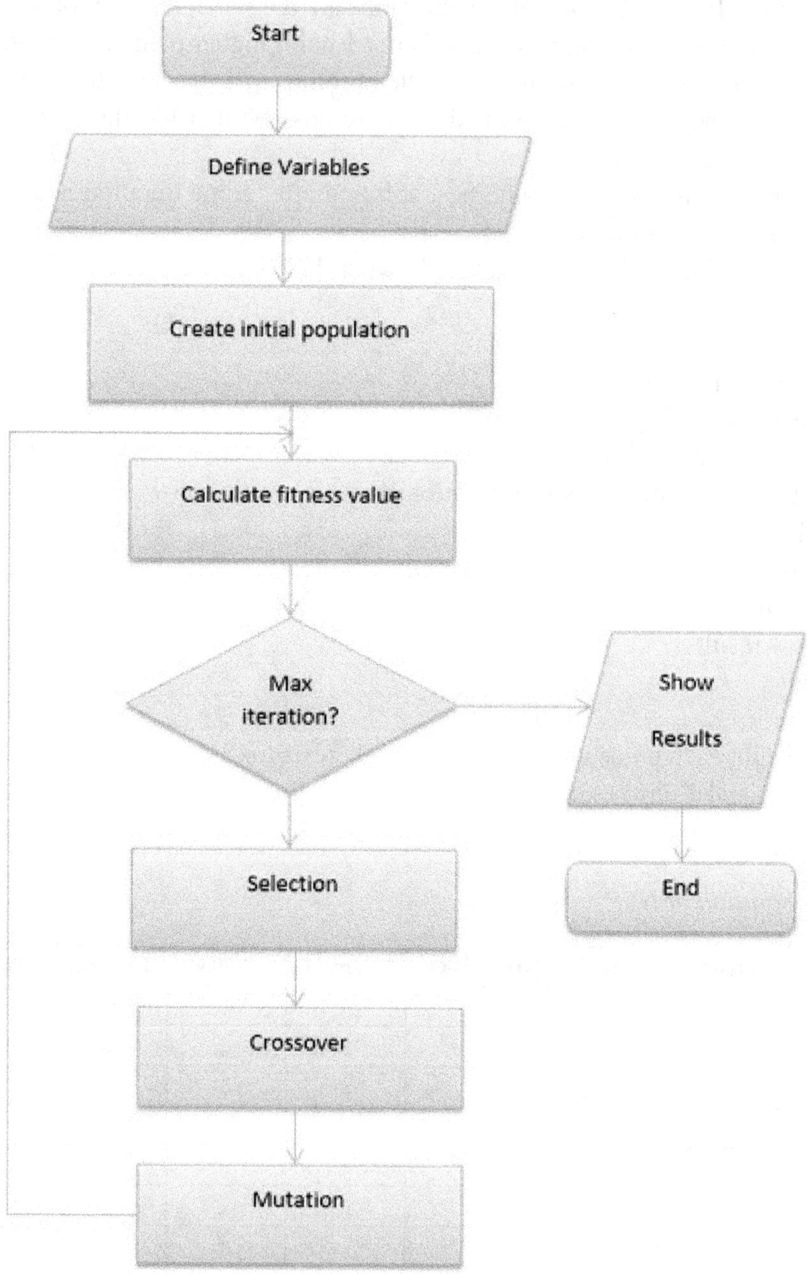

CONCLUSION

There are multiple solutions for NSP. This paper studied the method of the coding (Microsoft Visual Studio 2012 C# Programming Language) and the genetic operations via Genetic Algorithm with the absolute constraints for NSP. The exchange of shifts was done to satisfy the absolute constraints in the coding and after the genetic operations. It can be said that Genetic Algorithm is an effective method for nurse (or any other personnel) scheduling problems.

REFERENCES

Back, T. Applications of evolutionary algorithms, 5th ed. Germany: Dortmund, 1993.

Begur, S. V., Miller, D. M., & Weaver, J. R. (1997). An Integrated Spatial Dss For Scheduling And Routing Homehealth-Care Nurses. *Interfaces*, *27*(4), 35–48. doi:10.1287/inte.27.4.35

Bertrand, D. (2010). Les services de soins infirmiers domicile en 2008. *Etudes et rsultats*, *739*. Retrieved from http://drees.social-sante.gouv.fr/IMG/pdf/er739.pdf

Cai, X., & Li, K. N. (2000). A Genetic Algorithm For Scheduling Staff Of Mixed Skills Under Multi-Criteria. *European Journal of Operational Research*, *125*(2), 359–369. doi:10.1016/S0377-2217(99)00391-4

Chaiyaratana, N., & Zalzala, A. (1997). Recent developments in evolutionary and genetic algorithms: theory and applications. In P. Fleming & S. Zalzala (Eds.), *Genetic algorithms in engineering systems 2: innovations and applications* (pp. 270–277). Letchworth: Omega Print & Design. doi:10.1049/cp:19971192

Chang-Chun, T., & Li, S. H. A. (2009). A Two-Stage Modeling With Genetic Algorithms For The Nurse Scheduling Problem. *Expert Systems with Applications*, *36*(5), 9506–9512. doi:10.1016/j.eswa.2008.11.049

Cheng, E., & Rich, J. L. (1998). A home health care routing and scheduling problem. PSU. Retrieved from http://citeseerx.ist.psu.edu/viewdoc/summary

De Jong, K. (1993). Genetic Algorithms are NOT function optimizers. In D. Whitley (Ed.), *Foundations of Genetic Algorithms 2* (pp. 5–17). San Mateo, CA: Morgan Kaufmann Publishers.

Deb, K. (1996). *Genetic algorithms for function optimization* (pp. 4–31). Genetic Algorithms and Soft Computing.

Decerle, J., Grunder, O., Hassani Hajjam El, A., & Barakat, O. (2017). A General Model For The Home Health Care Routing And Scheduling Problem With Route Balancing. *IFAC Papers On Line*, *50-1*(1), 14662–14667. doi:10.1016/j.ifacol.2017.08.1907

Eveborn, P., Flisberg, P., & R¨onnqvist, M. (2006). Laps carean operational system for staff planning of home care. *European Journal of Operational Research*, *171*(3), 962–976. doi:10.1016/j.ejor.2005.01.011

Fogel, D. (1998). *Evolutionary computation: the fossil record*. New York: IEEE Press. doi:10.1109/9780470544600

Harris, M. D. (2015). *Handbook of home health care administration*. Jones & Bartlett Publishers.

Holland, J. (1976). *Adaptation in natural and arti6cial systems*. Ann Arbor, MI: University of Michigan Press.

Luke, S. (2015). *Essentials of Metaheuristics* (2nd ed.). Lulu. Retrieved from http://cs.gmu.edu/sean/book/metaheuristics/

Mankowska, D. S., Meisel, F., & Bierwirth, C. (2014). The Home Health Care Routing And Scheduling Problem With Interdependent Services. *Health Care Management Science*, *17*(1), 15–30. doi:10.100710729-013-9243-1 PMID:23780750

Ran, L., Xie, X., Vincent, A., & Carlos, R. (2013). Heuristic Algorithms For a Vehicle Routing Problem With Simultaneous Delivery And Pickup And Time Windows in Home Health Care. *European Journal of Operational Research*, *230*(3), 475–486. doi:10.1016/j.ejor.2013.04.044

Rasmussen, M. S., Justesen, T., Dohn, A., & Larsen, J. (2012). The home care crew scheduling problem: Preference based visit clustering and temporal dependencies. *European Journal of Operational Research*, *219*(3), 598–610.

Sana, F., Malek, M., & Jalel, E. (2017). General Variable Neighborhood Search For Home Healthcare Routing And Scheduling Problem With Time Windows And Synchronized Visits. *Electronic Notes in Discrete Mathematics*, *58*, 63–70. doi:10.1016/j.endm.2017.03.009

Uwe, A., & Dowsland, K. A. (2004). An Indirect Genetic Algorithm For A Nurse-Scheduling Problem. *Computers & Operations Research*, *31*(5), 761–778. doi:10.1016/S0305-0548(03)00034-0

Yong, S., Toufik, B., & Olivier, G. (2017). A Home Health Care Routing Problem with Stochastic Travel and Service Time. *IFAC PapersOnLine*, *50-1*, 13987–13992.

Chapter 3
A Review on Optimization Modeling of Hybrid Energy Systems

Marwa Mallek
Faculty of Economics and Management of Sfax, Tunisia

Jalel Euchi
College of Business and Economics, Qassim University, Tunisia

Yacin Jerbi
National School of Engineers of Sfax (ENIS), Tunisia

ABSTRACT

Hybrid energy systems (HESs) are an excellent solution for electrification of remote rural areas where the grid extension is difficult or not economical. Usually, HES generally integrate one or several renewable energy sources such as solar, wind, hydropower, and geothermal with fossil fuel powered diesel/petrol generator to provide electric power where the electricity is either fed directly into the grid or to batteries for energy storage. This chapter presents a review on the solution approaches for determining the HES systems based on various objective functions (e.g. economic, social, technical, environmental and health impact). In order to take account of environmental and health impacts from energy systems, several energy optimization model was developed for minimizing pollution and maximizing the production of renewable energy.

DOI: 10.4018/978-1-7998-0268-6.ch003

INTRODUCTION

The energy consumption is always increasing in the world. This energy increment cannot be sustained on conventional energy sources productions which rely on exhausting fossil fuels (IEA, 2017). Conventional fuel resources is a principal cause of greenhouse the gases, environmental and health impacts, renewable energy sources production sound feasible solution (e.g. solar Photovoltaic, Solar Thermal, Wind Turbine, Biomass, Hydropower and geothermal) and preserve the rise in energy demand (Inglesi, 2016). However, the problem of renewable energy sources is mainly their dependence on weather, climatic changes and the unpredictable nature. The solution is to a couple of sources of renewable energy and conventional energy of supply and forms a hybrid system. In addition, HES is an electrical system, comprising than one or more conventional energy sources and at least one renewable energy sources, while minimizing fuel consumption (Adefarati & Bansal, 2016). This system may or may not be connected to the National Grid (Twaha & Ramli, 2018). To efficiently utilize the resources for Hybrid energy system, economic, reliable and environment optimization is required, which can be done using diverse techniques of operations research (e.g. optimization approaches, multi-criteria decision making, simulation, and hybrid techniques).

ENERGY SOURCES

Energy is obtained from many sources, such as fossil fuel energy like petroleum, coal, and natural gas and renewable sources like solar Photovoltaic, Solar Thermal, Wind Turbine, Biomass, Hydropower and geothermal. These energy sources are converted to electric where the electricity is either fed directly into the Grid or to storage batteries.

Solar Energy

Solar energy can be converted into electricity by solar photovoltaic (SPV) and solar thermal (STH). The nature of Photovoltaic power system depends on the geographical location. Solar panels are connected either in parallel or in series based on the required current and voltage. On the one hand, SPV system is the direct converting solar radiation into current electricity using semiconductors that exhibit the photovoltaic effect (Overstraeten et al., 1986). On the other hand, STH systems collect and concentrate sunlight to produce the high-temperature heat needed to generate power (Asif, 2017).

Wind Turbine Energy

Wind turbines work by converting the rotational kinetic energy in the turbine of the wind into electrical energy. It can be classified into two types based on the horizontal axis and vertical axis about which the turbine rotates. In addition, this turbine that rotate around a horizontal axis are most common while vertical-axis turbines are less frequently used (Babu, 2013).

Biomass Energy

Biomass can be considered a renewable energy source based on the carbon cycle such as wood, crops, and algae. It can be converted into biogas or into liquid biofuels for the production of energy. It is the only renewable energy source that releases CO_2 (Carbon dioxide) in use (Goffé & Ferrasse, 2019).

Hydropower Energy

Generally, hydroelectric energy comes from the force of water (river, waterfall, stream, wave, etc.). It is rated a renewable energy source since the water cycle is constantly renewed by the sun (Sharma et al., 2019).

Geothermal Energy

Geothermal energy is energy derived from the original formation of the planet, from radioactive decay of minerals, from volcanic activity, and from solar energy absorbed at the surface (Kakkar et al., 2012).

Fossil Fuel Energy

Fossil fuels come from the living matter, remains of plants or animals. They contain big percentages of carbon like petroleum, coal, and natural gas. They are currently the most used energy source in the world with a rate of 86.8% (IEA, 2017).

ELECTRICITY DISTRIBUTION

Electric power distribution systems are a one or mix of both nonrenewable and renewable resources established near the consumer's emplacement. There are many research related to design, minimize cost, minimize emissions and configuration of hybrid Electric power distribution systems connected to the distribution networks or to the national grid systems. The National Grid is a network of public electricity that distributed energy production around the country and into houses and businesses. This chapter presents a review of the solution approaches for HES, considering both stand-alone and grid-connected systems (National Grid). Stand-alone systems which are producing power are not connected to a National Grid but instead, are utilized to charge a bank of batteries. Stand-alone systems comprise the majority of photovoltaic installations in remote regions of the world because they are the most cost-effective choice for applications far from the national grid (Kaundinya et al., 2009). There are several disadvantages forcing to throw away the extra energy generated such as excess battery costs and low capacity to store electricity

HYBRID ENERGY SYSTEM

The problems with renewable energy sources are known, they are intermittent, expensive and often not predictable. In recent years, HES are becoming popular on energy systems for providing electricity in remote areas due to advances in renewable energy sources and rise in cost of fossil fuels. Fig.1. shows the representation of HES consisting of different energy sources, energy consumption, grid connection, and battery bank system.

OPTIMIZATION OBJECTIVES FOR HES

This chapter presented the relevant papers with two categories, single-objective and multi-objective optimization problem. Some papers used optimization objectives to optimize HES (Singh et al., 2016). Several energy system models represented as optimizing a hybrid energy problem with a single objective function, the prime objective is the total cost of HES, while in multi-objective function, the other objectives (e.g. technical, social, political, environmental and health impact). The economic objectives which includes minimization the Net Present Cost of energy, minimization the annualized cost, minimization the initial investment cost, minimization the total net present cost and other cost-linked optimization. Technical optimizations are discussed in several energy problems such as maximizing the production of renewable energy, highest reliability, minimization energy losses, and other technical-linked optimization. In the environment and health objectives which include higher reliability and less emission. Various social objectives are discussed to optimize energy systems such as maximize job creation, maximize the Human Development Index and other environment-linked optimization. Political

Figure 1. Hybrid Energy System

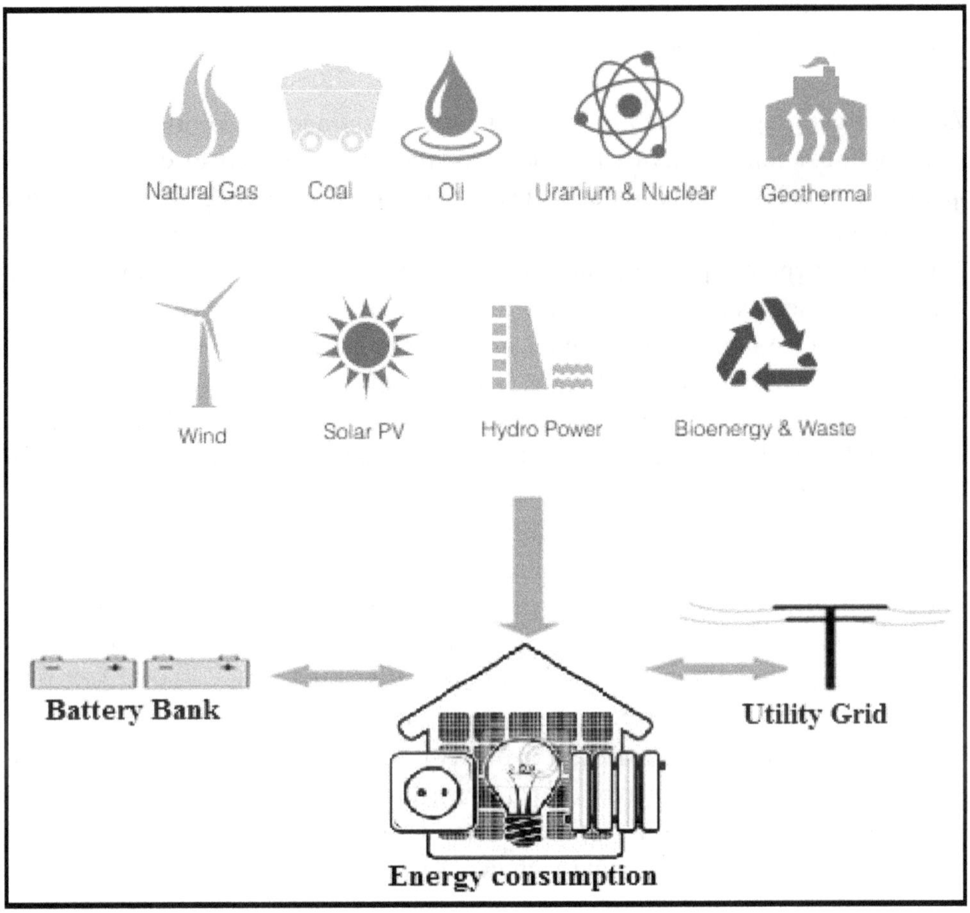

acceptance refers to renewable energy sources contribute to support government policy on technological development and its compatibility with the legislative and administrative situation (Haddad et al., 2017).

OPTIMIZATION METHODS APPLIED TO HES

The diverse methods available for the optimization or evaluation of HES can be extensively classified into five categories, i.e., optimization methods, multi-criteria decision making, software tools and hybrid approaches.

Optimization Methods

Mathematical Program

Mathematical program (MP) is applied to solve continuous and discrete variable based optimization problems. It which has already been used to optimize HES operation includes various models such as linear programming (LP), nonlinear programming (NLP), integer programming (IP), mixed-integer linear programming (MILP) and dynamic programming (DP). Table 1 shows a brief summary of the studies published using Mathematical programs for optimization energy systems.

The work of Ashok (2007) applied an NLP for getting the optimal combination of community based HES in Indian. The mathematical model was formulated for optimal sizing of the wind-photovoltaic- micro-hydropower hybrid system at minimum life cycle cost. Saif et al. (2010) formulated an LP of wind-photovoltaic-diesel-battery HES with two objectives: minimizing total cost and minimizing total CO2 emissions. The paper of Riffonneau et al. (2011) proposed a DP to improve HES using grid-connected photovoltaic with storage. The study of Supriya & Siddarthan (2011) developed an LP to improve HES using grid-connected wind-photovoltaic energy system with the minimum life cycle cost while meeting the energy balance condition. The work of Theo et al. (2016) proposed a MILP to optimal sizing of on-grid HES with the minimum net present value of the overall energy production cost. In reality, it is difficult to use a mathematical program to solve such optimization of hybrid energy systems problems. Genetic algorithm, particle swarm optimization, simulated annealing approach, and Tabu search are examples of these novel searching-techniques.

Genetic Algorithm

Genetic algorithm (GA) is an evolutionary method that simulates the principles of natural evolution to solve optimization problems (Holland, 1975). Therefore the literature review includes many researchers based on GA (we refer the reader to the paper of Euchi (2017)) for building energy systems. Table 2 shows a brief summary of the studies published using GA approaches for optimization energy system.

In addition, the paper of Hong et al. (2012) applied GA to determine optimal sizes for wind, photovoltaic, and diesel was determined to minimize cost. Similarly, the studies of Bilal et al. (2013) and Tegani et al. (2013) used Multi-Objectives GA approach to optimal sizing a stand-alone hybrid wind-photovoltaic-diesel system with minimizing the Levelized Cost of Energy and the CO2 emission. Shadmand & Balog (2014) proposed a Genetic Algorithm for multi-objective optimization is to simultaneously maximize the power availability and minimize the cost of HES.

Table 1. Summary of Mathematical programs for Optimization HES

Author	method	Objectif	Energy sources									Best configuration
			WT	SPV	STH	BI	HY	GE	FF	BT	GC	
Eke et al. (2005)	LP	Economic	X	X						X		WT+SPV+BT
Ashok (2007)	NLP	Economic	X	X			X		X	X	X	WT+HY+BT
Saif et al. (2010)	LP	Economic Environmental	X	X					X	X		WT+SPV+FF+BT
Riffonneau et al. (2011)	DP	Economic Technical		X						X	X	SPV+BT+GC
Supriya & Siddarthan (2011)	LP	Economic	X	X							X	WT+GC
Huneke et al. (2012)	LP	Economic	X	X					X	X		SPV+FF+BT
Torres et al. (2014)	LP	Economic		X						X	X	SPV+BT+GC
Theo et al. (2016)	MILP	Economic	X	X		X				X	X	WT+SPV+BI+BT +GC

WT: Wind Turbine; SPV: Solar Photovoltaic; STH: Solar Thermal; BI: Biomass; HY: Hydropower; GE: Geothermal; FF: Fossil Fuel; BT: Battery; GC: Grid-connected.

Table 2. Summary of Genetic Algorithm for Optimization HES

Author	Method	Objectif	Energy sources									Best configuration
			WT	SPV	STH	BI	HY	GE	FF	BT	GC	
Nafeh (2011)	GA	Economic	X	X						X		WT+SPV+BT
Hong et al. (2012)	GA	Economic	X	X					X			WT+SPV+FF
Merei et al. (2013)	GA	Economic	X	X					X	X		WT+SPV+FF+BT
Bilal et al. (2013)	GA	Economic Environmental	X	X					X	X		WT+SPV+FF+BT
Tegani et al. (2013)	GA	Economic Environmental	X	X					X	X		WT+SPV+FF+BT
Shadmand & Balog (2014)	GA	Economic Technical	X	X						X	X	WT+SPV+BT +GC
Tégani et al. (2014)	GA	Economic	X	X						X		WT+SPV+BT
Kumar & Bhusan (2014)	GA	Economic	X	X						X		WT+SPV+BT
Bilal et al. (2015)	GA	Economic Environmental	X	X					X	X		WT+SPV+FF+BT
Gokul et al. (2017)	GA	Economic	X	X					X	X		WT+SPV+BT

WT: Wind Turbine; SPV: Solar Photovoltaic; STH: Solar Thermal; BI: Biomass; HY: Hydropower; GE: Geothermal; FF: Fossil Fuel; BT: Battery; GC: Grid-connected.

The work of Bilal et al. (2015) used Multi-Objectives GA approach to design and optimize a stand-alone hybrid wind-photovoltaic-diesel-battery system in Senegal. The paper of Gokul et al. (2017) developed optimal Size methodology of a wind-Photovoltaic-diesel-battery HES by using GA.

Particle Swarm Optimization

The work of Eberhart and Kennedy (1995) developed a new optimization approach using the study of bird and fish movement behavior. Many types of research proposed that for hybrid energy system problems, the PSO algorithm can be a good approach for resolving these problems.

Table 3 shows a brief summary of the studies published using Particle swarm optimization for optimization energy system.

Also, the work of Ardakani et al. (2010) applied PSO to optimize HES which comprised of wind, photovoltaic and battery storage for certain region of Iran. Bashir & Sadeh (2012) developed a HES based on wind–photovoltaic with battery system for minimize the Net Present Cost applying PSO method. Maleki et al. (2015) optimized a HES with Photovoltaic-wind-battery power system using PSO method. The study of Mohamed et al. (2016) used PSO to obtain the optimum size of a wind-photovoltaic-diesel-battery based hybrid system for Saudi Arabia. Sawle et al. (2017) used PSO to optimize sizing of a wind-photovoltaic-biomass-battery-diesel HES with a cost of energy is minimized.

Ant Colony Algorithm

Ant Colony Algorithm (ACA) was introduced by the work of Dorigo (1992) in his Ph.D. (Dorigo & Gambardella, 1997). This algorithm was aiming to search for an optimal path in a graph, based on the behavior of ants in searching of the shortest path among their nests and source of food (Euchi et al., 2016). In the literature review, the researchers have observed some researchers that use the ACA to solve the optimization problems of optimal HES design. Table 4 shows a brief summary of the studies published using Ant colony algorithm for optimization energy system.

Suhane et al. (2014) applied ACA to optimize sizing of a wind- photovoltaic HES with the minimum total cost which is the sum of total Investment cost, Operational and maintenance cost, and replacement cost. The paper of Fetanat & Khorasaninejad (2015) used ACA based integer programming applied for optimal sizing of the hybrid wind-photovoltaic energy system with the minimum total cost. Vijay & Durga (2017) proposed an ACA for optimal placement and design of hybrid wind- photovoltaic energy system with minimum cost.

Table 3. Summary of Particle Swarm Optimization methods for optimization HES

Author	Method	Objectif	Energy sources									Best configuration
			WT	SPV	STH	BI	HY	GE	FF	BT	GC	
Ardakani et al. (2010)	PSO	Economic	X	X						X		WT+SPV+BT
Bashir & Sadeh (2012)	PSO	Economic	X	X						X		WT+SPV+BT
Amer et al. (2013)	PSO	Economic	X	X						X		WT+SPV+BT
Pirhaghshenasvali & Asaei (2014)	PSO	Economic	X	X					X	X		WT+SPV+FF+BT
Paliwal et al. (2014)	PSO	Economic	X	X					X	X		WT+SPV+FF+BT
Askarzadeh et al. (2015)	PSO	Economic	X	X						X		WT+SPV+BT
Maleki et al. (2015)	PSO	Economic	X	X						X		SPV+BT
Mohamed et al. (2016)	PSO	Economic	X	X					X	X		WT+SPV+FF+BT
Shang et al. (2016)	PSO	Economic	X	X					X	X		WT+SPV+FF+BT
Maleki et al. (2017)	PSO	Economic	X	X	X				X		X	WT+SPV+STH + FF+GC
Sawle et al. (2017)	PSO	Economic	X	X		X			X	X		WT+SPV+BI+FF +BT

WT: Wind Turbine; SPV: Solar Photovoltaic; STH: Solar Thermal; BI: Biomass; HY: Hydropower; GE: Geothermal; FF: Fossil Fuel; BT: Battery; GC: Grid-connected.

Table 4. Summary of Ant Colony Algorithm method for Optimization HES

Author	Method	Objectif	Energy sources									Best configuration
			WT	SPV	STH	BI	HY	GE	FF	BT	GC	
Suhane et al. (2014)	ACA	Economic	X	X						X		WT+SPV +BT
Fetanat & Khorasaninejad (2015)	ACA	Economic	X	X						X		WT+SPV+BT
Vijay & Durga (2017)	ACA	Economic	X	X								WT+SPV

WT: Wind Turbine; SPV: Solar Photovoltaic; STH: Solar Thermal; BI: Biomass; HY: Hydropower; GE: Geothermal; FF: Fossil Fuel; BT: Battery; GC: Grid-connected.

Table 5. Summary of Simulated Annealing method for Optimization HES

Author	Method	Objectif	Energy sources									Best configuration
			WT	SPV	STH	BI	HY	GE	FF	BT	GC	
Ekren & Ekren (2010)	SA	Economic	X	X						X		WT+SPV +BT
Agarwala & Kumarb (2012)	SA	Economic Environmental		X					X	X		SPV+FF+BT

WT: Wind Turbine; SPV: Solar Photovoltaic; STH: Solar Thermal; BI: Biomass; HY: Hydropower; GE: Geothermal; FF: Fossil Fuel; BT: Battery; GC: Grid-connected.

Simulated Annealing

Due to the complexity of the resulting mathematical programming approach, it is necessary to utilize simulation methods to model the energy systems such as Simulated annealing (SA). It is an algorithmic approach to solve combinatorial optimization problems (Kirkpatrick et al., 1984). Table 5 shows a brief summary of the studies published using simulated annealing for optimization energy system.

The work of Ekren and Ekren (2010) applied SA to optimize sizing of a wind-photovoltaic-battery HES to minimize total Net Present Cost in Turkey. The paper of Agarwala and Kumarb (2012) applied SA to determine optimal sizes for hybrid photovoltaic-diesel-battery energy system. However, few studies have analyzed the HES by Simulation Annealing.

Tabu Search

Tabu Search (TS) originally developed by Glover, which is an iterative approach that starts from a random initial solution and tries to find a better solution escaping local optima (Glover & Laguna, 1999; Euchi & Chabchoub, 2009). Up to now, there are few researches has been developed a TS in HES. For example, the work of Katsigiannis and Georgilakis (2008) applied TS to determine optimal design for hybrid wind-photovoltaic-diesel-battery energy system with minimum cost.

MULTI-CRITERIA DECISION MAKING

Efficiency evaluation of energy systems can be a challenging task, where there are multiple factors. Multi-criteria decision making (MCDM) techniques have become increasingly popular in decision making aid for energy sector because of the multi-dimensionality of energy systems and the complexity of different objectives (Shmelev et al., 2016; Elleuch & Frikha, 2018; Elleuch et al., 2019). Some of the MCDM methods that can be used are:

- Analytic Hierarchic Process (AHP);
- Preference Ranking Organization Method for Enrichment Evaluations (PROMETHEE)
- Technique for Order Performance by Similarity to Ideal Solution (TOPSIS)
- Multi-Criteria Optimization and Compromise Solution (VIKOR)
- Data Envelopment Analysis (DEA)
- Etc

Table 6 shows a brief summary of the studies published using MCDM methods for evaluation energy system.

The study of Papadopoulos & Karagiann (2008) utilized an Electra III method to evaluate four renewable energy sources and decide the best scenario giving to the criteria such as economic feasibility, stability, and CO2 emissions. The paper of Brand and Missaoui (2014) apply the VIKOR method to evaluate five power mix scenarios power generation in Tunisia. Al Garni et al. (2016) used AHP to evaluate five renewable energy sources: solar, wind, biomass, and geothermal in Saudi Arabia according to various criteria economic, technical, environmental, social and political. The ranking results show that photovoltaic is the most favorable technologies. The work of Haddad et al. (2017) used AHP to evaluate and sustainability ranking of renewable energy sources in Algerian.

Software Tools For Hybrid Systems

The simulation is the best common practice, which saves more time and cost for simulating, optimizing and sizing of HES. Several software tools are available for this purpose like HOMER, HYBRID 2, EnergyPLAN, SOMES, TRNSYS16, HOGA, RETScreen. It is inferred from the literature that best applied software tools found in the literature review is Hybrid optimization method for electric renewable (HOMER). HOMER simulates diverse renewable energy source configurations and shorted them on the basis of single objective function for minimizing Net Present Cost (Himri et al., 2008, Askari & Ameri, 2012; Khan et al., 2017). Grid-connection is also considered in HOMER design procedure (Koussa et al., 2011; El-Tous, 2012; Adaramola, 2014; Nurunnabi & Roy, 2015; Usman et al., 2018; Al Garni et al., 2018; Ahmad et al., 2018; Amit et al., 2018). Table 7 shows a brief summary of the studies published using software tools for optimization energy system.

Table 6. Summary of MCDM method for evaluation HES

Author	Method	Objectif	Energy sources									Best configuration
			WT	SPV	STH	BI	HY	GE	FF	BT	GC	
Papadopoulos & Karagiannidis (2008)	ELECTRE III	Economic Technical Environmental	X	X		X		X				WT
Tsoutsos et al. (2009)	PROMETHEE	Economic Technical Environmental Social	X	X		X						WT+SPV+BI
Amer & Daim (2011)	AHP	Economic Technical Environmental Social Political	X	X	X	X						BI
San Cristóbal (2011)	VIKOR	Economic Technical Environmental Social	X	X	X	X	X					BI
Demirtas (2013)	AHP	Economic Technical Environmental Social	X		X	X	X	X				WT
Malik et al. (2014)	AHP	Economic Technical Environmental Social Political	X	X					X	X		SPV+FF

continues on following page

Table 6. Continued

Author	Method	Objectif	Energy sources									Best configuration
			WT	SPV	STH	BI	HY	GE	FF	BT	GC	
Brand and Missaoui (2014)	TOPSIS	Economic Technical Environmental Social	X	X	X				X		X	WT+SPV+STH +GC
Ahmad and Tahar (2014)	AHP	Economic Technical Environmental Social	X	X		X	X				X	SPV+GC
Al Garni et al. (2016)	AHP	Economic Technical Environmental Social Political	X	X	X	X		X			X	SPV+GC
Haddad et al. (2017)	AHP	Economic Technical Environmental Social Political	X	X	X	X	X	X			X	SPV+GC
Lee and Chang (2018)	VIKOR	Economic Technical Environmental Social	X	X		X	X	X			X	HY+GC

WT: Wind Turbine; SPV: Solar Photovoltaic; STH: Solar Thermal; BI: Biomass; HY: Hydropower; GE: Geothermal; FF: Fossil Fuel; BT: Battery; GC: Grid-connected.

Table 7. Summary of few software tools for Optimization HES

Author	Software	Objectives	Energy sources									Best configuration
			WT	SPV	STH	BI	HY	GE	FF	BT	GC	
Himri et al. (2008)	HOMER	Economic	X						X			WT+ FF
Koussa et al. (2011)	HOMER	Economic	X	X							X	WT+SPV+GC
Dufo-López et al. (2011)	HOGA	Economic Environmental	X	X					X	X		WT+SPV+ FF +BT
Panayiotou et al. (2012)	TRNSYS	Economic	X	X						X		SPV+BT
Askari & Ameri (2012)	HOMER	Economic	X	X						X		SPV+BT
El-Tous (2012)	HOMER	Economic		X							X	SPV+GC
Anayochukwu & Nnene (2013)	HOMER	Economic		X					X	X		SPV+ FF +BT
Vani & Khare (2013)	HOMER	Economic	X	X					X	X		WT+SPV+ FF +BT
Sinha & Chandel (2014)	RETScreen	Economic	X	X						X		WT+SPV+BT
Ma et al. (2014)	HOMER	Economic	X	X						X		WT+SPV+BT
Adaramola (2014)	HOMER	Economic		X							X	SPV+GC
Malik et al. (2014)	HOMER	Economic	X	X					X	X		WT+ FF +BT
Olatomiwa et al. (2015)	HOMER	Economic	X	X					X	X		SPV+ FF +BT
Nurunnabi & Roy (2015)	HOMER	Economic	X	X						X	X	WT+SPV+GC
Sawle & Gupta (2015)	HOMER	Economic	X	X					X	X		WT+SPV+BT
Wicaksana et al. (2016)	HOMER	Economic		X					X	X		SPV+ FF +BT
Maatallah et al. (2016)	HOMER	Economic	X	X					X	X	X	WT+SPV+ FF
Khan et al. (2017)	HOMER	Economic	X	X					X	X		WT+SPV+ FF+BT
Usman et al. (2018)	HOMER	Economic		X					X	X	X	SPV+GC

continues on following page

Table 7. Continued

Author	Software	Objectives	Energy sources									Best configuration
			WT	SPV	STH	BI	HY	GE	FF	BT	GC	
Al Garni et al. (2018)	HOMER	Economic		X							X	SPV+GC
Ahmad et al. (2018)	HOMER	Economic	X	X		X					X	WT+SPV+BI+GC
Amit et al. (2018)	HOMER	Economic		X						X	X	SPV+GC
Fulzele & Daigavane (2018)	HOGA	Economic	X	X						X		WT+SPV+BT

WT: Wind Turbine; SPV: Solar Photovoltaic; STH: Solar Thermal; BI: Biomass; HY: Hydropower; GE: Geothermal; FF: Fossil Fuel; BT: Battery; GC: Grid-connected.

Table 8. Summary of Hybrid approaches method for Optimization HES

Author	Method	Objectif	Energy sources									Best configuration
			WT	SPV	STH	BI	HY	GE	FF	BT	GC	
Katsigiannis et al. (2012)	RT /RS	Economic	X	X		X			X	X		WT+SPV+FF +BT
Rojas & Yusta (2015)	VIKOR/ AHP	Economic Technical Environmental Social	X	X			X		X	X	X	SPV+HY+BT
Yahiaoui et al. (2016)	HOMER/ EP	Economic Technical Environmental		X					X	X		SPV+FF+BT
Diemuodeke et al. (2018)	HOMER/ TOPSIS	Economic Technical Environmental Social	X	X					X	X		-WT+SPV+FF+BT -WT+SPV+BT
Vishnupriyan & Manoharan (2018)	HOMER/ AHP	Economic Technical Environmental		X							X	SPV+GC

WT: Wind Turbine; SPV: Solar Photovoltaic; STH: Solar Thermal; BI: Biomass; HY: Hydropower; GE: Geothermal; FF: Fossil Fuel; BT: Battery; GC: Grid-connected.

HYBRID APPROACHES

Hybridization is a method of combining two or more techniques (e.g. Euchi & Frifita (2017), Elleuch et al. (2019)). In recent years, diverse authors have developed hybrid approaches to optimize HES. Table 8 shows a brief summary of the studies published using Hybrid approaches for optimization energy system.

The work of Katsigiannis et al. (2012) used SA and TS, for Optimal Sizing of Autonomous Power Systems with minimum cost. Rojas abd Yusta (2015) apply a combination of two multicriteria decision-making methods to evaluate several HES according to various factors with technical, economic, environmental and social criteria. Yahiaoui et al. (2016) used PSO-simulation based method to optimal sizing of the hybrid wind-Photovoltaic-diesel system with three objectives: minimizing the total cost of the system, the total CO2 emission, and Loss of load probability LLP. The studies of Cayir et al. (2018) implemented a combination of goal programming, fuzzy-TOPSIS, and AHP. It was applied to determinate of energy investment policy for Power Company. Vishnupriyan and Manoharan (2018) applied a techno-economic optimization model based on HOMER simulation and AHP method to improve a HES in Indian state.

Table 9. Summary of advantages and disadvantages of optimization methods.

Method	Advantages	Disadvantages
Mathematical program	-Easy to write code; -Simple and vast application.	-Constraints handing is not satisfactory; -It don't supply a global optimal solution; -Computational time more; -Often trap in local maxima or minima.
Optimization Algorithm (GA, PSO, ACA, SA,TS)	-Find global optima; -Less computational time; -Attain global optimum with relatively computational simplicity; -Vast application; -Easily available in literature; -Suitable for a number of parameters; -More efficient; -Better ability to handle constraints.	-Training procedure required; -Not easy to code, complex structure; for more number of parameter response time increase; -Solution clumps together in similar group; -Long time to come out from local optima. -Premature convergence;
Multi-criteria decision making	-Easy to use; scalable; Analysis can easily adjust to fit many sized problems; -Can adapt to changes in environment; -Capable of handling multiple inputs and outputs; -Simple; allows for any type of weight assignment technique; -Takes uncertainty and vagueness into account.	-Sensitive to inconsistent data; -Needs a lot of input; preferences need to be precise; -Procedure may not be convenient in distribution networks organization.
Software tool	-Easy to use; -Simple, straightforward; -Freely and commercially available; -Professional training not required; -Suitable for multi-objective or mono objective.	-Black box approach; -Algorithm and calculations are not accessible for utilization Simulation one configuration at one time.
Hybrid approaches	-Better convergence; -More competitive as single technique;	-Hard to analyze; -Complex; -Less literature available.

Advantages and Disadvantages of Optimization Methods

Optimization methods applied to hybrid energy system have many benefits but it has various limits.

LOCATION SPECIFIC STUDIES

The HES studies are presently going worldwide, some specific locations where the studies are being carried out include, Egypt (Kamel, 2005), Tunisia (Brand & Missaoui, 2014), Senegal (Bilal et al., 2013), Algeria (Haddad et al., 2017), India (Vani & Khare, 2013), Australia (Clarke et al., 2015), Japan (Ren et al., 2009), Taiwan (Lee & Chen, 2009), Saudi Arabia (Al-Nory & Brodsky., 2014), Malaysia (Theo et al., 2016), Pakistan (Ahmad et al., 2018), mexico (Torres et al., 2014), Texas (Shadmand & Balog, 2014), Nicaragua (Ranaboldo et al., 2015), Crete (Koutroulis & Kolokotsa, 2010), Romania (Catalina et al., 2011), France (Panayiotou et al., 2012), Spain (Carroquino et al., 2015), Switzerland (Lauinger et al., 2016), Turkey (Buyukozkan & Guleryuz, 2016). A summary of location-specific studies for optimization HES have been reported in Table 10.

DESALINATION SPECIFIC STUDIES

In the literature, recently much effort has been dedicated to developing and enhancing systems for hybrid reverse osmosis (RO) desalination that use various energy technologies from solar Photovoltaic, Solar Thermal, wind, geothermal, grid connection diesel, battery power or other sources. However, we present some studies of energy systems modeling such as wind energy (Miranda & Infield, 2003; Dehmas et al., 2011), Photovoltaic energy systems (Georgiou et al., 2015 ; Ahmad et al., 2015; Esfahani & Yoo, 2016), Photovoltaic/wind (Cherif & Belhadj, 2011), wind/battery (Bourouni et al., 2011; Caldera et al., 2016; Cabrera et al., 2018), Photovoltaic/battery (Clarke et al., 2015 ; Monnot et al., 2018; Mostafaeipour et al., 2019), wind/Photovoltaic/battery (Koutroulis & Kolokotsa, 2010; Zhang et al., 2018), Photovoltaic /diesel (Bilton et al., 2011;), wind/Photovoltaic/diesel (Setiawan et al., 2009; Novosel et al., 2015; Lai et al., 2016), Photovoltaic/diesel/battery (Wu et al., 2018), wind/Photovoltaic/diesel/battery (Gökçek, 2018; Padrón et al., 2019), wind/Grid (Kershman, 2003), Photovoltaic/Grid (Voivontas et al., 2001; Jones et al., 2016) and Photovoltaic/wind/Grid/diesel (Rheinländer et al., 2003). Table 11 shows a brief summary of the studies published for optimization energy system in desalination plants.

Table 10. Summary of some location specific for Optimization HES

Continent	Country	Applications				Approaches / software	Author
		Domestic	Industry	Commercial	Agriculture		
Africa	Egypt				X	HOMER	Kamel (2005)
	Tunisia		X			GA	Bourouni et al. (2011)
	Senegal	X		X		GA	Bilal et al. (2013)
	tunisia		X			TOPSIS	Brand & Missaoui (2014)
	Algeria	X	X			AHP	Haddad et al. (2017)
Asia	India			X		LP/DELPHI	Iniyan & Sumathy (2003)
	Australia			X		HOMER	Dalton et al. (2009)
	Japan	X				LP /AHP, PROMETHEE	Ren et al. (2009)
	Taiwan			X		PSO	Lee & Chen (2009)
	Saudi Arabia		X			NPL	Al-Nory & Brodsky (2014)
	India	X				HOMER	Vani & Khare (2013)
	Australia		X			PSO, HOMER	Clarke et al. (2015)
	Malaysia	X	X			MILP	Theo et al. (2016)
	Iran		X			GA	Janghorban & Yoo (2016)
	Jordan				X	HOMER	Jones et al. (2016)
	Iran	X				PSO	Maleki et al. (2017)
	India	X		X		HOMER/AHP	Vishnupriyan & Manoharan (2018)
	Pakistan	X		X		HOMER	Ahmad et al. (2018)

continues on following page

Table 10. Continued

Continent	Country	Applications				Approaches / software	Author
		Domestic	Industry	Commercial	Agriculture		
America	Mexico	X				LP	Torres et al. (2014)
	Texas	X				GA	Shadmand & Balog (2014)
	Nicaragua	X				HOMER	Ranaboldo et al. (2015)
Europe	Crete	X				GA	Koutroulis & Kolokotsa (2010)
	France	X				ELECTRE III	Catalina et al. (2011)
	France	X				TRNSYS	Panayiotou et al. (2012)
	Spain				X	GA	Carroquino et al. (2015)
	Switzerland	X				LP	Lauinger et al. (2016)
	Turkey	X				Fuzzy AHP/Fuzzy TOPSIS	Buyukozkan & Guleryuz (2016)

Table 11. Summary of various approaches to improve HES in desalination plants

Author	Method	Objectif	Energy sources									Best configuration
			WT	SPV	STH	BI	HY	GE	FF	BT	GC	
Koutroulis & Kolokotsa (2010)	GA	Economic	X	X						X		WI+SPV+BT
Bourouni et al. (2011)	GA/ HOMER	Economic	X	X						X		WI+BT
Menshsari et al. (2013)	ACA	Economic	X	X			X		X	X		WI+SPV+ FF +BT
Al-Nory & Brodsky (2014)	NLP	Economic	X	X				X			X	WI+SPV+GE+GC
Al-Nory & El-Beltagy (2014)	LP	Economic	X	X				X			X	WI+SPV+GE+GC
Askarzadeh et al. (2015)	GA	Economic	X	X					X	X		WI+SPV+BT
Georgiou et al. (2015)	AHP, PROMETHEE	Economic Technical Environmental Social	X	X					X	X		SPV
Clarke et al. (2015)	PSO, HOMER	Economic Environmental		X						X		SPV+BT
Esfahani & Yoo (2016)	GA	Economic		X								SPV
Jones et al. (2016)	HOMER	Economic		X					X		X	SPV+GC
Gökçek (2018)	PSO/HOMER	Economic	X	X					X	X		WI+SPV+ FF +BT
Zhang et al. (2018)	SA	Economic	X	X						X		WI+SPV+BT
Wu et al. (2018)	TS	Economic		X					X	X		SPV+FF+BT

WT: Wind Turbine; SPV: Solar Photovoltaic; STH: Solar Thermal; BI: Biomass; HY: Hydropower; GE: Geothermal; FF: Fossil Fuel; BT: Battery; GC: Grid-connected.

Koutroulis & Kolokotsa (2010) applied GA to determine optimal sizes desalination systems power-supplied by wind, photovoltaic and battery was determined to minimize cost. Georgiou et al. (2015) used AHP and PROMETHEE to evaluate five alternatives energy generation developed in a desalination unit in Jordan. Gökçek (2018) used HOMER software to evaluate seven alternatives (off-grid) power systems (wind-photovoltaic-diesel-battery) to provide electricity for an RO system to meet the fresh water demand on Bozcaada Island, Turkey. Wu et al. (2018) applied TS to optimal sizing of a reverse osmosis desalination based on photovoltaic and diesel energy plant for growing potable water availability and meeting the electrical load demand in Iran.

CONCLUSION

In the current era of sustainable development, energy planning has become complex due to the involvement of multiple benchmarks like economic, technical, social, environmental and Political. This chapter presents a review of the solution approaches for determining the HES systems, considering two principal classifications are stand-alone and grid-connected systems. There are various modeling and optimization techniques of operations research used on HES systems, containing of optimization approaches, multi-criteria decision making, simulation, and hybrid approaches. This study encompasses the selected journal papers published especially in the last ten years. Other approaches will be considered in future research to improve HES. For our future works would be necessary to better adapt the innovative hybrid approaches to optimize HES with various factors such as economic, social, technical, environmental and health impact.

REFERENCES

Adaramola, M. S. (2014). Viability of grid-connected solar PV energy system in Jos, Nigeria. *International Journal of Electrical Power & Energy Systems*, *61*, 64–69.

Adefarati, T., & Bansal, R. C. (2016). Integration of renewable distributed generators into the distribution system: A review. *IET Renewable Power Generation*, *10*(7), 873–884.

Agarwala, N., & Kumarb, A. (2012). Sizing Analysis and Cost Optimization of Hybrid Solar-Diesel-Battery Based Electric Power Generation System Using Simulated Annealing Technique. *Distributed Generation & Alternative Energy Journal*, *27*(3), 26–51.

Ahmad, J., Imran, M., Khalid, A., Iqbal, W., Ashraf, S. R., Adnan, M., ... Khokhar, K. S. (2018). Techno-economic analysis of a wind-photovoltaic-biomass hybrid renewable energy system for rural electrification: A case study of Kallar Kahar. *Energy*, *148*, 208–234.

Ahmad, N., Sheikh, A. K., Gandhidasan, P., & Elshafie, M. (2015). Modeling, simulation and performance evaluation of a community scale PVRO water desalination system operated by fixed and tracking PV panels: A case study for Dhahran city, Saudi Arabia. *Renewable Energy*, *75*, 433–447.

Ahmad, S., & Tahar, R. M. (2014). Selection of renewable energy sources for sustainable development of electricity generation system using the analytic hierarchy process: A case of Malaysia. *Renewable Energy*, *63*, 458–466.

Al Garni, H., Kassem, A., Awasthi, A., Komljenovic, D., & Al-Haddad, K. (2016). A multicriteria decision-making approach for evaluating renewable power generation sources in Saudi Arabia. *Sustainable Energy Technologies and Assessments*, *16*, 137–150.

Al Garni, H. Z., Awasthi, A., & Ramli, M. A. M. (2018). Optimal design and analysis of grid-connected photovoltaic under different tracking systems using HOMER. *Energy Conversion and Management*, *155*, 42–57.

Al-Nory, M., & El-Beltagy, M. (2014). An energy management approach for renewable energy integration with power generation and water desalination. *Renewable Energy*, *72*, 377–385.

Al-Nory, M. T., & Brodsky, A. (2014). Towards Optimal Decision Guidance for Smart Grids with Integrated Renewable Generation and Water Desalination. *Proceedings of the IEEE 26th International Conference on Tools with Artificial Intelligence*. IEEE.

Amer, M., & Daim, T. U. (2011). Selection of renewable energy technologies for a developing county: A case of Pakistan. *Energy for Sustainable Development*, *15*(4), 420–435.

Amer, M., Namaane, A., & M'Sirdi, N. K. (2013). Optimization of Hybrid Renewable Energy Systems (HRES) Using PSO for Cost Reduction. *Energy Procedia*, *42*, 318–327.

Amit, K. P., Md. Rakibul, H., Narruttam, K. R., & Md. Mostafizur, R. K. (2018). Economic Analysis of a Grid Connected PV Systems: A Case Study in Khulna. *European Journal of Engineering Research and Science*, *3*(7).

Anayochukwu, A. V., & Nnene, E. A. (2013). Simulation and Optimization of Photovoltaic/Diesel Hybrid Power Generation Systems for Health Service Facilities in Rural Environments. *Electronic Journal of Energy and Environment*, *1*(1), 57–70.

Ardakani, F. J., Riahy, G., & Abedi, M. (2010). Design of an optimum hybrid renewable energy system considering reliability indices. *Proceedings of the 18th IEEE Iranian Conference on Electrical Engineering (ICEE)* (pp. 842-847). IEEE.

Ashok, S. (2007). Optimized model for community-based hybrid energy system. *Renewable Energy*, *32*(7), 1155–1164.

Asif, M. (2017). Fundamentals and Application of Solar Thermal Technologies. In Encyclopedia of Sustainable Technologies (pp. 27–36). Academic Press. doi:10.1016/b978-0-12-409548-9.10093-4

Askari, I. B., & Ameri, M. (2012). Techno-economic Feasibility Analysis of Stand-alone Renewable Energy Systems (PV/bat, Wind/bat, and Hybrid PV/wind/bat) in Kerman, Iran. *Energy Sources. Part B, Economics, Planning, and Policy*, *7*(1), 45–60.

Askarzadeh, A., & dos Santos Coelho, L. (2015). A novel framework for optimization of a grid-independent hybrid renewable energy system: A case study of Iran. *Solar Energy*, *112*, 383–396.

Babu, N. R., & Arulmozhivarman, P. (2013). Wind Energy Conversion Systems-A Technical Review. *Journal of Engineering Science and Technology*, *8*(4), 493–507.

Bashir, M., & Sadeh, J. (2012). Optimal sizing of hybrid wind/photovoltaic/battery considering the uncertainty of wind and photovoltaic power using Monte Carlo. *Proceedings of the 11th IEEE International Conference on Environment and Electrical Engineering (EEEIC)* (pp. 1081-1086). IEEE.

Bilal, B. O., Nourou, D., Kébé, C. M. F., Sambou, V., Ndiaye, P. A., & Ndongo, M. (2015). Multi-objective optimization of hybrid PV/wind/diesel/battery systems for decentralized application by minimizing the levelized cost of energy and the CO2 emissions. *International Journal of Physical Sciences*, *10*(5), 192–203.

Bilal, B. O., Sambou, V., Ndiaye, P. A., Kébé, C. M. F., & Ndongo, M. (2013). Study of the Influence of Load Profile Variation on the Optimal Sizing of a Standalone Hybrid PV/Wind/Battery/Diesel System. *Energy Procedia*, *36*, 1265–1275.

Bilton, A. M., Wiesman, R., Arif, A. F. M., Zubair, S. M., & Dubowsky, S. (2011). On the feasibility of community-scale photovoltaic-powered reverse osmosis desalination systems for remote locations. *Renewable Energy*, *36*(12), 3246–3256.

Bourouni, K., Ben M'Barek, T., & Al Taee, A. (2011). Design and optimization of desalination reverse osmosis plants driven by renewable energies using genetic algorithms. *Renewable Energy*, *36*(3), 936–950.

Brand, B., & Missaoui, R. (2014). Multi-criteria analysis of electricity generation mix scenarios in Tunisia. *Renewable & Sustainable Energy Reviews*, *39*, 251–261.

Buyukozkan, G., & Guleryuz, S. (2016). Fuzzy Multi-Criteria Decision Making Approach for Evaluating Sustainable Energy Technology Alternatives. *International Journal of Renewable Energy Sources*, *1*, 1–6.

Cabrera, P., Carta, J. A., González, J., & Melián, G. (2018). Wind-driven SWRO desalination prototype with and without batteries: A performance simulation using machine learning models. *Desalination*, *435*, 77–96.

Caldera, U., Bogdanov, D., & Breyer, C. (2016). Local cost of seawater RO desalination based on solar PV and wind energy: A global estimate. *Desalination*, *385*, 207–216.

Carroquino, J., Dufo-López, R., & Bernal-Agustín, J. L. (2015). Sizing of off-grid renewable energy systems for drip irrigation in Mediterranean crops. *Renewable Energy*, *76*, 566–574.

Catalina, T., Virgone, J., & Blanco, E. (2011). Multi-source energy systems analysis using a multi-criteria decision aid methodology. *Renewable Energy*, *36*(8), 2245–2252.

Cherif, H., & Belhadj, J. (2011). Large-scale time evaluation for energy estimation of stand-alone hybrid photovoltaic–wind system feeding a reverse osmosis desalination unit. *Energy*, *36*(10), 6058–6067.

Clarke, D. P., Al-Abdeli, Y. M., & Kothapalli, G. (2015). Multi-objective optimization of renewable hybrid energy systems with desalination. *Energy*, *88*, 457–468.

Dalton, G. J., Lockington, D. A., & Baldock, T. E. (2009). Feasibility analysis of renewable energy supply options for a grid-connected large hotel. *Renewable Energy*, *34*(4), 955–964.

Dehmas, D. A., Kherba, N., Hacene, F. B., Merzouk, N. K., Merzouk, M., Mahmoudi, H., & Goosen, M. F. A. (2011). On the use of wind energy to power reverse osmosis desalination plant: A case study from Ténès (Algeria). *Renewable & Sustainable Energy Reviews*, *15*(2), 956–963.

Demirtas, O. (2013). Evaluating the Best Renewable Energy Technology for Sustainable Energy Planning. *International Journal of Energy Economics and Policy*, *3*, 23–33.

Diemuodeke, E. O., Addo, A., Oko, C. O. C., Mulugetta, Y., & Ojapah, M. M. (2018). Optimal Mapping of Hybrid Renewable Energy Systems for Locations Using Multi-Criteria Decision-Making Algorithm. *Renewable Energy*, 134, 461–477.

Dorigo, M., & Gambardella, L. M. (1997). Ant colony system: A cooperative learning approach to the traveling salesman problem. *IEEE Transactions on Evolutionary Computation*, *1*(1), 53–66.

Dufo-López, R., Bernal-Agustín, J. L., Yusta-Loyo, J. M., Domínguez-Navarro, J. A., Ramírez-Rosado, I. J., Lujano, J., & Aso, I. (2011). Multi-objective optimization minimizing cost and life cycle emissions of stand-alone PV–wind–diesel systems with batteries storage. *Applied Energy*, *88*(11), 4033–4041.

Eberhart, R., & Kennedy, J. (1995). A new optimizer using particle swarm theory. *IEEE MHS*, *95*, 39–43.

Eke, R., Kara, O., & Ulgen, K. (2005). Optimization of a wind/PV hybrid power generation system. *International Journal of Green Energy*, *2*(1), 57–63.

Ekren, O., & Ekren, B. Y. (2010). Size optimization of a PV/wind hybrid energy conversion system with battery storage using simulated annealing. *Applied Energy*, *87*(2), 592–598.

El Kafazi, I., Bannari, R., Adiba, E. B. E. I., Nabil, H., & Dragicevic, T. (2017). Renewable energies: Modeling and optimization of production cost. *Energy Procedia*, *136*, 380–387.

El-Tous, Y. (2012). A Study of a Grid-connected PV Household System in Amman and the Effect of the Incentive Tariff on the Economic Feasibility. *International Journal of Applied Science and Technology*, *2*(2).

Elleuch, M. A., Anane, M., Euchi, J., & Frikha, A. (2019). Hybrid fuzzy multi-criteria decision making to solve the irrigation water allocation problem in the Tunisian case. *Agricultural Systems*, *176*, 102644.

Elleuch, M. A., Elleuch, L., & Frikha, A. (2019). A hybrid approach for water resources management in Tunisia. *International Journal of Water*, *13*(1), 80.

Elleuch, M. A., & Frikha, A. (2018). Combining the PROMETHEE method and mathematical programming for multi-objective facility location problem. *International Journal of Multicriteria Decision Making*, *7*(3/4), 195.

Esfahani, I. J., & Yoo, C. (2016). An optimization algorithm-based pinch analysis and GA for an off-grid batteryless photovoltaic-powered reverse osmosis desalination system. *Renewable Energy*, *91*, 233–248.

Euchi, J. (2017). Genetic scatter search algorithm to solve the one commodity Pickup and Delivery Vehicle Routing Problem. *Journal of Modelling in Management, 12*(1), 2–18.

Euchi, J., & Chabchoub, H. (2009). Tabu Search metaheuristic embedded in Adaptive Memory Procedure for the Profitable Arc Tour Problem. *IFAC Proceedings Volumes, 42*(4), 990–995.

Euchi, J., & Frifita, S. (2017). Hybrid metaheuristics to solve the one to - many to - one problem: The case of distribution of soft drink in Tunisia. *Management Decision, 55*(1), 136–155.

Euchi, J., Moussi, R., Ndiaye, F., & Yassine, A. (2016). Ant Colony Optimization for Solving the Container Stacking Problem. *International Journal of Applied Logistics, 6*(2), 81–101.

Fetanat, A., & Khorasaninejad, E. (2015). Size optimization for hybrid photovoltaic–wind energy system using ant colony optimization for continuous domains based integer programming. *Applied Soft Computing, 31*, 196–209.

Fulzele, J. B., & Daigavane, M. B. (2018). Design and Optimization of Hybrid PV-Wind Renewable Energy System. *Materials Today: Proceedings, 5*(1), 810–818.

Georgiou, D., Mohammed, E. S., & Rozakis, S. (2015). Multi-criteria decision making on the energy supply configuration of autonomous desalination units. *Renewable Energy, 75*, 459–467.

Glover, F., & Laguna, M. (1999). *Tabu search*. US: Springer.

Goffé, J., & Ferrasse, J. H. (2019). Stoichiometry impact on the optimum efficiency of biomass conversion to biofuels. *Energy, 170*, 438–458.

Gökçek, M. (2018). Integration of hybrid power (wind-photovoltaic-diesel-battery) and seawater reverse osmosis systems for small-scale desalination applications. *Desalination, 435*, 210–220.

Gokul, B., Suresh, M., & Meenakumari, R. (2017). Optimal Sizing of Hybrid System for Standalone application using Genetic Algorithm. *World Journal of Engineering Research and Technology WJERT, 3*(2), 45–56.

Haddad, B., Liazid, A., & Ferreira, P. (2017). A multi-criteria approach to rank renewables for the Algerian electricity system. *Renewable Energy, 107*, 462–472.

Himri, Y., Stambouli, A. B., Draoui, B., & Himri, S. (2008). Techno-economical study of the hybrid power system for a remote village in Algeria. *Energy, 33*(7), 1128–1136.

Holland, J. (1975). *Adaptation in natural and artificial systems*. Cambridge, MA: MIT Press.

Hong, Y.-Yi., & Lian, R.-C. (2012). Optimal sizing of hybrid wind/PV/diesel generation in a stand-alone power system using a Markov-based genetic algorithm. *IEEE Transactions on Power Delivery*, *27*(2), 640–647.

Huneke, F., Henkel, J., González, J. A. B., & Erdmann, G. (2012). Optimisation of hybrid off-grid energy systems by linear programming. *Energy, Sustainability and Society*, *2*(1), 7.

IEA. (2017). *Key World Energy Statistics*. International Energy Agency.

Inglesi-Lotz, R. (2016). The impact of renewable energy consumption to economic growth: A panel data application. *Energy Economics*, *53*, 58–63.

Iniyan, S., & Sumathy, K. (2003). The application of a Delphi technique in the linear programming optimization of future renewable energy options for India. *Biomass and Bioenergy*, *24*(1), 39–50.

Janghorban, E. I., & Yoo, C. (2016). An optimization algorithm-based pinch analysis and GA for an off-grid batteryless photovoltaic-powered reverse osmosis desalination system. *Renewable Energy*, *91*, 233–248.

Jones, M. A., Odeh, I., Haddad, M., Mohammad, A. H., & Quinn, J. C. (2016). Economic analysis of photovoltaic (PV) powered water pumping and desalination without energy storage for agriculture. *Desalination*, *387*, 35–45.

Kakkar, V., & Nirmal, K.A., & Narendra, K. (2012). Geothermal energy: New prospects. *International Journal of Advances in Engineering and Technology*, 4(2).

Kamel, S. (2005). The economics of hybrid power systems for sustainable desert agriculture in Egypt. *Energy*, *30*(8), 1271–1281.

Katsigiannis, Y. A., & Georgilakis, P. S. (2008). Optimal sizing of small isolated hybrid power systems using Tabu search. *Optoelectron Adv. Mater.*, *10*(5), 1241–1245.

Katsigiannis, Y. A., Georgilakis, P. S., & Karapidakis, E. S. (2012). Hybrid simulated annealing–tabu search method for optimal sizing of autonomous power systems with renewables. *IEEE Transactions on Sustainable Energy*, *3*(3), 330–338.

Kaundinya, D. P., Balachandra, P., & Ravindranath, N. H. (2009). Grid-connected versus stand-alone energy systems for decentralized power. *Renewable & Sustainable Energy Reviews*, *13*(8), 2041–2050.

Kershman, S. A., Rheinländer, J., & Gabler, H. (2003). Seawater reverse osmosis powered from renewable energy sources - hybrid wind/photovoltaic/grid power supply for small-scale desalination in Libya. *Desalination*, *153*(1-3), 17–23.

Khan, M. J., Yadav, A. K., & Mathew, L. (2017). Techno-economic feasibility analysis of different combinations of PV-Wind-Diesel-Battery hybrid system for telecommunication applications in different cities of Punjab, India. *Renewable & Sustainable Energy Reviews*, *76*, 577–607.

Kirkpatrick, S. (1984). Optimization by simulated annealing: Quantitative studies. *Journal of Statistical Physics*, *34*(5–6), 975–986.

Koussa, S. D., Koussa, M., Belhamel, M., & Haddadi, M. (2011). Economic and environmental analysis for the grid-connected hybrid photovoltaic-wind power system in the arid region. *Energy Procedia*, *6*, 361–370.

Koutroulis, E., & Kolokotsa, D. (2010). Design optimization of desalination systems power supplied by PV and W/G energy sources. *Desalination*, *258*(1–3), 171–181.

Kumar, R. R., & Bhusan, R. B. (2014). Optimal Design of A Hybrid PV-Wind Energy System Using Genetic Algorithm (GA). *International Journal of Engineering Research & Technology*, *3*(1).

Lai, W., Ma, Q., Lu, H., Weng, S., Fan, J., & Fang, H. (2016). Effects of wind intermittence and fluctuation on reverse osmosis desalination process and solution strategies. *Desalination*, *395*, 17–27.

Lauinger, D., & Caliandro, P., Van Herle J., & Kuhn, D. (2016). A linear programming approach to the optimization of residential energy systems. *Journal of Energy Storage*, *7*, 24–37.

Lee, H. C., & Chang, C. T. (2018). Comparative analysis of MCDM methods for ranking renewable energy sources in Taiwan. *Renewable & Sustainable Energy Reviews*, *92*, 883–896.

Lee, T. Y., & Chen, C. L. (2009). Wind-photovoltaic capacity coordination for a time-of-use rate industrial user. *IET Renewable Power Generation*, *3*(2), 152–167.

Ma, T., Yang, H., & Lu, L. (2014). A feasibility study of a stand-alone hybrid solar–wind–battery system for a remote island. *Applied Energy*, *121*, 149–158.

Maatallah, T., Ghodhbane, N., & Ben Nasrallah, S. (2016). Assessment viability for hybrid energy system (PV/wind/diesel) with storage in the northernmost city in Africa, Bizerte, Tunisia. *Renewable & Sustainable Energy Reviews*, *59*, 1639–1652.

Maleki, A., Ameri, M., & Keynia, F. (2015). Scrutiny of multifarious particle swarm optimization for finding the optimal size of a PV/wind/battery hybrid system. *Renewable Energy*, *80*, 552–563.

Maleki, A., Rosen, M., & Pourfayaz, F. (2017). Optimal Operation of a Grid-Connected Hybrid Renewable Energy System for Residential Applications. *Sustainability*, *9*(8), 1314.

Malik, A., Al Badi, M., Al Kahali, A., Al Nabhani, Y., Al Bahri, A., & Al Barhi, H. (2014). Evaluation of renewable energy projects using multi-criteria approach. *Proceedings of the IEEE Global Humanitarian Technology Conference (GHTC)*. IEEE.

Menshsari, A., Ghiamy, M., Mousavi, M. M. M., & Bagal, H. A. (2013). Optimal design of hybrid water–wind–solar system based on hydrogen storage and evaluation of reliability index of a system using ant colony algorithm. *International Research Journal of Applied and Basic Sciences*, *4*(10), 3582–3600.

Merei, G., Berger, C., & Sauer, D. U. (2013). Optimization of an off-grid hybrid PV–Wind–Diesel system with different battery technologies using genetic algorithm. *Solar Energy*, *97*, 460–473.

Miranda, M. S., & Infield, D. (2003). A wind-powered seawater reverse-osmosis system without batteries. *Desalination*, *153*, 1–3.

Mohamed, M. A., Eltamaly, A. M., & Alolah, A. I. (2016). PSO-Based Smart Grid Application for Sizing and Optimization of Hybrid Renewable Energy Systems. *PLoS One*, *11*(8). PMID:27513000

Monnot, M., Carvajal, G. D. M., Laborie, S., Cabassud, C., & Lebrun, R. (2018). Integrated approach in eco-design strategy for small RO desalination plants powered by photovoltaic energy. *Desalination*, *435*, 246–258.

Mostafaeipour, A., Qolipour, M., Rezaei, M., & Babaee-Tirkolaee, E. (2019). Investigation of off-grid photovoltaic systems for a reverse osmosis desalination system: A case study. *Desalination*, *454*, 91–103.

Nafeh, A. E.-S. A. (2011). Optimal Economical Sizing Of A PV-Wind Hybrid Energy System Using Genetic Algorithm. *International Journal of Green Energy*, *8*(1), 25–43.

Novosel, T., Ćosić, B., Pukšec, T., Krajačić, G., Duić, N., Mathiesen, B. V., ... Mustafa, M. (2015). Integration of renewables and reverse osmosis desalination – Case study for the Jordanian energy system with a high share of wind and photovoltaics. *Energy*, *92*, 270–278.

Nurunnabi, M., & Roy, N. K. (2015). Grid-connected hybrid power system design using HOMER. *Proceedings of the International Conference on Advances in Electrical Engineering (ICAEE)*.

Olatomiwa, L., Mekhilef, S., Huda, A. S. N., & Ohunakin, O. S. (2015). Economic evaluation of hybrid energy systems for rural electrification in six geopolitical zones of Nigeria. *Renewable Energy*, *83*, 435–446.

Padrón, I., Avila, D., Marichal, G. N., & Rodríguez, J. A. (2019). Assessment of Hybrid Renewable Energy Systems to supplied energy to Autonomous Desalination Systems in two islands of the Canary Archipelago. *Renewable & Sustainable Energy Reviews*, *101*, 221–230.

Paliwal, P., Patidar, N. P., & Nema, R. K. (2014). Determination of reliability constrained optimal resource mix for an autonomous hybrid power system using Particle Swarm Optimization. *Renewable Energy*, *63*, 194–204.

Panayiotou, G., Kalogirou, S., & Tassou, S. (2012). Design and simulation of a PV and a PV–Wind standalone energy system to power a household application. *Renewable Energy*, *37*(1), 355–363.

Papadopoulos, A., & Karagiannidis, A. (2008). Application of the multi-criteria analysis method Electra III for the optimization of decentralized energy systems. *Omega*, *36*(5), 766–776.

Pirhaghshenasvali, M., & Asaei, B. (2014). Optimal modeling and sizing of a practical hybrid wind/PV/diesel generation system. *Proceedings of the 5th Annual International Power Electronics, Drive Systems, and Technologies Conference (PEDSTC 2014)*. Academic Press.

Ranaboldo, M., Domenech, B., Reyes, G. A., Ferrer-Martí, L., Pastor Moreno, R., & García-Villoria, A. (2015). Off-grid community electrification projects based on wind and solar energies: A case study in Nicaragua. *Solar Energy*, *117*, 268–281.

Ren, H., Gao, W., Zhou, W., & Nakagami, K. (2009). Multi-criteria evaluation for the optimal adoption of distributed residential energy systems in Japan. *Energy Policy*, *37*(12), 5484–5493.

Rheinländer, J., Perz, E. W., & Goebel, O. (2003). Performance simulation of integrated water and power systems — software tools IPSEpro and RESYSpro for technical, economic and ecological analysis. *Desalination*, *157*(1-3), 57–64.

Riffonneau, Y., Bacha, S., Barruel, F., & Ploix, S. (2011). Optimal Power Flow Management for Grid-Connected PV Systems with Batteries. *IEEE Transactions on Sustainable Energy*, *2*(3), 309–320.

Rojas-Zerpa, J. C., & Yusta, J. M. (2015). Application of multicriteria decision methods for electric supply planning in rural and remote areas. *Renewable & Sustainable Energy Reviews*, *52*, 557–571.

Saif, A., Elrab, K. G., Zeineldin, H. H., Kennedy, S., & Kirtley, J. L. (2010). Multi-objective capacity planning of a PV-wind-diesel-battery hybrid power system. *Proceedings of the IEEE International Energy Conference*. IEEE.

San Cristóbal, J. R. (2011). Multi-criteria decision-making in the selection of a renewable energy project in Spain: The Vikor method. *Renewable Energy*, *36*(2), 498–502.

Sawle, Y., & Gupta, S. C. (2015). A novel system optimization of a grid-independent hybrid renewable energy system for telecom base station. *International Journal of Soft Computing, Mathematics, and Control*, *4*(2), 49–57.

Sawle, Y., Gupta, S. C., & Bohre, A. K. (2017). Optimal sizing of standalone PV/Wind/Biomass hybrid energy system using GA and PSO optimization technique. *Energy Procedia*, *117*, 690–698.

Setiawan, A. A., Zhao, Y., & Nayar, C. V. (2009). Design, economic analysis and environmental considerations of mini-grid hybrid power system with reverse osmosis desalination plant for remote areas. *Renewable Energy*, *34*(2), 374–383.

Shadmand, M. B., & Balog, R. S. (2014). Multi-objective optimization and design of a photovoltaic-wind hybrid system for community smart DC microgrid. *IEEE Transactions on Smart Grid*, *5*(5), 2635–2643.

Shang, C., Srinivasan, D., & Reindl, T. (2016). An improved particle swarm optimisation algorithm applied to battery sizing for stand-alone hybrid power systems. *International Journal of Electrical Power & Energy Systems*, *74*, 104–117.

Sharma, S., Waldman, J., Afshari, S., & Fekete, B. (2019). Status, trends and significance of American hydropower in the changing energy landscape. *Renewable & Sustainable Energy Reviews*, *101*, 112–122.

Shmelev, S. E., & van den Bergh, J. C. J. M. (2016). Optimal diversity of renewable energy alternatives under multiple criteria: An application to the UK. *Renewable & Sustainable Energy Reviews*, *60*, 679–691.

Singh, S., Singh, M., & Kaushik, S. C. (2016). A review of optimization techniques for sizing of solar-wind hybrid energy systems. *International Journal of Green Energy*, *13*(15), 1564–1578.

Sinha, S., & Chandel, S. S. (2014). Review of software tools for hybrid renewable energy systems. *Renewable & Sustainable Energy Reviews*, *32*, 192–205.

Suhane, P., Rangnekar, S., & Mittal, A. (2014). Optimal Sizing of Hybrid Energy System using Ant Colony Optimization. *International Journal of Renewable Energy Research*, *4*(3).

Supriya, C. S., & Siddarthan, M. (2011). Optimization and sizing of a grid-connected hybrid PV-Wind energy system. *International Journal of Engineering Science and Technology*, *3*(5).

Tégani, I., Aboubou, A., Ayad, M. Y., Becherif, M., Saadi, R., & Kraa, O. (2014). Optimal Sizing Design and Energy Management of Stand-alone Photovoltaic/Wind Generator Systems. *Energy Procedia*, *50*, 163–170.

Tegani, I., Aboubou, A., Becherif, M., Ayad, M. Y., Kraa, O., Bahri, M., & Akhrif, O. (2013). Optimal sizing study of hybrid wind/PV/diesel power generation unit using genetic algorithm. *Proceedings of the 4th International Conference on Power Engineering, Energy and Electrical Drives*. Academic Press.

Theo, W. L., Lim, J. S., Wan Alwi, S. R., Mohammad Rozali, N. E., Ho, W. S., & Abdul-Manan, Z. (2016). A MILP model for cost-optimal planning of an on-grid hybrid power system for an eco-industrial park. *Energy*, *116*, 1423–1441.

Torres, D., Crichigno, J., Padilla, G., & Rivera, R. (2014). Scheduling coupled photovoltaic, battery and conventional energy sources to maximize profit using linear programming. *Renewable Energy*, *72*, 284–290.

Tsoutsos, T., Drandaki, M., Frantzeskaki, N., Iosifidis, E., & Kiosses, I. (2009). Sustainable energy planning by using multi-criteria analysis application on the island of Crete. *Energy Policy*, *37*(5), 1587–1600.

Twaha, S., & Ramli, M. A. M. (2018). A review of optimization approaches for hybrid distributed energy generation systems: Off-grid and grid-connected systems. *Sustainable Cities and Society*, *41*, 320–331.

Usman, M., Khan, M. T., Rana, A. S., & Ali, S. (2018). Techno-economic analysis of hybrid solar-diesel-grid connected power generation system. *Journal of Electrical Systems and Information Technology*, *5*(3), 653–662.

Vani, N., & Khare, V. (2013). Rural electrification system based on hybrid energy system model optimization using HOMER. Canadian Journal of Basic dan Applied Sciences, 1(1), 19-25.

VanOverstraeten, R., & Mertens, R. (1986). *Physics, technology and use of photovoltaics*. Bristol: Dam Hilger Ltd.

Vijay, R., & Durga, D. J. (2017). Optimal placement and sizing of wind-pv integrated power generation by ant colony optimization technique. *International Journal of Recent Trends in Engineering & Research*, *3*(5), 2455–1457.

Vishnupriyan, J., & Manoharan, P. S. (2018). Multi-criteria decision analysis for renewable energy integration: A southern India focus. *Renewable Energy*, *121*, 474–488.

Voivontas, D., Misirlis, K., Manoli, E., Arampatzis, G., & Assimacopoulos, D. (2001). A tool for the design of desalination plants powered by renewable energies. *Desalination*, *133*(2), 175–198.

Wicaksana, H., Muslim, M. M., Hutapea, S. F., Purwadi, A., & Haroen, Y. (2016). Design, implementation and techno-economic analysis of hybrid PV-Diesel for Off-grid system in Sebira Island. *Proceedings of the 2016 3rd Conference on Power Engineering and Renewable Energy (ICPERE)*. Academic Press.

Wu, B., Maleki, A., Pourfayaz, F., & Rosen, M. A. (2018). Optimal design of stand-alone reverse osmosis desalination driven by a photovoltaic and diesel generator hybrid system. *Solar Energy*, *163*, 91–103.

Yahiaoui, A., Benmansour, K., & Tadjine, M. (2016). Control, analysis, and optimization of hybrid PV-Diesel-Battery systems for the isolated rural city in Algeria. *Solar Energy*, *137*, 1–10.

Zhang, G., Wu, B., Maleki, A., & Zhang, W. (2018). Simulated annealing-chaotic search algorithm based optimization of reverse osmosis hybrid desalination system driven by wind and solar energies. *Solar Energy*, *173*, 964–975.

Chapter 4
A Variable Neighborhood Search Algorithm to Solve the Flow Shop-Scheduling Problem Through Blocking:
Variable Neighborhood Search (VNS)

Dalel Bouzidi
Sfax University, Tunisia

ABSTRACT

In this chapter, we deal with the flow shop-scheduling problem through blocking known to be difficult, where there is no space and a task remains blocked on a machine until the next machine is available. For this reason, we propose the heuristic approach to minimize the delay (tardiness) as an optimization criterion. This chapter proposes a VNS-based heuristic the solutions of which are compared to those of the metaheuristic Greedy Randomized Adaptive Search Procedure (GRASP). We have developed a heuristic-based VNS to get better solutions in a reasonable time. Finally, comparisons with optimal solutions for small problems have shown that all versions can give good results; it would be interesting to extend the ideas presented in this document to the blocking flow shop at minimizing the total delay.

DOI: 10.4018/978-1-7998-0268-6.ch004

INTRODUCTION

In this chapter, we are interested in solving the flow shop scheduling problem through blocking constraint. This solution consists in treating a set of tasks on a set of machines.

In a blocking situation, the machine remains blocked by a stain until its operation on the next machine is finished and leaves the machine. The range of different flow shop problems is very wide and close to real applications. According to (Hall et al., 1996), the blocking of the scheduling problems can be related to the production process itself in which there is no waiting.

For example, blocking can be found in the manufacture of concrete blocking, which does not allow stock in a few steps of manufacturing processes (Grabowski et al., 2000) and in a robotic cell where a task can block a machine while waiting for the robot to pick it up and move it to the next machine (Sethi et al., 1992), In addition, the constraint of blocking consists of industrial waste treatment and rail transport (Gandibleux et al., 2006).

The flow shop scheduling problem with blocking constraint is classified among the NP-difficult problems. As a result, and like many so-called difficult problems, the exact methods remain limited. In fact, the use of approached methods is more frequent for problem-solving, particularly metaheuristics, which represent a rapidly growing field. Similarly, they use generic techniques that can optimize a wide range of different problems without major changes in basic algorithms. The advantage of this type of method is to build a large number of possible solutions in a reasonable time, and reuse of the information collected during the research through the evaluation of the generated solutions.

For instance, the Greedy Randomized Adaptive Search Procedure (GRASP) was introduced by Ronconi et al. (2009) to reduce the objective of this section is to explore and justify the application of the VNS algorithm (variable neighborhood search) for the scheduling of flow shop type problems with blocking constraints. Therefore, we present our method to solve this problem with the purpose of minimizing the total scheduling delay.

PROBLEM DESCRIPTION

Let $J_1, J_2,\ldots,J_i,\ldots,J_n$ be the sequence to be evaluated, where J_i represents the task that occupies position i in the considered sequence, the, $M_1, M_2,\ldots, M_j,\ldots M_m$ the ordered sequence of machines, $P_{k,j}$ the processing time of task k on machine M_j, and d_k the due date of task k, $D_{J_i,0}$ the starting date of the task J_i on the first machine and

$D_{J_i,j}$ the starting date of the ask J_i on machine M_j. The departure dates of each task on each machine are given by the following expressions:

$$D_{J_1,0} = 0 \tag{1}$$

$$D_{J_1,j} = \sum_{q=1}^{j} p_{J_1,q} \qquad j = 1,\dots,m-1 \tag{2}$$

$$D_{J_i,0} = D_{J_{(i-1)},1} \qquad i = 2,\dots,n \tag{3}$$

$$D_{J_i,j} = \max\left(D_{J_i,j-1} + p_{J_i,j}, D_{J_{(i-1)},j+1}\right) \qquad i = 2,\dots,n \qquad j = 1,\dots,m-1 \tag{4}$$

$$D_{J_i,m} = D_{J_i,m-1} + p_{J_i,m} \qquad i = 1,\dots,n \tag{5}$$

$$T = \sum_{i=1}^{n} \max\left(D_{J_i,m} - d_{J_i,0}\right) \tag{6}$$

Since the completion time of tasks ($D_{J_i,j}$) is known, therefore, the total delay is given by:

Proposed Heuristic

LBNEH Performance

LBNEH: According to the LBNEH algorithm proposed by Ronconi, (2005) and Armentano et al., (2000) based on the tests performed by the authors, LBNEH is the best constructive procedure for the minimization of the total delay on a flow shop problem with a blocking constraint and unlimited storage capacity.

The GRASP performance proposed by (Ronconi et al., 2009).

The Basic version: In fact, several tests were carried out to select the components of the GRASP in its basic version therefore, the following parameters were chosen. Moreover, the construction phase consists of the FPD rule (the adaptation processing as well as the deadline which generates a list of priorities among the distribution tasks associated with a list called RCL (TE Restricted Candidate List) which has been previously defined while in other cases, it may vary from one iteration to another. As a consequence, the description of the construction phase is presented as follows:

Step 1: ket x= be an empty partial sequence.
Step 2: ket C= be all the tasks
Step 3: let c (e)=be the (e) for the candidates' tasks e ∈ C.
Step 4: Build the RCL using the selected Scheme Based on Scheme 1 $(RCL = \{e \in C|c(e) \le c^{min}(1+p)\}$, where p is a parameter in [0, ∝).
Step 5: Choose e from the RCL at random.
Step 6: Allocate job e at the end of the partial sequence x.
Step 7: Remove the selected job e from C.
Step 8: Compute c(e)=F_e for the candidate jobs e∈C.
Step 9: If x is not complete, go back to step 4.

Before using a local search, the solution is improved by the insertion procedure of the algorithm NEH. The local search utilizes the insertion move and first improvement strategy. The algorithm is executed until n local searches are completed or the maximum CPU time of the 1800s is reached.

GRASP with Path-Relinking

Path relinking was originally proposed by (Glover, 1996) as an intensification strategy that explores paths that connect high-quality solutions obtained by tabu search. (Laguna et al., 1999) the first presented the use of path relinking associated with GRASP as an intensification strategy. According to Resende et al., 2003 the application of Path relinking as an intensification procedure in each local optimum seems to be more effective than using it only as a post-optimization step. Therefore, for this implementation, a path is evaluated at each local optimum using a high-quality solution as an initial solution and the local optimum as the guide solution. This strategy was chosen because, according to (Ribeiro et al., 2002), if only one path is to be investigated, the best solutions are found when the relinking procedure starts from the best solution. They also observed that exploring two different paths for each pair of solutions takes about twice the time needed to explore only one of them, with hardly any improvement in the quality of the solution. The high-quality solution used is randomly selected from the set S, which is stored during the application of GRASP. Every local optimum is considered to be part of S and is included in this set if the value of the objective function is better than any element of the set.

In order to build the path connecting the initial solution x_i and the guide solution x_g, the symmetric difference between them, given by $\Delta(x_i,x_g)$ must be calculated. In this problem, this difference is defined as the number of jobs that are not at the same absolute position in the initial solution and in the guide solution. First, the procedure examines all possible insertion moves m∈(x_i,x_g) of the initial solution and selects the lowest cost solution. This move is made and is a new intermediate solution (x). If necessary, the best solution x^* is updated. The set of available moves $\Delta(x,x_g)$ is updated and a new iteration of the procedure begins with the current solution x. A similar search strategy is described by Resende et al., 2005). It should be noted that it is possible to connect x_i to x_g in up to m moves using insertion moves if each move is made of in an ordered way. However, if the moves are not ordered, it can be shown that more than m moves could be needed as one move can corrupt a previous one.

The steps below show the proposed path relinking strategy:

Step 1: When a local optimal x_{ls} is reached make $x_g=x_{ls}$.
Step 2: Choose the initial solution x_i from S and let iter = 1.
Step 3: Compute $\Delta(x_i,x_g)$ and make iter_max = $\Delta(x_i,x_g)$, where iter_max is the maximum number of iterations.
Step 4: Evaluate all moves $m \in \Delta(x_i,x_g)$
Step 5: Choose the move m with the lowest cost solution.
Step 6: Set $x_i = x_i \oplus m$ m, where $\oplus$ defines the insertion move execution.
Step 7: Let iter = iter +1.
Step 8: Let x^* = the best solution (x_i,x^*), where the best solution compares two feasible solutions and returns the best one.
Step 9: Compute $\Delta(x_i,x_g)$.
Step 10: If $\Delta(x_i,x_g)>0$ and iter≤ietr_max, go back step 4.

Solution Representation

The well-known job-based encoding is frequently used in the literature of the flow shop problem with blocking, in this representation; the $j^{éme}$ number in the permutation denotes the job located in position j. In order to guarantee the diversification in the solution, we use an initial random solution of P individuals uniformly distributed.

Initial Solution

In this part, we describe construction heuristics based on precedence rules from the literature, as well as their adaptations for the resolution of a problem considered. These heuristics have been proposed to solve the flow-shop with blocking with as criterion total tardiness.

The initial solution is generated by Earliest due date EDD: the jobs are sorted in ascending order of increasing due dates. In other words, priority is given to the most urgent tasks.

A Variable Neighborhood Search Algorithm

Variable neighborhood search VNS is a metaheuristic with two steps: a local search that generates a local optimum and a shaking step to escape.

We have developed two local searches based respectively on insertion and permutation neighborhood structures (Jarboui et al., 2009). Specifically, the permutation procedure of swapping all jobs two by two (algorithm 1). The insertion procedure starts when the local optimum is reached and all permutation possibilities are executed. It consists of making all possible insertion movements by inserting each job in all possible positions within the current solution (algorithm 2). Then we return to the permutation procedure with the improved solution as the current solution, if a local optimum is found, we reapply the permutation procedure until the lack of improvement in the solution.

If the solution obtained is the best, we replace this solution with the new solution and we reset the number of iterations to 0, if we increment, the number of iterations. As a result, we move to the developed perturbation phase to modify the current solution to k consecutive neighborhood-induced motions where we choose two distinct positions (i, j) randomly following the uniform distribution in the interval [1, n] of the best solution and the jobs are traded on these positions. The entire procedure is repeated until reaching the maximum number of iterations. They are presented pseudo-code of the algorithm is given in algorithm 3.

Algorithm 1: pseudo-code of swap local search procedure

```
Procedure swap local search (x_0)
x_best=x_0; //x_best is the best solution obtained by swap local search procedure
set i=1;
do
set j=i+1;
while (j≤n)
x' = Permuter the jobs in the positions i and j in x_best;
if (TT(x') < TT(x_best)) then //check the improvement of best solution
x_best = x';
i=i-1;
j=i+1;
else
j=j+1;
end if
end while
i=i+1;
```

```
if (i>n-1) then i←1;
until (no possible improvement)
return x_best;
end
```

Algorithm 2: pseudo-code of insert local search procedure

```
Procedure insert local search (x_0)
x_best=x_0; //x_best is the best solution obtained by insert local search procedure
Set i=1;
do
set j=1;
while (j≤n)
x' = Insert the jobs in the position i to position j in x_best;
if (TT(x') < TT(x_best)) then //check the improvement of the best solution
x_best = x';
i=i-1;
j=1;
else
j=j+1;
end if
end while
i=i+1;
if (i>n) then i=1;
until (no possible improvement)
return x_best
end
```

Algorithm 3: pseudo-code of VNS algorithm

```
Procedure VNS (x_0)
x_best=x_0; // x_best is the best solution obtained by VNS procedure
x_current=x_0;
do
do
x' = swap _local_ search (x_courant);
x_courant ← insert _local_search (x_0);
Until (no possible improvement)
if (TT(x_current)<TT(x_best)) then // check the improvement of the best solution
x_best=x_current;
end if
```

```
x_current=x_best
find i and j randomly and permute the jobs I the positions i and
j in solution current
until (stopping criterion is found)
return x_best;
end
```

Numerical Experiments

The codes were written in C ++ and the tests were conducted on an Intel® Pentium® Dual with a 2.3 GHz processor, Windows XP, and 512 Mb RAM. The VNS heuristic is evaluated by the percentage improvement ratio compared to the LBNEH algorithm proposed by (Ronconi, 2005) (Armentano et al., 2000) were considered, with m = 5, 10 and 20 and n = 20, 50, 100,200 and 500. The improvement PI is calculated using the following expression:

$$PI = \frac{T_{LBNEH} - T_{VNS}}{T_{LBNEH}} \times 100$$

where T_{LBNEH} and T_{VNS} are the values total tardiness obtained by the algorithm LBNEH and VNS respectively.

When $T_{LBNEH} = T_{VNS} = 0$ the improvement obtained by VNS in relation to LBNEH is defined as zero (as in all the other cases where $T_{LBNEH} = T_{VNS}$). When $T_{LBNEH} = 0$ et $T_{VNS} > 0$, the above expression suggests an improvement of - ∞. However, this case did not occur in the presented computational experiments.

The VNS metaheuristic is evaluated by the relative percent improvement over the metaheuristic GRASP base version and GRASP path relinking.

Table 1 shows the average percentage improvement of each class with 10 problems. The overall average percentage improvement of 34.65% was achieved by VNS.

In most cases, increasing the number of jobs with the same machine takes advantage of the performance of the VNS algorithm. PI max can be observed the best average results of PI min and PI moy, the Tmin column shows the average CPU time is the best of Tmax and T moy so the CPU time of VNS is better results than GRASP. The main exception is the case of job 500 and machine 20, probably because of the short CPU time allow to running the algorithm.

It should be noted that the basic version GRASP algorithm is faster, although better solutions can be found by the VNS algorithm.

Table 1. Percentage improvement of VNS compared to basic version GRASP and path re-edition path.

Instance n × m	GRASP version de base		GRASP path-relinking		VNS					
	PA	CPU temps (s)	PA	CPU temps (s)	PI min	PI moy	PI max	Tmin (s)	Tmoy (s)	Tmax (s)
20 × 5	42.24	0.10	44.42	0.11	55.91	55.43	54.74	0.20	0.65	2.03
20× 10	16.78	0.19	17.48	0.22	21.25	21.00	20.64	0.45	0 .80	1.79
20 × 20	9.68	0.31	9.09	0.34	10.06	9.95	9.88	0.91	1.22	1.58
50× 5	57.32	9.48	60.14	9.72	75.70	73.77	72.00	4.34	6.96	9.67
50 × 10	39.85	23.71	40.15	24.51	51.45	49.45	46.97	12.35	17.81	25.88
50 × 20	29.94	38.11	30.70	39.55	35.75	34.81	33.69	23.96	35.21	48.46
100× 5	59.56	308.84	59.95	317.87	85.61	84.22	82.64	31.41	58.40	91.75
100 × 10	45.94	730.46	46.66	755.73	65.51	63.77	62.15	82.48	148.08	232.26
100 × 20	33.90	1517.56	34.24	1576.46	48.90	46.97	44.09	182.85	377.20	653.60
200 × 10	40.44	1705.82	39.75	1676.97	70.05	68.24	66.49	974.93	1594.45	1800.01
200 × 20	28.76	1800.02	27.81	1803.66	48.65	75.02	46.05	1800 .01	1800.01	1800.01
500 × 20	11.38	1800 .02	9.57	1800.03	39.39	38.30	37.19	1800.01	1800.01	1800.01
Moyenne	34.65	661.22	35.00	667.10	50.65	51.74	48.04	409.49	464.73	538.92

CONCLUSION

This document is interested in flow shop type scheduling problems with blocking considering the total tardiness as optimization criterion where the buffer is zero.

In this thesis, the minimization of the total tardiness has been studied in a flow shop scheduling problem with blocking. We proposed a local search-based approach called VNS.

In a comparison of the VNS against the basic version GRASP algorithm, the proposed algorithm presented an average percentage improvement of 34.65%.

Then we developed a VNS based heuristics to get better solutions in a reasonable time. Finally, comparisons with optimal solutions for small problems have shown that all versions can give good results, it would be interesting to extend the ideas presented in this document to the flow shop with blocking to minimize the total tardiness.

REFERENCES

Jarboui, B., Eddaly, M., & Siarry, P. (2009). An estimation of distribution algorithm for minimizing the total flow time in permutation flow shop scheduling problems. *Computers & Operations Research, 36*(9), 2638–2646.

Armentano, V. A., & Ronconi, D. P. (2000). Minimização do Tempo Total de Atraso no Problema deFlowshop com Buffer Zero atravésde BuscaTabu. *Gestão & Produção, 7*(3), 352–363. doi:10.1590/S0104-530X2000000300011

Feo, T. A., & Resende, M. G. C. (1995). Greedy Randomized Adaptive Search Procedures. *Journal of Global Optimization, 6*(2), 109–133. doi:10.1007/BF01096763

Gandilleux, X., Jorge, J. S., & Martinez, N. (2006). Sauer 2006 premier retour d'experience sur le flow- shop bi objectif et hybride a deux etages avec une contrainte de blocage particuliere. *Proceedings of MOSIM'06*, Rabat, Maroc. Academic Press.

Glover, F. (1996). Tabu search and adaptative memory programing—advances, applications and challenges. In R. Barr, R. Helgason, & J. Kennington (Eds.), *Interfaces in computer science and operations research* (pp. 1–75). Dordrecht: Kluwer Academic Publishers.

Grabowski, J., & Pempera, J. (2000). Grabowski. J and J. Pempera. Sequencing of jobs in some production system. *European Journal of Operational Research, 125*(3), 535–550. doi:10.1016/S0377-2217(99)00224-6

Hall, N. G., & Sriskandarajah, C. (1996, May/June). A Survey of Machine Scheduling Problems with Blocking and No-Wait in Process. *Operations Research, 44*(3), 510–525. doi:10.1287/opre.44.3.510

Laguna, M., & Martí, R. (1999). GRASP, and path relinking for 2-layer straight line crossing minimization. *INFORMS Journal on Computing, 11*(1), 44–52. doi:10.1287/ijoc.11.1.44

Resende, M. G. C., & Ribeiro, C. C. (2003). Greedy randomized adaptative search procedures. In F. Glover & G. Kochenberger (Eds.), *Handbook of metaheuristics* (pp. 219–249). Kluwer Academic Publishers. doi:10.1007/0-306-48056-5_8

Resende, M. G. C., & Ribeiro, C. C. (2005). Grasp with path-relinking: recent advances and applications. In T. Ibaraki, K. Nonobe, & M. Yagiura (Eds.), *Metaheuristics: progress as real problem solvers* (pp. 29–63). Berlin: Springer. doi:10.1007/0-387-25383-1_2

Ribeiro, C. C., Uchoa, E., & Werneck, R. F. (2002). A hybrid grasp with perturbations for the steiner problem in graphs. *INFORMS Journal on Computing*, *14*(3), 228–246. doi:10.1287/ijoc.14.3.228.116

Ronconi, D. P. (2005). A branch-and-bound algorithm to minimize the makespan in a flowshop with blocking. *Annals of Operations Research*, *138*(1), 53–65. doi:10.100710479-005-2444-3

Ronconi, D. P., & Henriques, L. R. S. (2009). Ronconi.D,1, Luís R.S. Henriques Some heuristic algorithms for total tardiness minimization in a flowshop with blocking. *Omega*, *37*(2), 272–281. doi:10.1016/j.omega.2007.01.003

Sethi, S. P., Sriskandarajah, C., Sorger, G., Blazewicz, J., & Kubiak, W. (1992). Sequencing of parts and robot moves in a robotic cell. *International Journal of Flexible Manufacturing Systems, 4(3-4), 331-358.*

Section 2

Chapter 5
Optimization Approaches for a Home Healthcare Routing and Scheduling Problem:
A Real Case From Medellin, Colombia

Juan Carlos Rivera
https://orcid.org/0000-0002-2160-3180
Mathematical Modeling Research Group, Universidad EAFIT, Colombia

Victoria J. Zapata
Mathematical Modeling Research Group, Universidad EAFIT, Colombia

ABSTRACT

Welfare community projects, mainly related to health care, are essential for the development of societies. For this reason, the optimization of its resources through methodologies that support decision making becomes of interest for all stakeholders in order to reach the target users. In Colombia, particularly in the city of Medellin, several social projects are being developed seeking to provide health and other social services to vulnerable populations. The purpose of this chapter is to deal with a real application of the home health care routing and scheduling problem (HHCRSP), in which a set of health professionals grouped by teams should visit a set of users geographically scatter over the city. Here, it is proposed a mixed integer linear model and a heuristic solution approach. The mathematical model is based on vehicle routing problem with pickups and deliveries (VRPPD) with additional features related with the specific application and geographical conditions.

DOI: 10.4018/978-1-7998-0268-6.ch005

INTRODUCTION

Welfare community projects, mainly related to health care, are essential for the development of societies. For this reason, the optimization of its resources through methodologies that support decision making becomes of interest for all stakeholders in order to reach the target users. The population aging and the increase in the care requirements for chronic diseases have overtaken the health institutions capacity, generating a growing trend in home care. In Colombia, particularly in the city of Medellin, several social projects are being developed seeking to provide health services to vulnerable populations. One of these projects seeks to deliver attention to low-income disabled citizens, which are called users in the sequel, and their caregivers through four areas of health: psychology, nutrition, physiotherapy and nursing. This social project aims to give health services from each area to each user and the corresponding caregiver during a given horizon period. In that sense, professionals should visit home users by designing adequate routes to be performed by team each day.

In the field of Operations Research this problem is closely related to the Home Health Care Routing and Scheduling Problem (HHCRSP), which can be described as the problem in which a set of patients, dispersed on a geographical area, need care services, that is, home visits, which must be provided by professionals from a health service institution. The problem aims to define a set of routes to manage the group of patients. The objectives can vary and depend on each context and institution. Among the more common are the maximization of the patients served, as well as their level of satisfaction. On the other hand, operational performance measures can be sought such as cost, travel time or waiting times minimization, among others.

The HHCRSP is considered a variation of vehicle routing problem (VRP), which is a combinatorial optimization problem with multiple applications that has been extensively studied in the literature (Vidal et al. 2013). There is a wide range of applications that has led to proposing variants to the problem that include different characteristics and restrictions, which can be called attributes, seeking to obtain more detail of the system or decision making, which is known as multi-attribute vehicle routing problem (MAVRP) (Vidal et al. 2013). Many HHCRSP applications can be considered as MAVRP. The dimensions of this type of problem is an obstacle to the use of exact methods for the solution, so most of the authors propose heuristic methods.

The purpose of this chapter is to deal with a real application of the HHCRSP based on a social project from Medellin, Colombia. In this application a set of health professionals from different specialties of health should visit a set of users. This project has associated around 1,920 users, three teams of four professionals and a time horizon of five months, which applies around 7,680 visits and each professional must attend on average 5,8 users every day. Each user must be visited once by one professional of each of four specialties. The visits, from the different professionals, to each user are performed in such a way that two consecutive visits are separated by a period of at least four weeks. There are no precedence nor specific order between different areas of health. A vehicle is available for each team of professionals and it must leave them and pick them up to user homes. Professional also can move between user homes by walking as long as the distances does not exceed a maximum. A solution also includes to decide which transportation mode must be used. As the time is limited for the project and professionals time is scarcer, here it is used as objective function the minimization of the traveled time and waiting time by professionals, i.e. the time in which they are not on an appointment. Note that the number of professional can vary for every travel and it is not necessarily optimal to transport only one professional every time.

Here it is proposed a mathematical model and a heuristic solution approach. The mathematical model is based on VRP models with Pick up and Deliveries (VRPPD) and additional features coming from selective and resource constrained problem. Note that, as some travels can be done by walking, vehicles do not need to pick up and deliver professionals for every node. In addition, professionals have the role of resources due to they are available until they start a service and cannot be delivered to other user's homes until they finish the service in process and they have been picked up. The proposed solution methods contribute in the following decision making within the project:

- Assignment of visits that are performed by each of the health professionals, looking for a balance in the daily visit load of each one of them.
- Definition of the route order for each vehicle assigned to the teams.
- Definition of which transportation mode (vehicle or walking) should be used by the professional in the assigned route.
- Definition of the minimum time sufficient for the fulfillment of the attention goals, that is, to comply with the defined user coverage.

The mathematical model is a mixed integer linear program which is tested with a small instance while heuristic algorithm is tested with both, a small instance in order to compare its performance and large instances inspired on real case to evaluate it in more practical cases. The results are compared by using an efficiency measure based on the ratio between the time required to give service to all patients and the total time used by routes in the solution.

BACKGROUND

The first studies of HHCRSP are attributed to Begur et al. (1997), who developed a support system in spatial decision-making using a heuristic approach for daily nurses' scheduling and routing for a real case of home-health-care (the Visiting Nursing Association (VNA) of Birmingham, Alabama provides services to residents in several counties of central Alabama encompassing an area of 2,727 square miles). The heuristic approach is based on the savings algorithm and enhance the solution for each nurse based on TSP an using the nearest neighbor heuristic. They also mention a MILP formulation to optimize nurses' routes for a five-day routing problem.

Cisse et al. (2017) present a review of the recent models developed for the HHCRSP, defining the most relevant characteristics that are considered in these models, analyze them according to the restrictions and objective functions, and finally, discuss future research directions. They emphasize that the features considered in the existing HHCRSP models reflect the diversity of HHC operations and can be divided into three groups depending on whether they concern the HHC service organization, patients, or care workers. A given HHCRSP model results from the combination of features considered in the formulation of the problem. Each feature is formulated as either a constraint or a satisfaction. Table 1 show the different constraints used based on the three described groups. They also define the most frequently used criteria to evaluate a solution which are classified in four main types: minimize total routing cost, minimize the number of unassigned services, minimize the number of care workers and maximize satisfaction.

The developed models, by the particularities of each problem, are not easily comparable to each other. Nevertheless, the authors present below a brief review of papers with a greater similarity with the problem that is intended to solve, either by the restrictions or by the defined objective functions.

Table 1. Classification scheme based on constraints (Cisse et al., (2017)

Actors	Temporal constraints	Assignment constraints	Geographic constraints
HHC service organization	• Planning horizon • Frequency of decision	• Continuity of care	• Sectors/districts • Typology of HHC services provided
Patient	• Frequency of visits • Time windows • Temporal dependency • Disjunctive services	• Preferences	• Type of network between home locations
Care worker	• Contract type • Capacity/working hours	• Qualification/skill • Workload balancing	• Location of care workers

Trautsamwieser et al. (2011) address the Home Health Routing and Scheduling problem during times of natural disasters focused on the following objectives: to minimize the sum of driving times and waiting times and the dissatisfaction levels of patients and nurses. To achieve this, they defined seven aims for the objective function: travel time of professionals, extra work done, cost of unmet preferences, time windows of professionals and clients not met (soft restrictions), time not paid for transportation and service times covered by professionals with qualification levels above those required.

Liu et al. (2013) approach the vehicle scheduling problem for home health care logistics. It involves the delivery of medicines and medical devices from a defined depot to the patients' homes, the delivery of special medications from a hospital to patients, the withdrawal of laboratory samples, unused medications and patient's medical devices. The problem can be considered as a *Pick up and Delivery Vehicle Routing Problem with Time Windows (PDVPRTW)*, with four types of demands: delivery of medicines from pharmacy to patient, delivery from a hospital to patient, transfer of a patient to a depot and collection from a patient to a medical laboratory. Each patient is visited by a vehicle and each vehicle visits each node at most once. Two models MILP are proposed. Then a Genetic Algorithm (GA) and a Tabu Search (TS) metaheuristics are proposed. GA is based on a permutation chromosome, a Split procedure and local search. The TS is based on the attributes of patient route assignment, an increased cost function, re-optimization of routes and aspiration levels based on attributes.

Fikar et al. (2015) deliver a solution to a real scheduling and routing problem, in which a transport service takes professionals with different skill levels to the users and picks them up after the completion of their services. It is considered the possibility of assigning restrictions such as walking towards clients, interdependencies, time windows and obligatory rules of time of work and rest. The introduced matheuristic algorithm consists of two stages, identifying possible routes for walking and optimizing the transport system. The numerical studies presented are carried out with real-time instances of the Austrian Red Cross, an important provider of home care services in Austria. The results show that the implementation of treks and the grouping of trips into solution procedures substantially decreases the number of vehicles required.

Braekers et al. (2016) indicated that home care providers often face multiple conflicting goals such as minimizing their operating costs and maximizing the level of service offered to their customers by taking their preferences into account. They proposed a bi-objective mathematical model which includes nurses' qualifications, working regulations, overtime costs, travel costs depending on the mode of transportation, hard time windows and client preferences on visit times and nurses. A distinctive feature is that the scheduling problem for a single route is a bi-objective problem in itself, which considerably increases the difficulty of the problem. The first objective function minimizes the total cost, which consists in the route cost and the required overtime, and the second objective function minimizes customer dissatisfactions, which is measured by the deviation in the selected attendance time and nurse. They also propose a metaheuristic algorithm integrating an LNS (large neighborhood search) within the framework of a multi-directional local search.

Frifita and Masmoudi (2018) addressed the problem of scheduling and routing for home care to dependent people such as citizens who have difficulty leaving their homes by offering them social, medico-social, and medical services such as cleaning, cooking, shopping, hygiene assistance, nursing, etc. The problem is defined as an extension of the vehicle routing problems with time windows and synchronization constraints (VRPTW-S). The objective described is to design lower cost routes for home care workers who serve a group of geographically dispersed clients, respecting time windows and time-dependent restrictions, such as synchronization, disjunction and priority between visits. In the article is proposed the mathematical formulation for the new variant called Vehicle routing problems with time windows, time dependencies (synchronization, precedence and disjunction), multiple structures and problems of multiple specialties (VRPTW-TD-2MS). They developed three VNS methods to solve this problem in a reasonable calculation time: Variable neighborhood search (VNS), General variable neighborhood search (GVNS) and General variable neighborhood search with ejection chains (GVNS-EC).

Fathollahi-Fard et al. (2018) formulated a new bi-objective optimization model, defined as *Green Home Health Care (GHHC),* as a variation of VRPTW in which a balance between transport costs and environmental pollution is pursued when considering the rate CO2 emission released per unit of distance according to the transportation type. Four heuristics presented were considered to find the best tradeoff between two conflicting objective functions and to alleviate the drawbacks the authors proposed a number of memetic metaheuristics. The improvements involved of both modification and hybridization of Simulated Annealing (SA) as a well-known single-solution metaheuristic employed repeatedly in the literature as well as Salp Swarm Algorithm (SSA) as a recent nature-inspired swarm algorithm.

Xiao et al. (2018) formulated a mixed integer linear programming model of a home health care scheduling and routing problem with daily planning horizon with the objective of minimizing the total operation cost. The model includes the synchronization of several caregivers that must be assigned to the same patient in a given time window. The proposed model also represents multiple restrictions, such as working time, caregiver qualifications and patient preference, and flexible lunch break requirements.

Decerle et al. (2018) addressed a HHCRSP problem with time window (availability according to patient preferences) and synchronization (some visits may require the presence of two staff members simultaneously) constraints. They developed a mixed integer programming model and a memetic algorithm featuring two original crossover operators. The memetic algorithm is the hybridization of a genetic algorithm with a local search procedure. Decerle et al. (2019) addressed the same problem, HHCRSP with time windows and synchronization constraints, but with new restrictions that include workload balancing between caregivers. They developed a hybrid algorithm combining memetic and ant colony optimization algorithm and highlighted the efficiency of the proposed hybrid algorithm compared to other metaheuristics and commercial optimization solver. Decerle et al. (2019b) addressed the multi-objective home health problem, similar to those described earlier in this paragraph, with the aim of ensuring the applicability of the planning. The objectives considered in the proposed model are the minimization of the total working time of the caregivers, while maximizing the quality of service and minimizing the maximal working time difference among nurses and auxiliary nurses. A memetic algorithm is proposed for the solution of the problem.

Grenouilleau et al. (2019) addressed the HHCRSP in a one-week time horizon, where they take into account restrictions such as caregiver competencies, specialty, language, caregiver gender, patient availability (days and time windows), caregivers' work shifts, minimum and maximum amount of working time per day and week, and the repercussions of delays in travel time through a time- dependent distance matrix. The solution method is based on a set partitioning formulation and a large neighborhood search (LNS) framework. They proposed an algorithm that solves a linear relaxation of a set partitioning model of using the columns generated by the LNS. Then, a constructive heuristic is called to build an integer solution.

In the real base proposed problem, each group of professionals has a vehicle which must leave each professional to different user home, and then it must pick them up to leave them to other user home and so on until all appointments are concluded. It is permitted that the professional walks between two user's homes, as long as the distance between them below a defined maximum. Related with that, in the field of problems of pickup and delivery, Parragh et al. (2008) distinguish between two kinds of problems: the first class refers to situations in which all goods delivered must be loaded into one or more deposits and all the goods collected must be transported to one or more deposits. Problems in this class are often called vehicle routing problems with backhauls (VRPB). The second class includes all those problems in which goods (passengers) are transported between pick-up and delivery points (destinations) and are called vehicle routing problems with pickups and deliveries (VRPPD).

PROBLEM DEFINITION AND MATHEMATICAL FORMULATION

Problem Description

The government is interested on give health attention and support to low-income and disable population and their caregivers. The project defines three teams made up of four professionals from different areas of health: psychology, nutrition, physiotherapy and nursing. Nowadays, each team manually determines the assignment or set of patients, the order of the visits, the routes to be followed by the vehicle and the transportation modes between home patients.

Each team has a vehicle that transports them and a set of assigned users who must receive a total of four visits, one per health area. According to this description, it is identified that it is a vehicle routing problem with multiple periods where the visits of the different professionals to a user are intended to be distributed throughout the time horizon of the project. It also has multi modes of transport since travels between home users can be perform on a vehicle or walking if distance is close enough. In addition, as professionals must be left on each node and pick them up after attention, it can be also modeled as a pick up and delivery problem.

Tables 2 and 3 present examples of assigning to professionals. Table 2 depicts an example of the assigning of 60 users (U1 to U60), which are visited once for 3 days by 4 professionals (PR1 to PR4). For instance, user U1 is visited the first day by the professional PR1. Here we assume that, in order to complete a solution with four visits, once for each professional, it is possible to visit it once and the pattern of the first visit can be repeated with different professional assignments. For instance, Table 3 shows the same pattern assignment depicted in Table 2 with different professionals; i.e. user U1 is now visited the first day by the professional PR4.

Note that the number of users visited every day by each professional is not necessarily the same.

Each team, with the help of an address locator, identifies the users in a sector and defines the route for each professional considering the proximity between the users. There is a single point of departure or deposit for the vehicle and its professionals. According to the proximity of the users, professionals are left in each of their destinations. Considering that some of the journeys between users are short, professionals can go to their destinations walking. If required, professionals ask the vehicle to pick them up once the visit is over. It is possible that the vehicle has picked up another professional before or requires to pick up another professional just before taking them to their destinations (users), that is, there can be additional waiting times. The average attention time is 60 minutes for each user and each health area. At the end of the last user's attention, each professional is picked up by the vehicle in their locations to return to the starting point.

Table 2. Professionals scheduling for the first month and week

Week 1 - month 1											
Day 1				Day 2				Day 3			
PR1	PR2	PR3	PR4	*PR1*	PR2	PR3	PR4	*PR1*	PR2	PR3	PR4
U1	U6	U12	U17	U21	U26	U30	U36	U41	U46	U51	U56
U2	U7	U13	U18	U22	U27	U31	U37	U42	U47	U52	U57
U3	U8	U14	U19	U23	U28	U32	U38	U43	U48	U53	U58
U4	U9	U15	U20	U24	U29	U33	U39	U44	U49	U54	U59
U5	U10	U16		U25	U30	U34	U40	U45	U50	U55	U60
	U11					U35					

Table 3. Professionals scheduling for the second month, first week

Week 1 - month 2											
Day 1				Day 2				Day 3			
PR4	*PR1*	PR2	PR3	PR4	*PR1*	PR2	PR3	PR4	PR1	PR2	PR3
U1	U6	U12	U17	U21	U26	U30	U36	U41	U46	U51	U56
U2	U7	U13	U18	U22	U27	U31	U37	U42	U47	U52	U57
U3	U8	U14	U19	U23	U28	U32	U38	U43	U48	U53	U58
U4	U9	U15	U20	U24	U29	U33	U39	U44	U49	U54	U59
U5	U10	U16		U25	U30	U34	U40	U45	U50	U55	U60
	U11					U35					

Figure 1 depicts an example of the development of a route with 3 professionals and 7 users that require attention. Straight continuous lines represent the vehicle travels, dashed lines represent walking travels and curved lines indicates the travels performed in order to pick up a professional in a home user. In the example the vehicle leaves the deposit and delivers the professional PR1 in node 4 (U4), PR2 in node 1 (U1) and PR3 in node 2 (U2). Once the service time has ended, the vehicle must pick up PR1 in node 4, PR2 in node 1 and PR3 in node 2 to continue with their visits in nodes 3, 12 and 7, respectively. Note that professional PR1 once finished the attention in node 3 goes walking to node 24 (dashed line). The vehicle has a waiting time in node 7 (attention time) until the professional PR3 finishes, then the vehicle picks up PR2 and PR1 in nodes 12 and 24 respectively. Finally, after picking up all professionals, the vehicle finishes its route in the deposit.

Figure 1. Route example

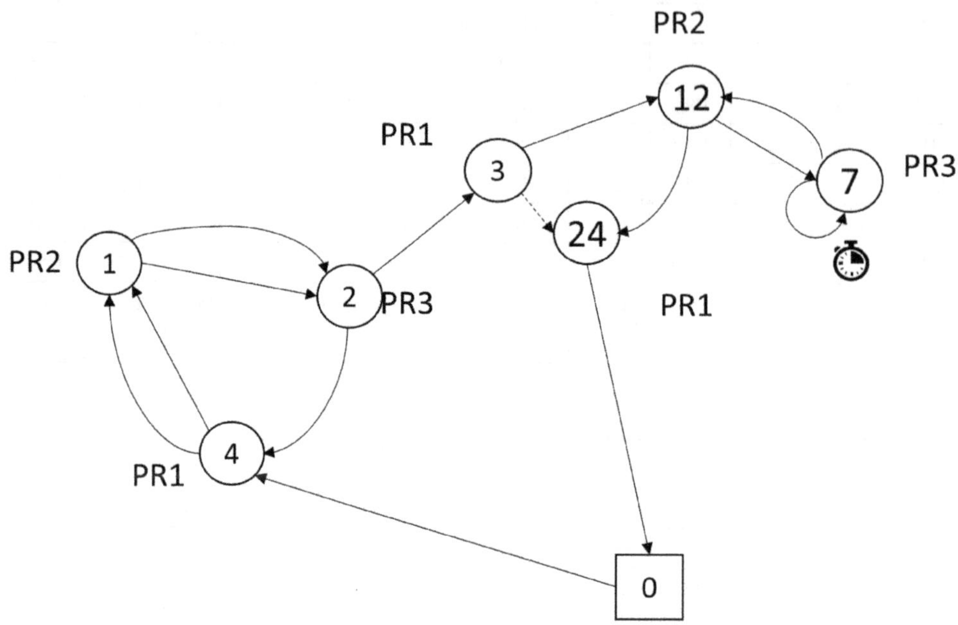

MATHEMATICAL DEFINITION

This chapter addresses a vehicle routing and scheduling problem whose purpose is to transport health professionals to different patients (users) homes, which means leaving and picking them up in different locations, seeking to minimize the spending time by professionals in transportation and waiting for a vehicle.

In order to model pick up and deliveries at patient homes, each node is represented by two separate nodes: one to deliver a professional an another to pick him up. Thus, the problem can be defined on a complete graph $G=(V,A)$ where $A=\{(i,j): i,j\in A, i\neq j\}$ is the set of arcs and $V=\{0, 1,\dots, n,\dots, 2\bullet n\}$ is the set of vertices. The vertex 0 represents the deposit, which is the starting and arrival point. The vertices $V\backslash\{0\}$ can be split on delivery nodes $V_d=\{1,2,\dots,n\}$ and pick up nodes $V_p=\{n+1, n+2_{,\dots,2\bullet n\}}$. Note that for each pair of nodes $(i,j+n)$ with $i\in V_d$ and $i+n\in V_p$ they have the same coordinates or geographical position. Each node $i\in V_d$ has a service time or attention time s which must be accomplished before a professional leaves that node. In addition, each arc $(i,j)\in A$ is characterized by a travel time τ_{ij} (transportation time between nodes i and j when it is performed by a vehicle) and a walking time w_{ij} (transportation time when a professional walks between nodes i and j). A professional only can walk between two nodes if the distance (or travel time) between them is less than the maximum accepted distance W.

Each user is visited by one of the professionals $p \in P$. In this context, professionals behave as renewable resources which are activated when a node is visited and cannot be assigned to another node until during the period of the service time. In that sense, it is assigned a demand q_i to each node i, being 1 for each node in V_d and -1 for each node in V_p. When a route is performed it is possible to guarantee that the number of professionals (load of the vehicle) is greater than zero and is less than the capacity Q, i.e. a maximum of Q professionals by team are assigned.

A solution is a collection of feasible routes, starting and finishing at the deposit, which visits all nodes such that the waiting and transportation time of professionals is minimized. A feasible route includes professional assignments and transportation modes decisions. Note that, given that exists a working time duration, routes cannot last more than that limit M.

It can be assumed, without loss of generality, that the set of routes contained on a solution can be organized to be performed during a number of days. For instance, if a solution is composed by nine routes and there are three teams available, three routes can be performed every day for three days.

Mixed Integer Linear Formulation

The HHCRSP defined in this chapter can be mathematically formulated as a mixed integer linear program (MILP). In the literature it can be found several mathematical models, however, they differ from specific features included on each study. To the best of our knowledge, there are not a mathematical model with the specific features dealt in this chapter. The mathematical model proposed for the problem under study is presented by Equations (1) to (34).

In this MILP, nodes represent users. But, as a vehicle visits each node twice (once to leave a professional and them to pick him/her up), copies of nodes are created in order to have a delivery node and a pickup node associated to each user. In a similar way, every delivery node demands the service of a professional and every pickup node allows to have a professional available for next users in the route. The last feature is modeled by defining a demand equal to 1 for delivery nodes and -1 for pickup nodes.

Finally, it is assumed that it is not necessary to define the routes for the total horizon period and all visits of all professional. Instead, the proposed MILP assures a visit of one professional for each user, and after that routes are performed, they can be repeated differing only on the professional assigned to each user.

In the sequel the subscripts, sets, parameters, decision variables, objective function and constraints are defined.

Subscripts

i: Represents the previous user location, i.e. origin of an arc.
j: Represents the next user location, i.e. destination of an arc.
k:: Represents a route.
p: Represents a professional.

Sets

$V_d=\{1,2,\ldots,n\}$: Set of delivery nodes.
$V_p=\{n+1,n+2_{,\ldots,}2\bullet n\}$: Set of pickup nodes.
$V = V_d \cup V_p \cup \{0\}$: Set of all available nodes, delivery nodes, pickup nodes and deposit.
$\mathcal{K} = \{1,2,\ldots,K\}$: Set of routes.
$P=\{1,2,\ldots,Q\}$: Set of professionals.

Parameters

τ_{ij}: Travel time in vehicle from node i to node j.
w_{ij}: Walking time from node i to node j.
s: Service time for the node j.
q_i: Demand of professionals in node i. q_i is equal to 1 for all $i\in V_d$, and -1 for all $i\in V_p$.
M: Maximum duration of the working day.
Q: Vehicle capacity i.e. number of professionals transported in the vehicle.
W: Maximum accepted walking time between nodes.

Decision Variables

$$x_{ij}^k = \begin{cases} 1, & if\ arc(i,j)\ is\ traversed\ by\ the\ route\ k \\ 0, & otherwise \end{cases}.$$

$$y_{ij}^k = \begin{cases} 1, & if\ arc(i,j)\ is\ performed\ by\ walking\ in\ the\ route\ k \\ 0, & otherwise \end{cases}.$$

$$z_i^p = \begin{cases} 1, & if\ node\ i\ is\ served\ by\ professional\ p \\ 0, & otherwise \end{cases}.$$

$$I_{ij}^{p} = \begin{cases} 1, & \begin{array}{c} \textit{if node } i \textit{ is served before node } j \textit{ by the same vehicle and} \\ \textit{both are served by same professional } p \end{array} \\ 0, & \textit{otherwise} \end{cases}$$

t_i: Arriving time to node *i*.
T_k: Ending time of route*k*.
l_{ij}^k : Load of vehicle *k* in the arc (*i,j*).

Mixed Integer Linear Formulation

$$\min F = \sum_{k \in \mathcal{K}} T_k \tag{1}$$

subject to:

$$\sum_{j \in V_d} x_{0j}^k \leq 1, \forall k \in \mathcal{K} \tag{2}$$

$$\sum_{j \in V_d} x_{0j}^1 = 1 \tag{3}$$

$$x_{0j}^k = 0, \quad \forall j \in V_p, \ k \in \mathcal{K} \tag{4}$$

$$x_{i0}^k = 0, \quad \forall j \in V_d, \ k \in \mathcal{K} \tag{5}$$

$$2 \cdot n \cdot \sum_{j \in V_d} x_{0j}^k \geq \sum_{i \in V} \sum_{j \in V_d} x_{ij}^k + \sum_{i \in V_p} \sum_{j \in V_d} y_{ij}^k, \quad \forall k \in \mathcal{K} \tag{6}$$

$$\sum_{j \in V_d} x_{0j}^k \leq \sum_{j \in V_d} x_{0j}^{k-1}, \forall k \in \mathcal{K}, \ k > 1 \tag{7}$$

$$\sum_{\substack{j \in V \\ i \neq i}} x_{ij}^k - x_{ji}^k = 0, \forall i \in V, k \in \mathcal{K} \tag{8}$$

$$\sum_{k\in\mathcal{K}}\sum_{\substack{i\in V\\ i\neq j}} x_{ij}^k + \sum_{k\in\mathcal{K}}\sum_{\substack{i\in V_p\\ i\neq j}} y_{ij}^k = 1, \quad \forall j \in V_d \tag{9}$$

$$\sum_{k\in\mathcal{K}}\sum_{\substack{j\in V\\ i\neq j}} x_{ij}^k + \sum_{k\in\mathcal{K}}\sum_{\substack{j\in V_d\\ i\neq j}} y_{ij}^k = 1, \quad \forall i \in V_p \tag{10}$$

$$\sum_{\substack{j\in V\\ j\neq i}} x_{ji}^k + \sum_{\substack{j\in V_p\\ j\neq i}} y_{ji}^k - \sum_{\substack{j\in V\\ j\neq i}} x_{i+n,j}^k - \sum_{\substack{j\in V_d\\ j\neq i}} y_{i+n,j}^k = 0, \quad \forall i \in V_d \tag{11}$$

$$w_{ij} \cdot y_{ij}^k \leq W, \quad \forall j \in V_d,\ i \in V_p, k \in \mathcal{K} \tag{12}$$

$$l_{ij}^k = Q \cdot x_{ij}^k, \quad \forall i, j \in V, i = 0 \text{ or } j = 0, k \in \mathcal{K} \tag{13}$$

$$l_{ij}^k \leq Q \cdot x_{ij}^k, \quad \forall i, j \in V, i, j > 0, k \in \mathcal{K} \tag{14}$$

$$\sum_{k\in\mathcal{K}}\sum_{\substack{j\in V\\ j\neq i}} l_{ji}^k - l_{ij}^k = \sum_{k\in\mathcal{K}}\sum_{\substack{j\in V\\ j\neq i}} q_i \cdot x_{ij}^k, \quad \forall i \in V \tag{15}$$

$$\sum_{p\in\mathcal{P}} z_i^p = 1, \quad \forall i \in V_d \tag{16}$$

$$z_j^p \geq z_{i-n}^p - 1 + \sum_{k\in\mathcal{K}} y_{ij}^k, \quad \forall i \in V_p, j \in V_d, p \in \mathcal{P} \tag{17}$$

$$I_{ij}^p \leq 1 - \sum_{k\in\mathcal{K}} x_{ij}^k, \quad \forall i, j \in V_d, p \in \mathcal{P} \tag{18}$$

$$I_{ij}^p \leq 1 - \sum_{k\in\mathcal{K}} y_{i+n,j}^k, \quad \forall i \in V_p, j \in V_d, p \in \mathcal{P} \tag{19}$$

$$I_{ij}^p + I_{ji}^p \geq z_i^p + z_j^p - 1 - n \cdot \sum_{v\in V} x_{vi}^k + x_{vi}^k, \quad \forall i, j \in V_d, i \neq j, k \in \mathcal{K}, p \in \mathcal{P} \tag{20}$$

$$t_i \geq \sum_{k \in \mathcal{K}} \tau_{0i} \cdot x_{0i}^k, \quad \forall i \in V_d \tag{21}$$

$$t_j \geq t_i + s + \tau_{ij} - M \cdot \left(1 - x_{ij}^k\right), \quad \forall i \in V_d, j \in V, k \in \mathcal{K} \tag{22}$$

$$t_{j+n} \geq t_j + s, \quad \forall j \in V_d \tag{23}$$

$$t_j \geq t_i + s + w_{i-n,j} - M \cdot \left(1 - y_{ij}^k\right), \quad \forall i \in V_p, j \in V_d, k \in \mathcal{K} \tag{24}$$

$$t_j \geq t_i + \left(s + \min\left\{w_{ij}, \tau_{ij}\right\}\right) \cdot I_{ij}^p - M\left(1 - I_{ij}^p\right), \quad \forall i \in V, j \in V_d, p \in \mathcal{P} \tag{25}$$

$$T_k \leq \sum_{j \in V_d} M \cdot x_{0j}^k, \quad \forall k \in \mathcal{K} \tag{26}$$

$$T_k \geq t_i + \tau_{i-n,0} - M \cdot \left(1 - x_{i0}^k\right), \quad \forall i \in V_p, k \in \mathcal{K} \tag{27}$$

$$x_{ij}^k \in \{0,1\}, \quad \forall i, j \in V, k \in \mathcal{K} \tag{28}$$

$$y_{ij}^k \in \{0,1\}, \tag{29}$$

$$l_{ij}^k \geq 0, \quad \forall i, j \in V, k \in \mathcal{K} \tag{30}$$

$$t_i \geq 0, \quad \forall i \in V \tag{31}$$

$$T_k \geq 0, \quad \forall k \in \mathcal{K} \tag{32}$$

$$z_i^p \in \{0,1\}, \quad \forall i \in V_d, p \in \mathcal{P} \tag{33}$$

$$I_{ij}^p \in \{0,1\}, \quad \forall i, j \in V_d, p \in \mathcal{P} \tag{34}$$

Equation (1) represents the objective function to be minimized. The main goal of the project is to minimize the time used by professional doing activities which are different to attend users, i.e. transportation and waiting for a vehicle or another professional. In that sense, for each professional it can be measured as the total time of routes less the time spent with a patient. Equation (35) sums up that time for all professional.

$$\min F = |P| \cdot \sum_{k \in K} T_k - s \cdot \sum_{i \in V_d} \sum_{p \in P} Z_i^p \tag{35}$$

Nevertheless, as all users must be visited, the second term in Equation (35) is constant and it can be reduced to Equation (1). That is, minimize the total time spent by professional doing activities which are different to attend users is equivalent to minimize the total length or duration of routes.

Equations (2) to (7) refers to start or finish of each route. Constraints (2) guarantee that a route has at most one initial arc, but not all available route need to be used. Constraint (3) ensures that the first route is used within the solution. Constraints (4) and (5) avoid some infeasible arcs: routes cannot start on a pickup node nor finish after a delivery node. The restrictions (6) indicate that arcs of a route k only can be used for active route, i.e. routes with an initial arc. When a route is activated the maximum number of delivery nodes visited is n. Constraints (7) ensures that the routes are assigned in order, i.e. a route cannot be used if previous route is not.

Equations (8) to (12) help to configure feasible routes. Constraints (8) ensure that vehicle visiting node i must leave it. Constraints (9) guarantee that all delivery nodes are visited once; the professional can arrive using the vehicle or by walking. Constraints (10) guarantee that all pick-up nodes are leaved once. Note that when a travel is performed by walking from node $i \in V_p$ to node $j \in V_d$, there is not arc leaving the node j and there is not arc arriving to node j. Constraints (11) guarantee consistency and integrality between flow in and flow out variables, including vehicle and walking travels. Constraints (12) indicate that only short distances, limited to W, can be performed walking.

Equations (13) to (15) are related to vehicle capacity and load of the vehicle; here load is referred to the number of professionals available in the vehicle to be left on visited nodes. Constraints (13) force to have one professional of each health area at the beginning and at the end of the routes. Q represents the total number of available professionals on teams, i.e. number of health areas. Constraints (14) guarantee that the number of professionals on traversed arcs (i,j) do not exceed Q. On the other hand, they must be zero for no traversed arcs. Constraints (15) ensure that when a vehicle arrives to a node i, the demand q_i can be accomplish, get in (q_i=-1) or get out (q_i=1) a professional.

Equations (16) to (20) limit decisions on assignments of professionals. Constraints (16) ensure that all delivery nodes have a professional assigned. Constraints (17) guarantee that the same professional p is assigned to nodes i and j if a professional travels between those patients homes by walking. In an opposite way, Constraints (18) avoids that a professional is assigned to two consecutive delivery nodes on a route. Constraints (19) indicate that if arc (i,j). is performed walking the corresponding delivery nodes must be assigned to the same professional. These constraints, contrary to (17), also indicates that node i is visited first which is used after to limit arrival times. Constraints (20) force to assign a visit order between two delivery nodes if they are visited by the same professional in the same route.

Equations (21) to (25) refer to arrival times at delivery and pickup nodes. Note that these constraints also avoid the presence of subtours. Restrictions (21) limit arrival times for first delivery node on each route. Constraints (22) limits the arrival time for two nodes consecutively visited by a vehicle. They differ, at least, on travel time and service time. Constraints (23) indicates that the difference between the arrival time to a delivery node and it corresponding pickup node is at least the service time. Similarly to Equation (22), constraints (24) limit the arrival time when a travel is performed by walking. Constraints (25) limit arrival time for nodes visited by the same professional.

Equations (26) and (27) are related to the length or duration of routes. Constraints (26) impose a maximum time duration for each route, i.e. the total duration of each rout must be less than a working day. Constraints (27) limit the finish of a route by its relation with the last visited pickup node.

Finally, constraints (28) to (34) represent the domain of the decision variables.

The total number of available routes K can be computed as the product between the number of available days and the number of teams.

MULTIPLE PHASES HEURISTIC APPROACH

This problem is considered a generalization of the VRP, that is defined by Lenstra and Rinnooy Kan (1981) as a NP-Hard problem since it cannot be optimally solved in polynomial time. Consequently, HHRSP is also considered as NP-Hard. Therefore, the proposed MILP can only be used to solve very limited size cases and a heuristic method is also proposed. The solution method is composed by four phases, as follows:

Phase One: Defines the group of users that are going to be visited by a route and the order in which they are going to be visited. In this phase, the savings algorithm (Clarke and Wright; 1964) is used looking for a routing for deliveries at each user.

Phase Two: Assigns the travels which professionals must perform by walking from one user's home to another. In this phase, a local search-based algorithm is used which replaces vehicle travels for slower walking travels if the walking distance is lower than a predefined value.

Phase Three: Defines the order to pick up the professionals from each user's homes. In this phase a best insertion algorithm is used.

Phase Four: Assigns the professionals to each group of visits. In this phase is used a greedy algorithm which assigns every time the professional with less assigned jobs or users. It also takes into account that when a travel is performed by walking, case in which both users must be serviced by the same professional.

The following describes each of the algorithms applied to each phase.

Phase One: The Savings Algorithm

Clarke and Wright (1964) proposed a heuristic method, known as the savings algorithm, which is the basis of many other solution algorithms for VRP and CVRP. This method starts with a state that involves as many routes as nodes has the problem. Each route starts and ends in the depot, (0,*i*,0). Then it is defined the savings as the difference between the time of carrying out these two routes separately and the time by joining them in a single route. After, a couple of routes with maximum saving are selected and a new route is created as the union of those routes and their associated savings are updated. The method is described in the following steps:

Step 1: For each user *i* build and calculate the time taken by the route (0,*i*,0)
Step 2: Calculate s_{ij} for each pair of users *i* and *j*

$$s_{ij} = \tau_{i0} + \tau_{0j} - \tau_{ij} \tag{36}$$

Step 3: Let $s_{i^*j^*} = max\left(s_{ij}\right)$ where the maximum is taken among the savings that have not yet been considered. Let r_{i^*} and r_{j^*} be the routes that contain the users i^* and j^* respectively. If i^* is the last user of r_{i^*} and j^* is the first user of r_{j^*} and the combination of r_{i^*} and r_{j^*} is feasible, combine them.

Step 4: Remove $s_{i^*j^*}$ from future considerations. If there are remaining savings to be evaluated, go to step 3, if not, finish.

Clarke and Wright (1964) proposed a parallel version and a sequential version of the savings algorithm. In the first, all the routes are built simultaneously, in the second the routes are built, as the name says, sequentially. The sequential version is used in this chapter.

Phase Two: Local Search-based Algorithm

This heuristic takes the solution obtained by the savings algorithm and try to improve it changing travels performed by vehicle for walking travels. This kind of moves reduces the time spent by professionals waiting for a vehicle.

The algorithm scans every visited node and evaluates if the distance between two consecutive nodes in the route can be done by walking. Remind that a travel can be performed walking if the distance w_{ij} is less than the maximum accepted distance W. In addition, as the visited nodes in the route are already defined by the savings algorithm, it is possible to impose a limit number of consecutive walking travels. This limit avoids to have a large number of nodes assigned to the same professional. Note that nodes in walking travels (origin and destination) are attended by the same professional. For instance, if a route obtained by savings algorithm has 12 nodes and there are four available professionals, a balanced assignment with 4 nodes per professional is desired.

The local search procedure is based on first improvement strategy, i.e. every time a travel satisfies the conditions, the transportation mode is changed from a vehicle travel to a walking travel. As only consecutive nodes are considered, the algorithm runs in linear time, $O(n)$.

Phase Three: Best Insertion Algorithm

Solomon (1987) proposed an extension of the savings algorithm and was the first to generalize a series of heuristic algorithms for the VRP solution with time windows, and developed the heuristic insertion structure, which has been widely used in the literature for solutions of different problems through heuristic methods. The best insertion algorithm consists of:

Step 1: Select an initial route with m users. One of the routes obtained after step two.
Step 2: Sort the users to insert. Here, the user to insert are the pickup nodes.
Step 3: For each user that has not yet been included in the route, do the following:

- Calculate the cost (in time terms) of inserting it in each feasible position.
- Insert in the position that generates the lowest cost.

Note that capacity constraint defines the feasible positions of a pickup node.

Figure 2. Best insertion sequence considering 5 delivery nodes and 3 professionals

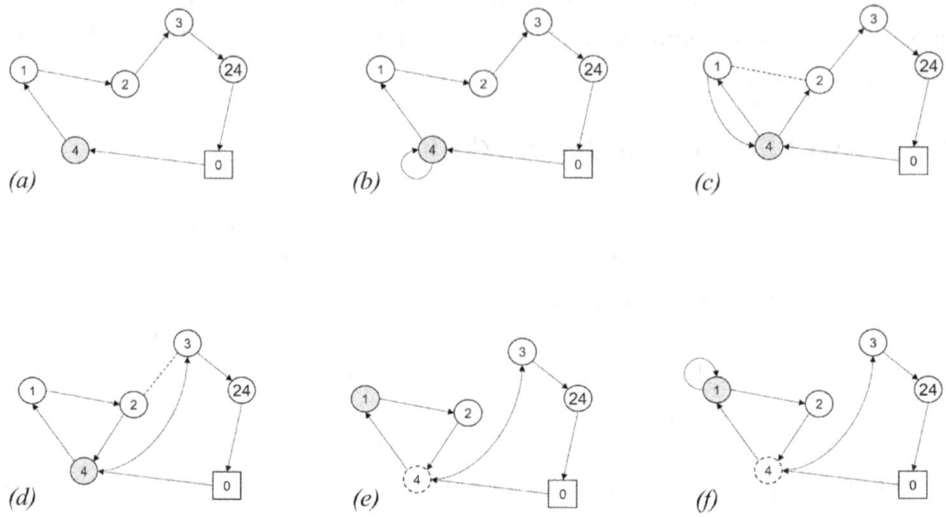

Figure 2 is an example of the sequence of best insertion algorithm, where it is defined a delivery route with tree different professionals. The sequence can be described as follows:

1. Figure 2shows the defined delivery route and the node (4) to define the pickup order.
2. Figure 2shows the first alternative for the pickup, that is, to wait until the first professional finishes the attention time to continue the route. It is implied that the other professionals are waiting in the vehicle to be "delivered".
3. Figure 2shows the second alternative where the professional in node 4 is pickup after the vehicle leaves the second professional in node 1. The arc (1,2) is eliminated and two new arcs are added, (1,4) and (4,2).
4. Figure 2shows the third alternative where the professional in node 4 is pickup after the vehicle leaves the third professional in node 2. The arc (2,3) is removed and arcs (2,4) and (4,3) are added. Note that it is not feasible to pick up the node 4 after 2 since there are only 3 professionals, and the solution would have four consecutive deliveries.
5. Figure 2shows the best alternative in time terms where the professional in node 4 is picked up after node 2 and the next node to define the pickup in the route is node 1 (alternative described by Figure 2(d)).
6. Figure 2shows the first alternative to pick up node 1, similar to alternative in Figure 2(b).

Phase Four: Assignment Algorithm

This algorithm finishes the routes construction by assigning professionals to each visited node in a route.

Given a feasible solution with pick up and deliveries from step three, this algorithm takes into account the available professionals and their number of assigned patients. The algorithm starts with zero assignments for each professional. When a delivery node is visited, it is chosen an available professional with the least number of assignments and that number is updated. The chosen professional is removed from the list of available professionals. When the delivery assigned node has walking travels after it in the route, the number of assignments takes into account the number of consecutive nodes with walking travels. On the other hand, if a pick up node is visited, the number of assignments does not change, but the corresponding professional is added to the list of available professionals.

COMPUTATIONAL EXPERIMENTS

In this section, both procedures are tested. MILP, due to the combinatorial behavior of the problems, is only tested with a very small instance. Heuristic approach is tested with larger instances. Due to the particularity of the problem, there are no available reference instances to test solutions, so the solution procedures are tested with instances based on the real case of study.

The first instance is defined by ten nodes including the departure point. The number of professionals is three and the working day duration is 8 hours. The maximum walking time is nine minutes. The MILP and the heuristic solution are proved in this instance where the results can be compared.

The second instance is defined by 30 nodes including the departure point, with the same parameters from instance 1. Only the heuristic solution is proved in this instance.

The third, fourth and fifth instances are defined by 101, 120 and 221 nodes respectively. In this instance the number of professionals is four, the working day and the maximum walking time are the same as previous instances. The heuristic solution in proved in this instance.

Computational results were gathered on an Intel Core i7-5600 U 2.6 GHZ Intel 12 GB RAM, -with Windows 10, 64 bits.

Results of MILP

The mathematical model is tested with the smaller instance (9 delivery nodes). It is coded in Python 2.7.10 running on Windows 10 and Gurobi 8.1 is used to solve it.

Figure 3 describes the best solution found, which only uses a single vehicle. The figure shows the delivery nodes in the top where nodes are ordered in non-decreasing order of arrival time, and pick up nodes are in the bottom in front of their respective delivery nodes. The arrows indicate the route followed by the vehicle. There are no walking travels. It is important no notice that Gurobi does not find an optimal solution after 3 running hours, and the reported gap between the best known solution and the best lower bound is 65.5%.

It can be defined the efficiency of a solution as the relation between the time required to give service to all patients and the total time used by routes in the solution as presented by Equation (37).

$$\frac{n \cdot s}{|P| \cdot T_k} \tag{37}$$

The efficiency of the solution presented in Figure 3 is 84.7%. That means that, on average, 84.7% of time professionals are servicing patients while 15.3% of time they spent time on transportation and waiting time.

Results of Heuristic Solution

The heuristic algorithm is also coded in Python 2.7.10 running on Windows 10. This algorithm is tested with 5 instances from 10 to 221 delivery nodes.

For the smaller instance, also tested with the MILP, Figure 4 depicts the solution found by the heuristic method in the same way presented for the MILP solution. As the solution found by MILP, only one vehicle is used. Nevertheless, as the proposed

Figure 3. MILP results scheme for a 9 patients' instance

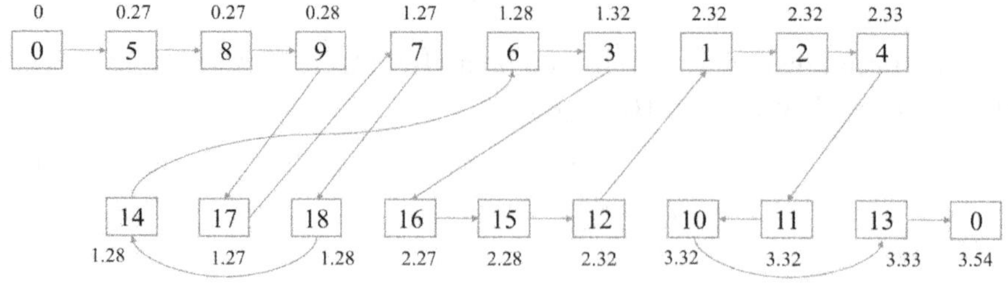

Figure 4. Heuristic results scheme for a 9 patients' instance

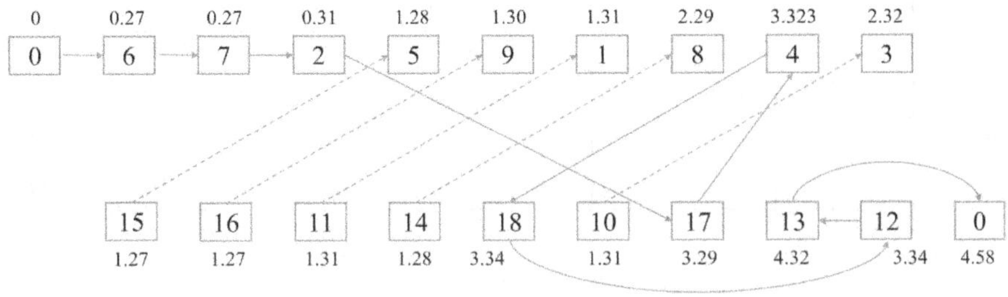

heuristic favors walking travels when it is feasible, this solution uses more times this transportation mode. The arrows indicate the route followed by the vehicle, and dashed arrows indicate the walking arcs performed by professionals.

Compared with the MILP solution, the heuristic one gets routes 1.26 times longer. In terms of efficiency, the heuristic is around 20% times less efficient than the MILP with 65.5%.

Table 4 summarizes the results for 5 instances. The first column indicates the method used to get a solution. Columns two and three represent the instances, the number of delivery nodes and the number of professionals respectively. Columns four to seven are related to the solution's features. Forth column shows the number of routes in the solution. Fifth column scores the average route length; this column equivalent to the objective function in presented by Equation (1) divided by the number of routes (column four). Sixth column presents the efficiency of the solutions, i.e. the percentage time spent for professionals on activities which do not include patient attention. Last column indicates the algorithm running time in seconds for each instance and method.

In these instances, the different routes defined in the solution allow only a few walking routes, particularly in instances 3 and 5. The results in terms of efficiency are not satisfactory in all instances. Some solutions have routes with a small number of delivery nodes, making difficult to assign professionals with a balanced load. Even though all the solutions are feasible and all restrictions are met. The solution efficiency decreases when the size of the problem increases. On the other hand, the running time increases with the number of patients.

It can be seen that there is a relationship between average route length and solution efficiency. For instance, for small instances (10 and 30 delivery nodes) the time per node is between 1.41 and 1.52 hours. The time per node for the solution found by MILP, which presents a greater efficiency, is around 1.21 hours. When this time is closer to $s=1$, the efficiency is greater. For larger instances, the time per node is between 2.84 and 4.1 hours.

Table 4. Results for 10 and 30 nodes instances

Solution method	Instance		Number of routes	Average route length	Solution efficiency	Running time (s)
	size	Number of professionals				
MILP	9	3	1	3.54	84.7%	10800.00
Heuristic	9	3	1	4.58	65.5%	0.01
Heuristic	29	3	2	6.80	71.1%	0.03
Heuristic	101	4	23	4.55	25.9%	0.57
Heuristic	120	4	14	6.10	17.8%	1.08
Heuristic	221	4	43	4.52	22.0%	9.43

FUTURE RESEARCH DIRECTIONS

The population aging and the increase in the care requirements for chronic diseases have overtaken the health institutions capacity, generating a growing trend in home health care mainly in Europe and the United States. Latin America is not indifferent to these phenomena but in a smaller proportion. Therefore, programs that involve home health care increasingly require tools that help decision-making, where the number of patients and the professionals required is increasing. Likewise, in the literature can be observed the growing interest in this type of problems in recent years.

The problem of routing and scheduling professionals with pickups and deliveries is considered a great application to different programs not only of home health care but also that offer different social services. This kind of models allow to give services to a geographically scattered population while reducing the required resources.

The results can show that there are opportunities to improve solution efficiency since average length is short for some instances. Different improvement heuristic algorithms and metaheuristics can be used in order to get more efficient solutions.

On the other hand, new features or objective functions can be considered. New objectives can include the minimization of the number of routes or days to cover all population, or monetary measures based on professional's salaries. New features can include time dependent travel times, time windows and stochastic events like cancelled appointments.

CONCLUSION

This chapter proposes a MILP that solves the problem of routing and scheduling for home health services with pickup and delivery for small instances. This model does not have practical uses since it cannot get optimal solutions even for instances with 9 delivery nodes, neither feasible solutions for instances with 29 delivery nodes.

The proposed four-phases heuristic approach finds feasible solutions faster, even for instances with 221 delivery nodes. It is important to notice that nowadays the problem is dealt manually, so the four-phases heuristic algorithm can be used to support that process.

The efficiency of the solution also depends on the instance complexity. Instances are based on real case where delivery nodes correspond to patient's homes and most of patients in this program are located at surroundings of the city. Efficiency of the solutions and routes lengths can be used to identify complex regions, difficult to include in routes with other nodes.

Finally, as stochastic events can occur during logistics operations, it is important to have fast methods able to reconstruct routes if some appointments are cancelled by patients, or variation on travels makes that the professionals cannot arrive to patient's homes within a working day.

REFERENCES

Begur, S., Miller, D., & Weaver, J. (1997). An Integrated Spatial DSS for Scheduling and Routing Home-Health-Care Nurses. *Interfaces*, *27*(4), 35–48. doi:10.1287/inte.27.4.35

Braekers, K., Hartl, R. F., Parragh, S. N., & Tricoire, F. (2016). A bi-objective home care scheduling problem: Analyzing the trade-off between costs and client inconvenience. *European Journal of Operational Research*, *248*(2), 428–443. doi:10.1016/j.ejor.2015.07.028

Cissé, M., Yalçındağ, S., Kergosien, Y., Şahin, E., Lenté, C., & Matta, A. (2017). Or problems related to home health care: A review of relevant routing and scheduling problems. *Operations Research for Health Care*, *13-14*, 1–22. doi:10.1016/j.orhc.2017.06.001

Clarke, G., & Wright, J. W. (1964). Scheduling of vehicles from a central depot to a number of delivery points. *Operations Research*, *12*(4), 568–581. doi:10.1287/opre.12.4.568

Decerle, J., Grunder, O., El Hassani, A., & Barakat, O. (2018). A memetic algorithm for a home health care routing and scheduling problem. *Operations Research for Health Care, 16*, 59–71. doi:10.1016/j.orhc.2018.01.004

Decerle, J., Grunder, O., El Hassani, A., & Barakat, O. (2019a). A hybrid memetic-ant colony optimization algorithm for the home health care problem with time window, synchronization and working time balancing. *Swarm and Evolutionary Computation, 46*, 171–183. doi:10.1016/j.swevo.2019.02.009

Decerle, J., Grunder, O., El Hassani, A., & Barakat, O. (2019b). A memetic algorithm for multi-objective optimization of the home health care problem. *Swarm and Evolutionary Computation, 44*, 712–727. doi:10.1016/j.swevo.2018.08.014

Fathollahi-Fard, A., Hajiaghaei-Keshteli, M., & Tavakkoli-Moghaddam, R. (2018). A bi-objective green home health care routing problem. *Journal of Cleaner Production, 200*, 423–443. doi:10.1016/j.jclepro.2018.07.258

Fikar, C., & Hirsch, P. (2015). A matheuristic for routing real-world home service transport systems facilitating walking. *Journal of Cleaner Production, 105*, 300–310. doi:10.1016/j.jclepro.2014.07.013

Frifita, S., & Masmoudi, M. (2019). VNS methods for home care routing and scheduling problem with temporal dependencies, and multiple structures and specialties. *International Transactions in Operational Research.*

Grenouilleau, F., Legrain, A., Lahrichi, N., & Rousseau, L. (2019). A set partitioning heuristic for the home health care routing and scheduling problem. *European Journal of Operational Research, 275*(1), 295–303. doi:10.1016/j.ejor.2018.11.025

Lenstra, J. K., & Kan, A. H. (1981). Complexity of vehicle routing and scheduling problems. *Networks, 11*(2), 221–227. doi:10.1002/net.3230110211

Liu, R., Xie, X., Augusto, V., & Rodriguez, C. (2013). Heuristic algorithms for a vehicle routing problem with simultaneous delivery and pickup and time windows in home health care. *European Journal of Operational Research, 230*(3), 475–486. doi:10.1016/j.ejor.2013.04.044

Parragh, S. N., Doerner, K. F., & Hartl, R. F. (2008). A survey on pickup and delivery problems. *Journal fur Betriebswirtschaft, 58*(1), 21–51. doi:10.100711301-008-0033-7

Solomon, M. M. (1987). Algorithms for the vehicle routing and scheduling problems with time window constraints. *Operations Research, 35*(2), 254–265. doi:10.1287/opre.35.2.254

Trautsamwieser, A., Gronalt, M., & Hirsch, P. (2011). Securing home health care in times of natural disasters. *OR-Spektrum*, *33*(3), 787–813. doi:10.100700291-011-0253-4

Vidal, T., Crainic, T. G., Gendreau, M., & Prins, C. (2013). Heuristics for multi-attribute vehicle routing problems: A survey and synthesis. *European Journal of Operational Research*, *231*(1), 1–21. doi:10.1016/j.ejor.2013.02.053

Xiao, L., Dridi, M., & El Hassani, A. (2018). Mathematical model for the home health care scheduling and routing problem with flexible lunch break requirements. *IFAC-PapersOnLine*, *51*(11), 334–339. doi:10.1016/j.ifacol.2018.08.305

KEY TERMS AND DEFINITIONS

Combinatorial Optimization: It is a subset of mathematical optimization that is related to operations research, algorithm theory, and computational complexity theory. It involves algorithmic techniques to solve discrete optimization problems within a finite set of possibilities.

Health Systems: It refers to the organization of people, institutions, resources and policies with the aim to improve the population health and deliver health services.

Heuristic Algorithms: It refers to a set of procedures or methods that search, fast and easily, good quality solutions for complex problems.

Mixed Integer Linear Programming: It involves optimization problems make up of linear functions where some decision variables are constrained to be integers and other are allowed to be continuous.

Multi Modal Transportation: It is a transport system which includes several ways to move material, goods or people from one or several origins to one or several destinations.

Pickup and Delivery: It is related to logistic services where material or people need to be collected at some sites (nodes) and others need to be delivered at other sites.

Vehicle Routing Problems: It is a classical combinatorial optimization problem where a set of vehicles need to visit once a set of nodes.

Chapter 6
An Application for Routing Ambulance via ACO in Home Healthcare

Şahin Inanç
Bursa Uludağ University, Turkey

Arzu Eren Şenaras
https://orcid.org/0000-0002-3862-4551
Uludag University, Turkey

ABSTRACT

In this study, rovers of ambulances were identified and determined quickly and practically via ant colony optimization. Non-intuitive methods can also be used to determine the routing, but when the number of nodes is large, and the number of operations is very large, the heuristic methods are more practical. The purpose of this work is to use ant colony optimization via C# for ambulance routing. The patients were served as soon as possible thanks to ambulance routing. In this the effectiveness of the ambulance has been increased. In this study, 12 nodes were selected as an application. The nodes were used to determine the route of the ambulance in-home health care.

INTRODUCTION

Home health care is growing in the French medical sector since demands increase. Organizations providing home care services are willing to optimize their activities in order to meet the increasing demand for home care. Consequently, research on this problem has appeared by the end of the 20th century. Most of the work being

DOI: 10.4018/978-1-7998-0268-6.ch006

application-based, the number of publications rises to cover the different variants of the problem. The problem is complicated by factors such as caregivers qualification, various patients demand, multiple home care offices, caregivers workload limitation, shared visits, patients availability and workload fairness among caregivers (Decerle et.al., 2017, Bertrand, 2010).

Home Health Care is a wide range of health care services that can be given in one's home for an illness or injury. In recent years, the health care industry has become one of the largest sectors of the economy in developed countries such as France, Germany, Australia, etc. Since the transportation cost is one of the most important spendings in the company activities, it is of great significance to optimize the vehicle routing problem in home health care company. According to a survey (Mankowska et al., 2014; Harris, 2015; Liu et al., 2013) of the home health care companies, each day, an HHC company carries out various logistics activities including the delivery of drugs or medical instruments from the pharmacy to patients, and pickup of the biological samples and waste from patients' home to the laboratory. A large number of patients are located in a town or village, and the task of a home health care company is to provide health care services to the patients at ones' homes one by one. The main operational process of the HHC can be summarized as three steps (Shi et al., 2017, p. 13987):

1. The HHC company collects information from the patients, this information may include: name, address, sex, type of the illness, symptom and other related information;
2. The HHC company plan to arrange the visited routes and assign nurses according to the information collected;
3. The nurses are scheduled to visit the patients. Each nurse is assigned to a planned route, and he/she has to carry out all of the service-related activities for the route. This nurse will drive the vehicle to visit the patients one by one according to the designed route.

Among the first papers about home health care, Begur et al. (1997) described a decision support system not taking into account time window and shared visits in opposite to Cheng and Rich (1998) who considered patients and care givers time window as well as multiple home care offices. They solved small instances with exact and heuristic approaches. Shared visits have been lately studied in the literature. Eveborn et al. (2006) developed a decision support system for an application in Sweden including shared visits who have also been studied by Rasmussen et al. (2012) using a branch-and-price algorithm or by Mankowska et al. (2014) using an adaptive variable neighborhood search algorithm as solving approaches (Decerle, 2017, p. 14662).

A SHORT LITERATURE REWIEV

Liu Ran et. al. (2013) studied a vehicle scheduling problem encountered in home health care logistics. Each patient is visited by one vehicle and each vehicle visits each node at most once. Patients are associated with time windows and vehicles with capacity. Two mixed-integer programming models were proposed. They proposed a Genetic Algorithm (GA) and a Tabu Search (TS) method. The GA is based on a permutation chromosome, a split procedure and local search. The TS were based on route assignment attributes of patients, an augmented cost function, route re-optimization, and attribute-based aspiration levels. These approaches were tested on test instances derived from existing VRPTW benchmarks.

Liu Ran et. al. (2014) proposed a Tabu Search method combined with different local search schemes including both feasible and infeasible local searches. The proposed approaches were tested on a range of instances derived from existing Vehicle Routing Problem with TimeWindow (VRPTW) benchmarks and benchmarks on special cases of their problem. Numerical results show that local search scheme starting with an infeasible local search with a small probability followed by a feasible local search with high probability is an interesting hybridization.

Shi et.al. (2017). studied a Home Health Care Routing problem with stochastic travel and service time is considered, and a stochastic programming model with recourse is proposed. Stochastic simulation method and hybrid genetic algorithm were integrated to solve the proposed model. Their study considers a Home Health Care Routing Problem with stochastic travel and service time, which comes from the logistics practice of the home health care company. A stochastic programming model with recourse (SPR) was proposed, the Hybrid Genetic Algorithm (HGA) and stochastic simulation method are integrated to solve the proposed model. Three series of experiments were carried out to evaluate the model.

Decerle et.al. (2017). proposed a general mixed-integer programming model for the home health care routing and scheduling problem with route balancing. The proposed model handles most of the known characteristics in order to be application-based independent. A memetic algorithm was proposed to evaluate the multi-objective approach on several instances and support decision-making. The impact of the focus on route balancing was analyzed on the behavior of the objectives.

ANT COLONY OPTIMIZATION (ACO)

In the early 1990s, ant colony optimization (ACO) was introduced by M. Dorigo and colleagues as a novel nature-inspired metaheuristic for the solution of hard combinatorial optimization (CO) problems. ACO belongs to the class of metaheuristics,

Figure 1. Natural Behaviors of Arts

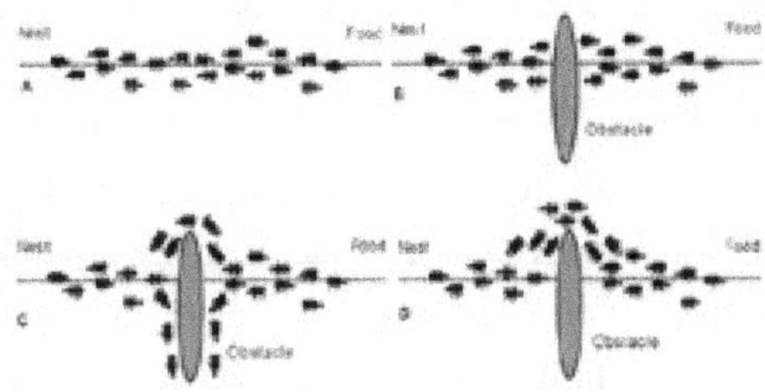

which are approximate algorithms used to obtain good enough solutions to hard CO problems in a reasonable amount of computation time. Other examples of metaheuristics are tabu search, simulated annealing, and evolutionary computation. The inspiring source of ACO is the foraging behavior of real ants. When searching for food, ants initially explore the area surrounding their nest in a random manner. As soon as an ant finds a food source, it evaluates the quantity and the quality of the food and carries some of it back to the nest. During the return trip, the ant deposits a chemical pheromone trail on the ground. The quantity of pheromone deposited, which may depend on the quantity and quality of the food, will guide other ants to the food source. As it has been shown in, indirect communication between the ants via pheromone trails enables them to find shortest paths between their nest and food sources. This characteristic of real ant colonies is exploited in artificial ant colonies in order to solve CO problems (Dorigo and Blum, 2005).

Ant colony algorithms were first proposed by Dorigo and colleagues as a multi-agent approach to difficult combinatorial optimization problems such as the traveling salesman problem and the quadratic assignment problem. There is currently much ongoing activity in the scientific community to extend and apply ant-based algorithms to many different discrete optimization problems. Recent applications cover problems such as vehicle routing, job shop scheduling, quadratic assignment problem, and so on (Kulatunga et. al., 2006).

ACO APPLICATION VIA C# FOR AMBULANCE ROUTING

This work was used to calculate the shortest path in this study, by passing through all the nodes according to the ant colony algorithm and providing a closed loop by returning to the starting point, provided that the dropped node does not come back. These types of problems are referred to as traveling salesman problems.

In this study, 12 nodes were selected as an application. The nodes were used to determine the route of the ambulance im home health care.

The problem is a traveling salesman type problem in which the aim is to create the shortest trip by visiting each node once. There are many ways to solve such problems.

When the number of nodes are too much instead of finding the optimal solution, generally it is preferred a solution that can be find in a reasonable time close to optimal solution with heuristic algorithms.

The solution of the ambulance routing problem was found by ant colony optimization for 12 different nodes. The distances between the nodes are shown in the table.

The ant colony algorithm is not necessary to find the solution of this problem consisting of 12 nodes, but it is an appropriate example to show how the algorithm works.

Ant Colony Optimization that used to solve the problem was developed in Microsoft Visual Studio. Net C # programming language.

Features of the computer used to run the software is Intel i5 2.4 GHz processor, 4GB RAM with Windows 10 Operating System.

The algorithm for routing ambulance via ant colony optimization is shown as below:

Ant Colony Optimization Algorithm:

1. Start
2. define iterationCount, antCount, tour, localSolution[], globalSolution, pheromone, etc.
3. Create tree structure for node connections
4. for I = 0 to iterationCount
5. for J = 0 to antCount
6. Generate random number between 0-1
7. if generated number is smaller than q0 select method1 else select method2

Method1: Select path with the most pheromone
Method2: Collect all possible paths
Divide all possible paths to total collected amount
Choose the path that has the greatest value

8. Store the path information into memory
9. if tour is impossible to complete go to step 6
10. localSolution[J] = tour
11. if tour is better than globalSolution then

globalSolution = tour

12. next I
13. Update pheromone value on paths using localSolution[]
14. Update pheromone value on paths using globalSolution
    13. next J
    14. Show the bestTour
    15. End

In practice, a cluster structure (array structure) is created for each node to which nodes can be traversed. Routes between the nodes are defined as array and initial pheromones are set to record pheromone information. Then, starting from the start node, each node transition is marked to not return the same node to the previous node again, and the next node is switched to the next node based on the pheromone values of the potential nodes that are to be passed next

Ant Colony Optimization parameters are; alpha = 1.23 (alpha indicates the importance of pheromone density), beta = 1.08 (the beta parameter indicating the importance of the path), evaporatipn = 0.08 (pheromone evaporation rate), $q_0 = 0.5$ (q_0 The parameter that determines the probability of choosing the path in which the pheromone is dense).

The shortest path is: 1-3-2-4-8-7-11-12-10-9-6-5-1
The total road is: 36.24

Table 1. Distances Between Patients for Ambulance Routing Problem

Nodes	1	2	3	4	5	6	7	8	9	10	11	12
1	0	4	3,61	9,22	3	6,32	9,22	7,21	9,49	10,82	12,04	12,73
2	4	0	2,24	5,39	4,24	6,32	6,71	4,47	9,06	9,22	9,43	10,3
3	3,61	2,24	0	6	2,24	4,12	5,66	3,61	7	7,48	8,49	9,22
4	9,22	5,39	6	0	8,06	8,06	4,47	3,61	9,22	7,62	6	7
5	3	4,24	2,24	8,06	0	3,16	6,71	5,1	6,32	7,81	9,43	10
6	6,32	6,32	4,12	8,06	3,16	0	5	4,47	3,16	5	7,28	7,62
7	9,22	6,71	5,66	4,47	6,71	5	0	2,24	5	3,16	2,83	3,61
8	7,21	4,47	3,61	3,61	5,1	4,47	2,24	0	5,83	5	5	9,06
9	9,49	9,06	7	9,22	6,32	3,16	5	5,83	0	3	6,08	6
10	10,82	9,22	7,48	7,62	7,81	5	3,16	5	3	0	3,16	3
11	12,04	9,43	8,49	6	9,43	7,28	2,83	5	6,08	3,16	0	1
12	12,73	10,3	9,22	7	10	7,62	3,61	9,06	6	3	1	0

Figure 2. Flowchart of Routing Ambulance Via ACO-1

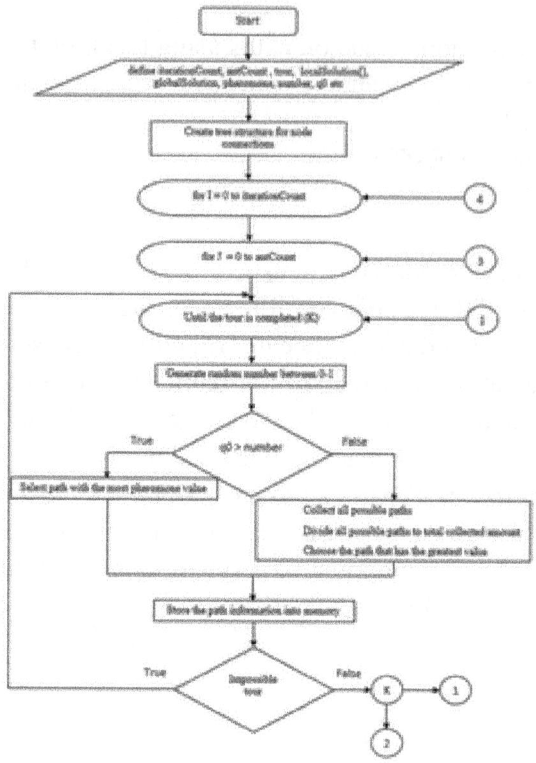

Figure 3. Flowchart of Routing Ambulance Via ACO-2

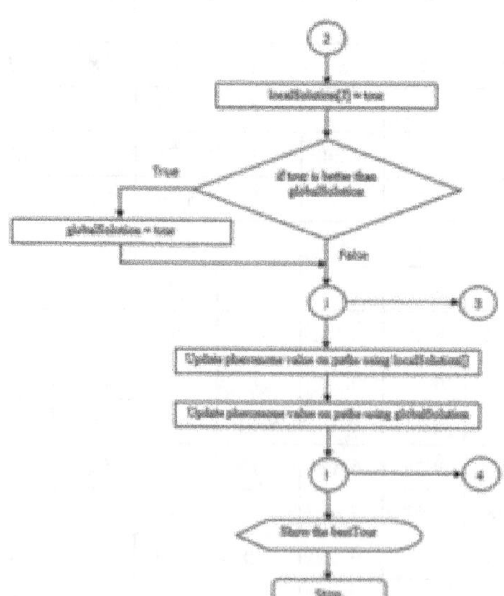

CONCLUSION

In this study, the shortest way for ambulance line was found using Ant colony optimization. The application is developed in C# programming language. Ant colony optimization technique is used for ambulance path planning problems. As a result, in this study ambulance ant colony optimization helped to determine and direct the route more practically and quickly. The advantage of this method arises especially when the number of nodes is large. It can be said that ACO is an effective optimization method for solving any problem that includes shortest way.

REFERENCES

Begur, S. V., Miller, D. M., & Weaver, J. R. (1997). An Integrated Spatial Dss For Scheduling And Routing Homehealth-Care Nurses. *Interfaces*, *27*(4), 35–48. doi:10.1287/inte.27.4.35

Bertrand, D. (2010). Les services de soins infirmiers domicile en 2008. *Etudes et rsultats*, *739*. Retrieved from http:// drees.social-sante.gouv.fr/IMG/pdf/er739.pdf

Cheng, E., & Rich, J. L. (1998). A home health care routing and scheduling problem. Retrieved from http://citeseerx.ist.psu.edu/viewdoc/summary

Decerle, J., Grunder, O., Hassani Hajjam El, A., & Barakat, O. (2017). A general model for the home health care routing and scheduling problem with route balancing. *IFAC Papers On Line*, *50-1*(1), 14662–14667. doi:10.1016/j.ifacol.2017.08.1907

Eveborn, P., Flisberg, P., & R¨onnqvist, M. (2006). Laps carean operational system for staff planning of home care. *European Journal of Operational Research*, *171*(3), 962–976. doi:10.1016/j.ejor.2005.01.011

Harris, M. D. (2015). *Handbook of home health care administration*. Jones & Bartlett Publishers.

Kulatunga, A. K. D., Liu, K., Dissanayake, G., & Siyambalapitiya, S. B. (2006). Ant colony optimization based simultaneous task allocation and path planning of autonomous vehicles. *Proceedings of the IEEE Conference on Cybernetics and Intelligent Systems*, Bangkok, Thailand. IEEE. 10.1109/ICCIS.2006.252349

Mankowska, D. S., Meisel, F., & Bierwirth, C. (2014). The Home Health Care Routing And Scheduling Problem With Interdependent Services. *Health Care Management Science*, *17*(1), 15–30. doi:10.100710729-013-9243-1 PMID:23780750

Marco, D., & Christian, B. (2005). Ant colony optimization theory: A survey. *Theoretical Computer Science*, *344*(2-3), 243–278. doi:10.1016/j.tcs.2005.05.020

Ran, L., Xie, X., & Thierry, G. (2014). Hybridization Of Tabu Search With Feasible And Infeasible Local Searchesfor Periodic Home Health Care Logistics. *Omega*, *47*, 17–32. doi:10.1016/j.omega.2014.03.003

Ran, L., Xie, X., Vincent, A., & Carlos, R. (2013). Heuristic algorithms for a vehicle routing problem with simultaneous delivery and pickup and time windows in home health care. *European Journal of Operational Research*, *230*(3), 475–486. doi:10.1016/j.ejor.2013.04.044

Yong, S., Toufik, B., & Olivier, G. (2017). A Home Health Care Routing Problem with Stochastic Travel and Service Time. *IFAC PapersOnLine*, *50-1*, 13987–13992.

Chapter 7
A Multi-Objective Model for the Simultaneous Planning Problems:
Dock Courtyard Formulations and a Case Study

Kallel Lobna
https://orcid.org/0000-0001-9016-5463
LOGIQ ISGI, University of Sfax, Sfax, Tunisia

Kamoun Hichem
MODELIS FSEG, University of Sfax, Sfax, Tunisia

Benaissa Mounir
REGIM ENIS, University of Sfax, Sfax, Tunisia

ABSTRACT

This chapter examines two of the most important operational problems in seaport terminals, first, the berth allocation problem (BAP) which finds an optimal assignment of ships to the berths that minimise the total waiting time of all ships. Then we consider the ships containers to storage areas assignment problem (SSAP) which finds an allocation of ship containers to storage area that minimises the travelling time and containers dispersion. In the first step, a mixed integer linear program model is designed to address the BA problem with the aim of minimising the ships stay time in the port (known as the scheduling theory by the flow time). In a second step, the output of the first model is used in another mixed integer linear program model to solve the SSA problem with a view at reducing both travelling time and containers dispersion while satisfying storage capacities for the case where the containers of one ship can be partitioned into two different and consecutive storage area when needed. The experimental part is conducted on a real case, namely the Tunisian port of Radès.

DOI: 10.4018/978-1-7998-0268-6.ch007

INTRODUCTION

Considered as an inter-modal interface in maritime Supply Chain, seaport container terminals play a primary role in maritime transportation. The process begins with a port allocation ship entering the dock where containers will be unloaded by shore cranes and transported by a Straddle Carrier (SC) or Reach Stacker (RS) to the storage area. Thus, the mode of transport changes from maritime to inland. Allocating berths for arriving containers is a key factor in promoting the efficiency of container handling as well as reducing the turnaround time and the congestion of a ship in the port. A practical way of enhancing the efficiency and competitiveness of the container terminals depends on the identification and resolution of several operational problems that usually occur in the port (Lobna, Hichem & Mounir, 2016). These optimization problems include Stowage Planning (Imai, Sasaki, Nishimura & Papadimitriou, 2016), Quay Crane Scheduling Lee, Wang, & Miao, 2008), Yard Truck Scheduling, Yard Crane Scheduling (Lee, Cao & Meng, 2007), Storage Allocation (Lee, Chew, Tan & Han, 2006) and Berth Allocation (Imai, Nishimura & Papadimitriou, 2001).

In practice, most ships are unproductive while they are stuck in a port. Accelerating the handling operation and improving the assignment of ships to berths and the containers to the storage areas are equally important to reduce the waste of time. Therefore, an efficient berth allocation at the seaport terminal is highly crucial for reducing the time spent by ships in the port and enhancing the competitiveness of ports. Further minimizing ships' stay time and reducing congestion in ports has become a vital priority for seaport terminals (Lobna, Hichem & Mounir, 2016).

It should be noted that each berth can handle one ship at the same time and that the handling time of a ship depends on the distance between the berth and the storage area. Thus, we must consider the availability of berths and cranes responsible for unloading of the ship.

Due to the importance of choosing the berths and the storage areas, we have dedicated this paper to deal with the Berth Allocation Problem (BAP) and the Assignment of Ship Containers to the Storage Area Problem (SSAP). These problems have been extensively scrutinized in the following papers: (Lobna, Hichem & Mounir, 2016; Imai, Nishimura & Papadimitriou, 2001; Zeinebou & Abdellatif, 2014; Zeinebou & Abdellatif, 2013; Peter & Kozan, 2001), which serve as a background for our paper.

This paper examines the BAP and the SSAP with the aim of minimizing ships' stay time in the port and the traveling time of containers unloaded between the berth and the storage area as well as decreasing the dispersion of each ship's containers in the storage areas. To address these problems, we present two mathematical models solved using CPLEX.

The outline of the paper including a review of the literature which is provided in Section 2. In section 3 a description of the BAP and its mathematical model are presented. Section 4 presents The SSAP problem, its mathematical model. A real-life example from the port of Rades, in Tunisia is studied in Section 5. Finally, concluding remarks and directions for future research are suggested in Section 6.

LITERATURE REVIEW

The substantial increase of international trade dependent on maritime transport, and more particularly containerization, has placed the maritime container shipping industry at the centre of the global economy. Consequently, competition between ports has become fiercer with a view to improving the customer service. Chief among the performance measures of customer service is the berthing time of container carrying ships that accounts for a considerable proportion of its journey (Peter & Kozan, 2001). Shipping lines are mainly concerned with the waiting time and berthing time of the ships at the port. Nevertheless, the docking time for all the ports must be as small as possible to service all the ships efficiently. This will consequently satisfy customer requirements and reduce the costs and congestion in the port (Lee, Cao, Shi & Chen, 2009) as well.

In order to reduce the overall time spent in the port, two steps should be taken. First, it is essential to reduce the time in which the ships stay in the port (known in the Scheduling Theory by the flow time). This problem is conceptualized in the literature as the Berth Allocation Problem (BAP). Second, both the travelling time of a container from the berth until the storage area and the dispersion of containers need to be minimized. Thus, the aim is to reach an optimal assignment of berths containers to the storage areas (SSA).

However, in practice, the BAP consists in assigning all the ships to berths along the dock, but when we assign these ships, we must take into consideration some constraints such as the depth of water for ships berthing, the preferred docking area, etc. (Zeinebou & Abdellatif, 2014). Worth mentioning is that the BAP exists in a static version, in which the arrival times of ships are known in advance, and a dynamic version, where ships do not follow a schedule.

The BAP has been thoroughly studied in the literature. Some researchers (Imai, Nishimura & Papadimitriou, 2001; Pierre & Ceyda, 2003; Zeinebou & Abdellatif, 2014; Xu, Li, & Joseph, 2012; Imai, Nishimura & Papadimitriou, 2001; Imai, Nishimura, Papadimitriou, 2003; Monaco & Sammarra, 2007;, Hansen, Oguz & Mladenovic, 2008; Golias, Boile & Theofanis, 2009) presented the discrete BAP as a platform of a finite set of places. Others (Kim & Moon, 2003; Guan & Cheung; 2004; Imai, Sun, Nishimura & Papadimitriou, 2005; Moorthy & Teo, 2006; Lee, Chen & Cao, 2010) argued that ships can dock anywhere on the quay in the continuous BAP.

These researchers have investigated several techniques in an attempt to find a better solution to the BAP (or SAB) and SSAP. Many approximate methods have been used, namely Heuristics, Meta-Heuristics and hybridization procedures. For example, Zeinebou and Abdellatif (2014) proposed a mathematical model to minimize the time spent by the ships in the port and the distance travelled by containers of berth to the storage area. Different meta-heuristics have been used to solve this problem such as Genetic Algorithm, Simulated Annealing and their Hybridization. Barros et al. (2011) addressed the BAP using a Heuristic based on simulated annealing. Arango et al. (2011) developed a Heuristic procedure based on a genetic algorithm to solve a non-linear problem while Zhen et al. (2011) designed a Meta-Heuristic approach to solve a model that decides on uncertainties for the BAP.

Lai and Shih (1992) proposed heuristic algorithms for a BAP on the assumption of the FCFS (First Come First Served) allocation strategy. Kim and Kim (2002) devised a method for determining the optimal amount of storage space and the optimal number of transfer cranes for handling import containers. Lee et al. (2008) proposed an integrated model for yard truck scheduling and storage allocation for import containers. This problem was formulated as a MIP with the objective of minimizing the makespan of operations. A Genetic Algorithm and a dedicated heuristic algorithm were developed to solve the problem.

Preston and Kozan (2001) formulated a mathematical optimization model to minimize the time spent during the transfer of containers from the storage area to the ship and vice versa. A Genetic Algorithm was used to address this problem. Kim and Kim (1999) determined optimal routes for a single SC to retrieve containers, which need to be loaded on a ship from the stock, more efficiently. Their objective was to minimize the total travel time of the SC. As for Zhang et al. (2003), they studied the Storage Space Allocation Problem in the storage yards of a terminal so that the total transportation distance for moving containers between blocks and ship berthing locations is reduced.

Vacca et al. (2012) dealt with the simultaneous optimization of berth allocation and quay crane assignment in seaport container terminals. They presented a model based on an exponential number of variables that is solved using Column generation and an exact branch-and-price algorithm in order to produce optimal integer solutions to the problem. Lee et al. (2009) devised an approach that integrates the problems of Yard Truck Scheduling and Storage Allocation, Their work sought to minimize the weighted sum of total delay of requests and the total travel time of yard trucks. A hybrid algorithm was presented to solve this problem. Moussi et al. (2015) examined the Container Stacking Problem and suggested a model that would determine the optimal storage strategy for various container-handling schedules. This problem deployed an efficient hybrid ant colony and simulated annealing.

Our work seeks to minimize the flow time of all the ships in the port, decrease the traveling time of containers unloaded between the berth and the storage area, and reduce the dispersion of containers in the storage area. In light of the seminal work of Zeinebou and Abdellatif (2014), we propose two mathematical models in this paper. The BAP model aims to decrease the flow time of all the ships in the port and can be used for both the static and dynamic berth allocation cases where ships' ready time and berths' availability are different from zero. A succinct description of the model is provided in Kallel et al.

Compared with that adopted by Zeinebou and Abdellatif (2014), our model has distinct additional characteristics. In fact, our model finds independent optimal solutions for both the BAP and SSA problems. A new formulation of the BA problem where the flow time is modelled as a variable is presented. Only the import part of the SSA problem is considered. Besides the minimisation of the dispersion of containers in the storage areas is guaranteed in the SSAP model.

Considerable effort has been made in order to solve many optimization problems using approximate methods (Heuristics and Meta-Heuristics) or Enumerative methods. Yet, heuristic and meta-heuristic methods did not guarantee optimality, provided only approximate solution searching through the set of feasible solutions, and were usually time-consuming, especially for large problems. More recently, optimization problems have been classified according to their computational complexity and the difficulty to find the optimal solution.

Finding an Optimal Assignment for the BAP

In this section, we present a mathematical model (introduced in a previous paper (Lobna, Hichem & Mounir, 2016)) that is designed to minimize the flow time of all the ships in the port and to reduce the waiting time and overall length of stay for all ships in the port.

Based on the work of Zeinebou and Abdellatif (2014), we present in this section a mathematical model, where we consider that both the ready time and availability of ships are different from zero. We notice that this model can solve the static and dynamic versions of BAP at the same time.

This mathematical model takes into account the following hypotheses:

- The planning process is considered at the same time as static (SBAP) (the arrival times of all the ships are known in advance) or dynamic (DBAP) (all the ships may come after the start of the scheduled plan).
- Each berth can accommodate only one ship at the same time.
- Each ship can be assigned to only one berth.
- The processing time of the ship remains unchangeable for all berths.
- Physical restrictions on the docks considered here are water depth and berth length.
- When a ship is assigned to a dock post, it will remain in office until the end of its stay in the port.

1. Parameters and Decision variables:
   a. Parameters:
      i: is the index of available berths, i (= 1…….I) ∈ B
      j: is the index of entering ships, j (=1…..T) ∈ V
      k: is the index of the service order; in each berth, the number of the service order is equal to the number of Ships, k (=1…. T) ∈ O.
      B: the set of available berths.
      V: the set of entering ships.
      O: the set of the service order.
      P_j: processing time of ship j.
      r_j: realise date (ready time) which corresponds to the date of availability for the treatment of ship j.
      S_i: 'set up /*availability*', which corresponds to the date of availability of the berth i.
      W_i: depth of the water berth i.
      E_j: draft of the ship's j water.
      Q_i: length of berth i.
      L_j: length of ship j.
   b. Decision Variables
      F_{ijk}: Flow time of ship j assigned in berth i in order k.

$$X_{ijk} = \begin{cases} 1, & \textit{if the shipjis assigned to berthi in order k} \\ 0, & \textit{otherwise} \end{cases}$$

C_{ijk}: '*Completion time*', which corresponds to the end date of the execution of the ship j on the berth i in the order k. according to formula $C_{ijk} = F_{ijk} + (r_j * X_{ijk})$

Then, the mathematical model is outlined as follows

$$G = \text{Min} \sum_{i \in B} \sum_{j \in V} \sum_{K \in O} F_{ijk} \tag{1}$$

$$\sum_{i \in B} \sum_{K \in O} X_{ijk} = 1; \forall j \in V \tag{2}$$

$$\sum_{j \in V} X_{ijk} \leq 1; \forall i \in B, k \in O \tag{3}$$

$$F_{ijk} \geq C_{it(k-1)} - \left(r_j * X_{ijk}\right) + \left(P_j * X_{ijk}\right); \quad \forall i \in B, j \in V, k \in O, t \in V \text{ and } t \neq j \tag{4}$$

$$F_{ijk} \geq (P_j * X_{ijk}); \quad \forall i \in B, j \in V, k \in O \tag{5}$$

$$F_{ijk} = C_{ijk} - (r_j * X_{ijk}); \quad \forall i \in B, j \in V, k \in O \tag{6}$$

$$\left(W_i - E_j\right) X_{ijk} \geq 0; \quad \forall i \in B, j \in V, k \in O \tag{7}$$

$$\left(Q_i - L_j\right) X_{ijk} \geq 0; \quad \forall i \in B, j \in V, k \in O \tag{8}$$

$$C_{it0} = S_i; \quad \forall i \in B, t \in V \tag{9}$$

$$X_{ijk} \in \{0,1\}; \quad \forall i \in B, j \in V, k \in O \tag{10}$$

- The objective function (1) aims to reduce the processing time and waiting time for all the ships in the port.
- Constraint (2) ensures that all ships are served on a berth in a given service order.
- Constraint (3) ensures that each berth can only accommodate one ship at a time (i.e. a dock cannot accommodate two ships or more at the same time. It can only accommodate one single ship).

- Constraint (4) gives the value of the flow time of the ship *j* on the berth *i* according to the order k, where $Cit(k\text{-}1)$ is greater than rj that is to say the end date of the execution of the ship *t* exceeds the availability date of the ship *j*.
- Constraint (5) gives the value of the flow time of the ship *j* on the berth *i* according to the order *k*, when rj is greater than $Cit(k\text{-}1)$ that is to say the beginning date of the execution of the ship *j* exceeds the completion time of the ship *t* ordered in the position *(k-1)*.
- Constraint (6) stands for the relation between the flow time and completion time.
- Constraint (7) ensures compatibility between the depth of the water and the berth requested by the ship.
- Constraint (8) ensures compatibility between the length of the ship and the berth length.
- Constraint (9) gives the initial value of the completion time $Cit0$ and is equal to S_i.
- Constraint (10) defines the decision variables.

The output of this first problem is used as one of the inputs to the second problem in the following section. Therefore, the output of this problem presents the result of assigning ship *j* in berth *i* in order *k* given by X_{ijk} for the import ships part only. We will use this result as a parameter in the second model. However, our choice to treat each of the problems BAP and SSAP independently allows us to choose any method for the BAP such as FCFS (First Come First Served) or any other method while we can use their results as input in the SSAP model.

AN OPTIMAL SHIPS CONTAINERS TO STORAGE AREAS ASSIGNMENT PROBLEMS (SSAP)

The Mathematical Model

In this part, we propose a mathematical model that aims to minimize the time required to transfer all the containers between the berths and the storage areas, and minimize the dispersion of all the containers in the ship to the storage areas.

Our model assumes the following hypotheses:

- The planning process is considered as static that is the arrival times of all the ships are known in advance.

- The first mathematical model (presented in Section 3) is used to determine the set of service ships orders according to the processing /handling time of the ship on the berth and is given by X^*_{ij} for import ships.
- Each berth can accommodate only one ship at the same time.
- Each ship is assigned to one berth.
- We focus on the operations of the containers unloaded in storage area and arriving from different terminals.
- Each Reach Stacker (RS) can carry only one container per path at the same time.
- The velocity of the RS is constant and identical for all the RSs used in the transfer of containers on the various berths.
- We do not consider the congestion of RSs during their trips from the dock to the storage areas.
- The distance between the berths and the storage areas is determined by the port authorities.
- The travelling time of a container is presented by the travelling time of a container berth to the storage area while using the RS. This includes the time of loading and unloading a container at the beginning and at the end of the path.

1. Parameters and Decision variables
   a. Parameters

      i: The index of available berths, i (= 1…I)∈ B

      j: The index of entering ships, j (=1…T) ∈ V

      z: The index of storage areas, z (=1…A) ∈ D

      c: The index of moving containers, c (=1…C)∈ F

      n: The index of the RS to use, *n* (= 1…..N) ∈ E

      B: The set of available berths.

      V: The sets of entering ships.

      D: The set of storage areas with A=|D|, (A is equal to the cardinality of D).

      D1: The set of storage areas with D1 = {1, 3, 5, …, A-2} ∈ D, if A is odd.

      D1: The set of storage areas with D1 = {1, 3, 5, …, A-1} ∈ D, if A is even.

      D2: The set of storage areas with D2 = {D\ D1\ {A}} = {2, 4, 6, …, A-1} ∈ D, if A is odd.

      D2: The set of storage areas with D2 = {D\ D1} = {2, 4, 6, …, A} ∈ D, if A is even.

      F: The set of containers.

      V^n: The velocity of the RS.

***lock*:** This is the time required for the RS to hold on to a container before taking up. It is also called locking time (or unload time). It is equal to the release time (also called load time) of a container after moving.

d_{iz}: The distance between the berth i and the storage area z.

C_j: The number of containers unloaded from the ship j.

T_{iz}: The traveling time of a container from the berth i until the storage area z, (Also called locking time *(lock)*) is equal to the time required for an RS to hold on to a container before taking up. This is also equal to the release time of a container after moving *(lock)* + the distance between the berth i and the storage area z (d_{iz}) divided by the velocity of the RS used to move the container (V^n).

The traveling time is given by the formula:

$$T_{iz} = lock + (d_{iz}/V^n) + lock$$

Traveling time of a container:

$$X^*_{ij} = \begin{cases} 1, & \text{if the ship } j \text{ is assigned to berth } i \\ 0, & \text{otherwise} \end{cases}$$

(Solution given by the first Mathematical Model).

Q_z: The total capacity of each storage area z.
M: A very large number.

We propose for all j: $C'_j = MC_j$ we want to try to find a solution where each ship is assigned to the same storage area. If the ship with fewer containers is not capable of being divided, on the other hand, the vessel with the largest number of containers is attempted to allocate it to a single storage area.

b. Decision Variables

Y_{jz}=1 if the containers associated with the ship j will be discharged in the storage area z.*0* otherwise.

YY_{jz}=1 if the containers associated with the ship j that will be discharged in the storage area z *and* $z+1$, *0* otherwise, for $z \in$ D1.

We have added ZZ_{jz} for the linearization of a non linear product ($CC_{jz}*YY_{jz}$).

ZZ_{jz}=The number of containers associated with the ship j that will be discharged in the storage area z if YY_{jz}=1.

$\boldsymbol{C_{jz}}$: The number of containers associated with the ship j that will be discharged in the storage area z, if Y_{jz}=1.

$\boldsymbol{CC_{jz}}$: The number of containers associated with the ship j that will be discharged in the storage area z, if YY_{jz}=1.

This problem can be converted into a binary linear program by inserting a suitable objective function. The linear program (F) is defined as follows:

$$F = Min\sum_{i\in B}\sum_{j\in V}\sum_{z\in D}T_{iz} * C_j * X_{ij}^* * Y_{jz} + \sum_{i\in B}\sum_{j\in V}\sum_{z\in D1}\left(T_{iz} + T_{i(z+1)}\right)/2 * C_j' * X_{ij}^* * YY_{jz} \tag{11}$$

Subject to:

$$C_{jz} \le C_j + M\left(1 - Y_{jz}\right); \quad \forall j \in V,\ z \in D \tag{12}$$

$$C_{jz} + M\left(1 - Y_{jz}\right) \ge C_j; \quad \forall j \in V,\ z \in D \tag{13}$$

$$CC_{jz} + CC_{j(z+1)} \le C_j + M\left(1 - YY_{jz}\right); \quad \forall j \in V,\ z \in D1 \tag{14}$$

$$CC_{jz} + CC_{j(z+1)} + M\left(1 - YY_{jz}\right) \ge C_j; \quad \forall j \in V,\ z \in D1 \tag{15}$$

$$\sum_{z\in D} Y_{jz} + \sum_{z\in D1} YY_{jz} = 1; \quad \forall j \in V \tag{16}$$

$$\sum_{j\in V} C_j * Y_{jz} + \sum_{j\in V} ZZ_{jz} \le Q_z; \quad \forall z \in D1 \tag{17}$$

$$ZZ_{jz} \le CC_{jz} + M\left(1 - YY_{jz}\right); \quad \forall j \in V,\ z \in D1 \tag{18}$$

$$ZZ_{jz} + M\left(1 - YY_{jz}\right) \ge CC_{jz}; \quad \forall j \in V,\ z \in D1 \tag{19}$$

$$ZZ_{jz} \leq M * YY_{jz}; \quad \forall j \in V,\ z \in D1 \tag{20}$$

$$\sum_{j \in V} C_j * Y_{jz} + \sum_{j \in V} ZZ_{jz} \leq Q_z; \quad \forall z \in D2 \tag{21}$$

$$ZZ_{jz} \leq CC_{jz} + M\left(1 - YY_{j(z-1)}\right); \quad \forall j \in V,\ z \in D2 \tag{22}$$

$$ZZ_{jz} + M\left(1 - YY_{j(z-1)}\right) \geq CC_{jz}; \quad \forall j \in V,\ z \in D2 \tag{23}$$

$$ZZ_{jz} \leq M * YY_{j(z-1)}; \quad \forall j \in V,\ z \in D2 \tag{24}$$

$$\sum_{j \in V} C_j * Y_{jz} \leq Q_z; \quad z = A;\ si\ A\ estimpair \tag{25}$$

$$Y_{jz}, YY_{jz} \in \{0,1\}; \quad \forall j \in V,\ z \in D \tag{26}$$

$$C_{jz}, CC_{jz}, ZZ_{jz} \in \mathbb{R}; \quad \forall j \in V,\ z \in D \tag{27}$$

- In the objective function (11), we attempt mainly to reduce the traveling time of all the containers discharged from the berth until the storage areas. Similarly, when we assign ships to the storage areas, we minimize the dispersion of the containers from the ships on the various storage areas in such a way that minimizes the time that the ships spend at the docks.
- Constraints (12) and (13) ensure that all the containers c_j are assigned to one storage area z when Y_{jz} is equal to 1.
- Constraints (14) and (15) ensure that all the containers c_j are assigned to two storage areas z and $(z+1)$, when YY_{jz} is equal 1.
- Constraint (16) ensures that each ship j is assigned to one single storage area z, or to two storage areas z *and* $(z+1)$.
- Constraint (17) ensures that all the containers are unloaded to all the ships j and assigned to one storage area z, or to two storage areas z *and* $(z+1)$. Containers must not exceed the total capacity of the storage area z (for all odd number of z).

- Constraints (18) and (19) ensure that all the containers CC_{jz} are assigned to a storage area ZZ_{jz} when YY_{jz} is equal to1.
- Constraint (20) ensures that if YY_{jz} is equal to zero, then ZZ_{jz} is equal to zero too.
- Constraint (21) ensures that all the containers are unloaded to all the ships *j* and assigned to one storage area z, or to two storage areas(z-*1) and z* must not exceed the total capacity of the storage area *z,* (for all peer number of z).
- Constraints (22) and (23) ensure that all the containers CC_{jz} are assigned to a storage area ZZ_{jz} when $YY_{j(z-1)}$ is equal to 1.
- Constraints (24) ensure that if $YY_{j(z-1)}$ is equal to zero, then ZZ_{jz} is equal to zero too.
- Constraint (25) ensures that all the containers are unloaded to all the ships *j* and assigned to one storage area z, must not exceed the total capacity of the storage area *z, and z=A* if A is odd.
- Constraint (26) and (27) defines the decision variables.

Simultaneous Planning Problems Dock-Courtyard: Port of Radès in Tunisia

In this section we propose to solve the simultaneous planning problems Docks-Courtyard using our two mathematical models presented in section 3 and 4.

Experimental Data from the Port of Radès

During the data collection period at the port of Radès, the ship unloading operation begins from the container ship already docked at the berth with a quay crane and then placed on the dock.

The capacity of each storage area reserved for containers in the port of Radès is presented in Table 1 (this capacity is given by the Office of the Merchant Marine and Port:OMMP).

In the following section we will present the results of allocation and storage of the containers of each ship from the berth to the storage area by comparing them with the methodology for allocating containers in the storage areas carried out by STAM.

Table 1. The capacity for each storage area reserved for containers

Storage Area	Storage Capacity
A	500 EVP
B	1400EVP
C	800 EVP
D	2200 EVP
E	800 EVP
F	2400 EVP
H	2300 EVP

Table 2. The travelling time in minutes between the berth and the storage area

T_{iz}	Storage area A	Storage area B	Storage area C	Storage area D	Storage area E	Storage area F	Storage area H
Berth 1	14.04	14.21	13.64	14.25	13.08	13.61	13.93
Berth 2	13.50	13.69	13.13	13.75	13.34	13.41	13.81
Berth 3	13.08	13.22	13.10	13.41	13.75	13.69	14.12

RESULTS AND BENCHMARKING

From the data collected at the port of Radès for the month of December we will first start our assignment of containers to storage areas by taking the date of 01/12/2016 as a start date of the assignment. Then, every 10 days, the same principle is applied to the allocation of the containers to the storage areas, taking into account the number of EVP available in each storage area.

In this section we will use the results of assignment and allocation of import ships to berths noted X_{ij}^* obtained from the model of Kallel et al.(2016).

1. First planning of containers assignment to storage area (during the period from 01/12/2016 until 10/12/2016)

At the beginning of our first assignment plan, we should calculate the number of EVP available in each storage area noted in our mathematical model by $Q_{z'}$, based on the last results of the allocation of the containers to the storage areas of the last ships for the month of November. The actual remaining EVP capacity in each storage area on 01/12/2016 is reported. This data is presented in Table 3.

Table 3. Capacity of the storage areas in evp on the date of 01/12/2016

	Storage area A	Storage area B	Storage area C	Storage area D	Storage area E	Storage area F	Storage area H
Capacity of the storage area	410	870	618	1756	674	1624	1469

Then in Table 4 we will present the number of containers to be unloaded from each ship. The total of the containers to be unloaded for each ship is calculated in EVP (20 ‘).

The results of the first assignment of ships to berths during the period from 01/12/2016 until 10/12/2016 are:

$$X_{13}^{*}=1,\ X_{16}^{*}=1,\ X_{22}^{*}=1,\ X_{27}^{*}=1,\ X_{31}^{*}=1,\ X_{35}^{*}=1 \text{ and } X_{34}^{*}=1.$$

Table 4. Number of containers to be discharged in evp on the date of 01/12/2016

Stopover number	Ship number	Consignee	Name of ship entering	Date of arrival of ship in the harbor	Number of containers to be unloaded for each ship C_j				
					20'P	20'V	40'P	40'V	Total in EVP
6558	1	CMA	KARINA	02/12/2016 17:30	0	0	0	0	0
6542	2	MSC	REECON EMRE	03/12/2016 00:40	200	0	225	0	650
6537	3	MAERSK	PASSAT	03/12/2016 15:00	85	10	215	0	525
6561	4	MAERSK	AVERA	05/12/2016 07:00	88	10	281	0	660
6552	5	GENMAR	HEINZ SCHEPPERS	07/12/2016 07:00	82	0	43	0	168
6569	6	CMA	NICOLA	07/12/2016 22:00	79	0	88	0	255
6553	7	ASA	ALLEGRO	08/12/2016 07:00	106	0	263	0	632
					Total				2890

The experimental tests were conducted on a personal computer with 2.2 GHz, core 2 Duo processor and 3 GB of RAM. The Integer Linear Programming solver used is CPLEX 12.2. The following assignment results are obtained in 0.063 seconds:

$Y_{11} = 1, Y_{26} = 1, Y_{35} = 1, Y_{42} = 1, Y_{51} = 1, Y_{66} = 1$ and $Y_{76} = 1$
$C_{11} = 0, C_{26} = 650, C_{35} = 525, C_{42} = 660, C_{51} = 168, C_{66} = 255$ and $C_{76} = 632.$

The objective function is equal to 38447 minutes.

It should be noted that the containers of the same ship are assigned to a single storage area. The containers of ship 1 and those of ship 5 are assigned to storage area 1, ships 2, 6 and 7 are assigned to storage area 6. Storage areas 1, 2, 3, 5.6 and 7 presented in the results correspond to storage area A, B, C, D, E, F and H of the port of Radès.

It can also be seen that out of seven available storage areas the containers of the seven ships could be assigned to only four storage area (1, 2, 5 and 6), not assignment in storage areas 3, 4 and 7, subsequently minimizing the dispersion of containers to storage areas and reducing the travelling time of berths to storage areas.

2. Second planning of containers assignment to storage area (during the period from 11/12/2016 until 20/12/2016)

For our second assignment plan, the number of EVP available in each storage area (this data provided by STAM and OMMP) for each zone on 11/12/2016 are presented in Table 5.

Then in Table 6 we will present the number of containers to be unloaded for each ship.

The result of the second assignment of ships to berths during the period from 11/12/2016 until 20/12/2016 are:

$X^*_{12} = 1,\ X^*_{21} = 1,\ X^*_{33} = 1$ and $X^*_{34} = 1.$

Table 5. Capacity of the storage areas in evp on the date of 11/12/2016

	Storage area A	Storage area B	Storage area C	Storage area D	Storage area E	Storage area F	Storage area H
Capacity of the storage area	353	463	538	1291	321	718	702

Table 6. Number of containers to be discharged in evp on the date of 11/12/2016

Stopover number	Ship number	Consignee	Name of ship entering	Date of arrival of ship in the harbor	Number of containers to be unloaded for each ship C_j				
					20'P	20'V	40'P	40'V	Total in EVP
6545	1	GREEN T	MAX CAVALIER	13/12/2016 15:40	108	0	139	0	386
6595	2	MSC	GRAND	14/12/2016 00:40	223	0	216	0	655
6575	3	SEAWAVE	JSR CAPILA	15/12/2016 13:00	34	0	19	0	72
6597	4	MAERSK	JSP SLIDUR	20/12/2016 16:00	110	0	274	0	658
					Total				1771

The assignment results obtained in 0.047 seconds are as follows:

$Y_{13} = 1$, $Y_{26} = 1$, $Y_{31} = 1$ and $Y_{44} = 1$.
$C_{13} = 386$, $C_{26} = 655$, $C_{31} = 72$ and $C_{44} = 658$.

the objective function is equal to 23747 minutes

This result shows that all the containers of the same ship are assigned to a single storage area.

It can also be seen that out of the seven available storage areas, the containers could be assigned to only four storage areas (1, 3, 4 and 7), which subsequently allows minimizing the dispersion of containers to storage areas and decrease the traveling time in berths to storage areas.

3. Third planning of containers assignment to storage area (during the period from 21/12/2016 until 31/12/2016)

For our third assignment plan, the number of EVP available in each storage area for each zone on 21/12/2016) are presented in Table 7.

Table 7. Capacity of the storage areas in evp on the date of 21/12/2016

	Storage area A	Storage area B	Storage area C	Storage area D	Storage area E	Storage area F	Storage area H
Capacity of the storage area	0	527	0	674	0	159	598

It can be seen from this table that storage areas A, C and E are saturated due to the non-delivery of containers during the last period (formality papers, conveyor, scanning of the container, weighing of the container, etc.) and also a poor organization of containers in the storage areas.

Then in Table 8 we will present the number of containers to be unloaded for each ship on the date of 21/12/2016

In a first step, we used the model H to assign all the containers of the same ship to a single storage area (presented in section 4), but it proved impossible. Therefore, we were obliged to use the model that allows F to allocate the containers of the same ship in two consecutive storage areas (presented in section 3).

The result of the third assignment of ships to berths during the period from 21/12/2016 until 31/12/2016 are:

$X_{11}^{*}=1$, $X_{22}^{*}=1$ and $X_{33}^{*}=1$.

The assignment results obtained in 0.049 seconds are as follows:

$Y_{26} = 1, YY_{16} = 1, YY_{17} = 1, YY_{32} = 1$ and $YY_{34} = 1.$
$C_{26} = 137, CC_{16} = 22, CC_{17} = 586, CC_{32} = 527$ and $CC_{34} = 168.$
$ZZ_{16} = 22, ZZ_{17} = 586, ZZ_{32} = 527$ and $ZZ_{34} = 168.$

The objective function is equal to 19516 minutes.

It can be seen from this result that the containers of the same ship assigned in a single zone are only those of the ship 2, while those of the ships 1 and 3 are assigned to two successive storage areas

Table 8. Number of containers to be discharged in evp on the date of 21/12/2016

Stopover number	Ship number	Consignee	Name of ship entering	Date of arrival of ship in the harbor	Number of containers to be unloaded for each ship C_j				
					20'P	**20'V**	**40'P**	**40'V**	**Total in EVP**
6615	1	MAERSK	PASSAT	21/12/2016 08:00	104	0	252	0	608
6610	2	GENMAR	HEINZ SCHEPPERS	21/12/2016 11:06	55	0	41	0	137
6638	3	MSC	MANDO	23/12/2016 00:40	199	0	248	0	695
					Total				**1771**

Note also that, out of the seven storage areas available, the containers were allocated to only four storage areas (2, 4, 6 and 7). On the other hand, a first assignment has been registered since our first planning in favor of storage areas 7 due to the saturation of certain storage areas such as storage areas 1, 3 and 5 and also the travelling time to this storage area.

After presenting in this section the result of the allocation of the containers to the storage areas, we will compare in the following section our results obtained with those carried out by STAM at the port of Radès.

Benchmarking

After illustrating the results of our allocation of containers from the same ship to the storage areas during the month of December, we will compare them with the results achieved by STAM.

According this result, it will be noted that the available capacity of the storage areas at the date of 01/12/2016 has been respected by STAM when the various containers are allocated to the storage areas. This capacity was also respected at the time of the assignment of the containers of ships 5, 4, 7 and 8 on 11/12/2016. On the other hand, the storage capacity available on 21/12/2016 for zone D (excess of 199 EVP), zone F (excess of 392 EVP) and zone H (excess of 278 EVP) was not respected by STAM, which obliged it to place the containers at three levels (storage areas) (in principle at the port of Radès the stowage of the containers in the storage area is done at two levels only in order to facilitate the delivery and the transhipment of the containers with the exception of the empty containers).

This stowage of three-levels containers in storage areas could be explained not only by the delay in delivery to customers of containers in the various import zones, given the increased time spent on customs formalities (customs declaration, weighing, scanning, etc.) but also by a bad storage of the containers in the blocks.

These assignment data realized by STAM can be illustrated in figure 1.

This figure shows a great dispersion of the containers of the same ship when they are assigned to storage areas, sometimes reaching four zones, for the ship 4, 8, 11, 13 and 14. This could be due to a bad policy of allocating containers and the lack of consideration of travelling time when allocating the containers from the berth to the storage area, which subsequently generates an increase in the transfer time of all containers.

However, our results of allocation of containers to the storage areas obtained by our modeling summarizing the three allocation plans during the month of December carried out at the port of Radès.

Figure 1. Result of assignment of the containers of the ships to the storage areas carried out by STAM for the month of December

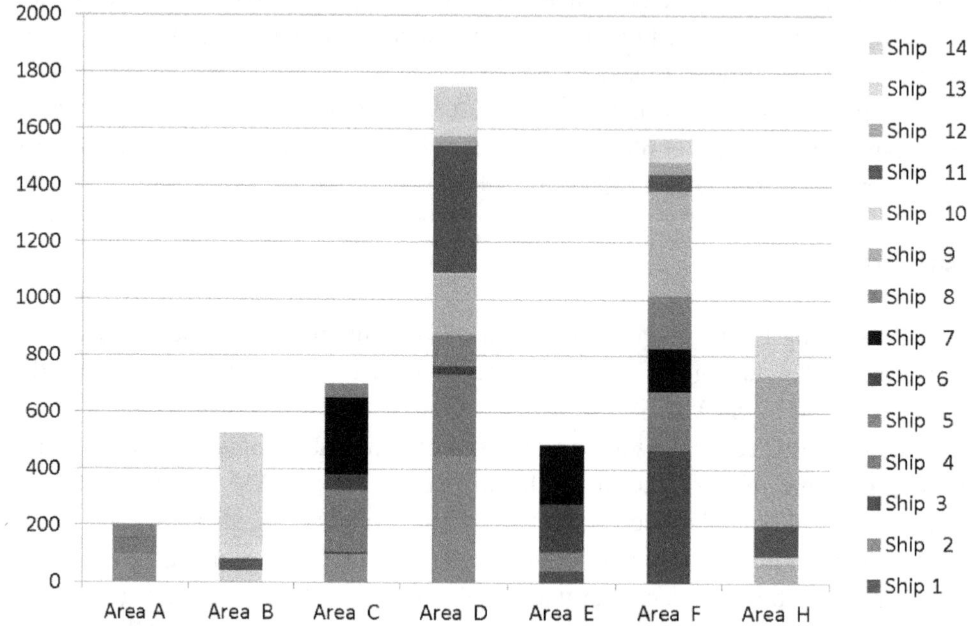

It can be seen that during the allocation of the containers belonging to incoming ships in December, the available capacity of the storage areas was well respected for the three planning periods, namely: 01/12/2016, on 11/12/2016 and finally on 21/12/2016.

Our results for the allocation of containers from the same ship to the storage areas during the month of December (according to the three allocation plans already presented) can be presented in (figure 2).

This figure shows a decrease in the dispersion of the containers when they are assigned to the storage areas, which go beyond one storage areas only for ships 12 and 14. This generates a decrease in the total transfer time of all containers.

Also, we can notice a decrease in the time of transfer of the containers to the storage areas at the port of Rades. This decline is confirmed by a simple comparison between the results of our modeling of transfer and storage of containers with the actual results carried out at the port of Radès by the port authorities. The total time spent transferring containers from ships to the storage areas has decreased by 211 minutes, which saves time when unloading and allocating the containers to the storage areas.

Figure 2. Result of assignment of the containers of the ships to the storage areas carried out by our model for the month of December

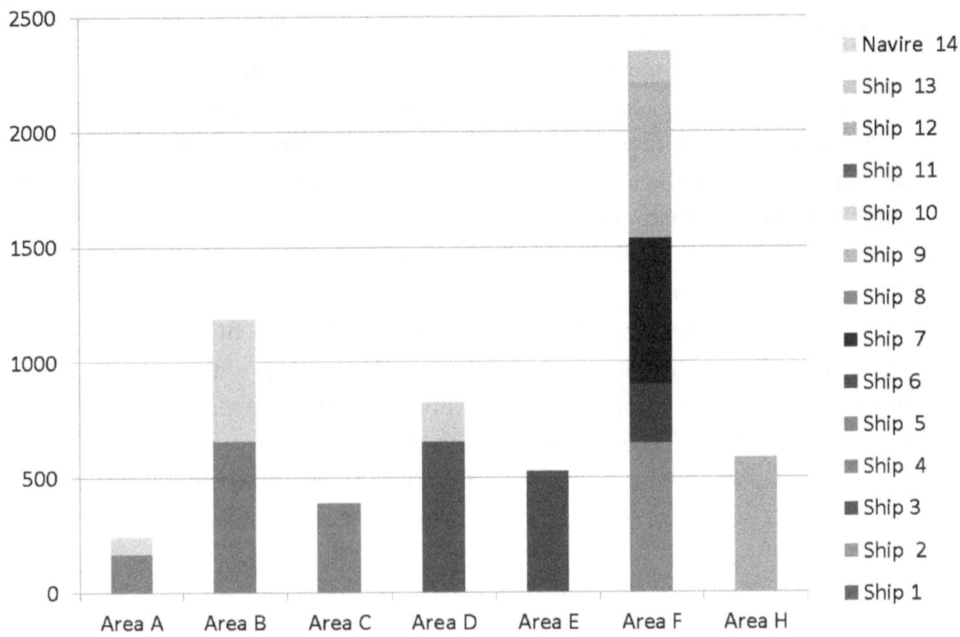

In light of the above results, we conclude that our mathematical models (presented in sections 3 and 4) reduce the time required to transfer containers to storage areas and their dispersion. They also make it possible to minimize and optimize the unloading time of all ships in the port, which has a significant impact on the length of stay of ships at the berths and consequently in the port.

CONCLUSION AND PERSPECTIVES

In this paper, we have investigated the Berth Allocation Problem and the Ships Containers Assignment to the Storage Area (SSA) problems. Two mathematical models are developed with the aim of minimizing the total flow time of the ships and the overall travelling time of containers unloaded between the berth and the storage areas and the reduction of the dispersion of containers in the storage areas. Unfortunately, however, these models are too huge to be used when the number of berths and storage areas is very high.

New research directions can be identified in light of the following remarks:

- These models are limited because when the problem size increases it becomes difficult to optimally solve the associated assignment problem; either approximate methods Heuristics or Meta-Heuristics can be used. Enumerative methods cannot be used as they take too much time.
- Velocity and the number of RS can be changed according to their states.
- The proposed model can be improved by adding the containers loaded in the ships in the case of export.
- These models can be improved by adding the sum of the set up for all containers in the storage areas.
- For the SSA problem we allowed limited possibilities of two partitions of ship containers to two storage area. Enumerating all possible partitions can be considered. Also three or more partitions can be allowed.
- Extend the application of the SSA to other large port terminals.
- Take into account the environmental and social constraints during the assignment containers from the berth until the storage area.

REFERENCES

Zhen, L., Lee, L. H., & Chew, E. P. (2011). A Decision Model for Berth Allocation Under Uncertainty. *European Journal of Operational Research*, *212*(1), 54–68. doi:10.1016/j.ejor.2011.01.021

Arango, C., Corts, P., Munuzuri, J., & Onieva, L. (2011). Berth Allocation Planning in Seville inland Port by Simulation and Optimisation. *Advanced Engineering Informatics*, *25*(3), 452–461. doi:10.1016/j.aei.2011.05.001

Barros, V. H., Costa, T. S., Oliveira, A., Luiz, A., & Lorena, N. (2011). Model and Heuristic for Berth Allocation in Tidal Bulk Ports with Stock level Constraints. *Computers & Industrial Engineering*, *60*(4), 606–613. doi:10.1016/j.cie.2010.12.018

Golias, M., Boile, M., & Theofanis, S. (2009). Berth Scheduling by Customer Service Differentiation: A Multiobjective Approach. *Transportation Research Part E, Logistics and Transportation Review*, *45*(6), 878–892. doi:10.1016/j.tre.2009.05.006

Guan, Y., & Cheung, R. K. (2004). The berth allocation problem: Models and solution methods. *OR-Spektrum*, *26*(1), 75–92.

Hansen, P., Oguz, C., & Mladenovic, N. (2008). Variable Neighborhood Search for Minimum Cost Berth Allocation. *European Journal of Operational Research*, *131*(3), 636–649. doi:10.1016/j.ejor.2006.12.057

Imai, A., Nishimura, E., & Papadimitriou, S. (2001). The Dynamic Berth Allocation Problem For a Container Port. *Transportation Research Part B: Methodological*, *35*(4), 401–417. doi:10.1016/S0191-2615(99)00057-0

Imai, A., Nishimura, E., & Papadimitriou, S. (2003). Berth allocation with service priority. *Transportation Research Part B: Methodological*, *37*(5), 437–457. doi:10.1016/S0191-2615(02)00023-1

Imai, A., Sasaki, K., Nishimura, E., & Papadimitriou, S. (2006). Multiobjective Simultaneous Stowage and Load Planning For a Container Ship with Container Rehandle in yard Stacks. *European Journal of Operational Research*, *171*(2), 373–389. doi:10.1016/j.ejor.2004.07.066

Imai, A., Sun, X., Nishimura, E., & Papadimitriou, S. (2005). Berth Allocation in a Container Port: Using Continuous Location Space Approach. *Transportation Research Part B: Methodological*, *39*(3), 199–221. doi:10.1016/j.trb.2004.04.004

Kim, K. H., & Kim, H. B. (2002). The optimal sizing of the storage space and handling facilities for import containers. *Transportation Research*, *36*(9), 821–835. doi:10.1016/S0191-2615(01)00033-9

Kim, K. H., & Moon, K. C. (2003). Berth Scheduling by Simulated Annealing. *Transportation Research*, *37*, 541–560.

Kim, K. Y., & Kim, K. H. (1999). A routing algorithm for a single straddle carrier to load export containers onto a containership. *International Journal of Production Economics*, *59*(1-3), 425–433. doi:10.1016/S0925-5273(98)00108-X

Lai, K. K., & Shih, K. (1992). A study of container berth allocation. *Journal of Advanced Transportation*, *26*(1), 45–60. doi:10.1002/atr.5670260105

Lee, D.-H., Cao, J. X., & Shi, Q. (2008). Integrated model for truck scheduling and storage allocation problem at container terminal. *Proceedings of the International research Board 87th Annual Meeting*, Washington DC. Academic Press.

Lee, D. H., Cao, J. X., Shi, Q., & Chen, J. H. (2009). A Heuristic Algorithm for Yard truck Scheduling and Storage Allocation Problem. *Transportation Research Part E, Logistics and Transportation Review*, *45*(5), 810–820. doi:10.1016/j.tre.2009.04.008

Lee, D.-H., Cao, J. X., Shi, Q., & Chen, J.-H. (2009). Heuristic algorithm for yard truck scheduling and storage allocation problems. *Transportation Research Part E, Logistics and Transportation Review*, *45*(5), 810–820. doi:10.1016/j.tre.2009.04.008

Lee, D. H., Cao, Z., & Meng, Q. (2007). Scheduling of two Transtainer Systems For Loading Outbound Containers in Port Container Terminals with Simulated Annealing Algorithm. *International Journal of Production Economics*, *107*(1), 115–124. doi:10.1016/j.ijpe.2006.08.003

Lee, D. H., Chen, J. H., & Cao, J. X. (2010). The Continuous Berth Allocation Problem: A Greedy Randomized Adaptive Search Solution. *Transportation Research Part E, Logistics and Transportation Review*, *46*(6), 1017–1029. doi:10.1016/j.tre.2010.01.009

Lee, D. H., Wang, H. Q., & Miao, L. X. (2008). Quay Crane Scheduling With non-interference Constraints in Port Container Terminals. *Transportation Research Part E, Logistics and Transportation Review*, *44*(1), 124–135. doi:10.1016/j.tre.2006.08.001

Lee, L. H., Chew, E. P., Tan, K. C., & Han, Y. (2006). An Optimization Model for Storage Yard Management in Transshipment Hubs. *OR-Spektrum*, *28*(4), 539–561. doi:10.100700291-006-0045-4

Lobna, K., Hichem, K., & Mounir, B. (2016). A Decision Support Model for Ships to Berths Allocation Problem and Physical Flows in a Container Terminal. *Proceedings of the 5th IEEE Int. conf. on Advanced Logistics and Transport, IEEE ICALT'2016*, Krakow, Poland. IEEE.

Monaco, F. M., & Sammarra, M. (2007). The Berth Allocation Problem: A Strong Formulation Solved by a Lagrangean Approach. *Transportation Science*, *41*(2), 265–280.

Moorthy, R., & Teo, C. P. (2007). Berth management in container terminal: the template design problem. In *Container Terminals and Cargo Systems* (pp. 63–86). Springer.

Moussi, R., Euchi, J., Yassine, A., & Ndiaye, N. F. (2015). A hybrid ant colony and simulated annealing algorithm to solve the container stacking problem at seaport terminal. *International Journal of Operational Research*, *24*(4), 399–422. doi:10.1504/IJOR.2015.072723

Peter, P., & Kozan, E. (2001). An approach to Determine Storage location of containers at sea port Terminals. *Computers & Operations Research*, *28*, 983–995.

Pierre, H., & Ceyda, O. (2003). *A Note on Formulations of Static and Dynamic Berth Allocation Problems*. Les Cahiers du GERAD.

Preston, P., & Kozan, E. (2001). An approach to determine storage locations of containers at seaport terminals. *Computers & Operations Research*, *28*(10), 983–995. doi:10.1016/S0305-0548(00)00020-4

Vacca, I., Salani, M., & Bierlaire, M. (2012). An exact algorithm for the integrated planning of berth allocation and quay crane assignment. *Transportation Science*, *47*(2), 148–161. doi:10.1287/trsc.1120.0428

Xu, D., Li, C. L., & Joseph, T. L. (2012). Berth allocation with time dependent physical limitations on vessels. *European Journal of Operational Research*, *216*(1), 47–56. doi:10.1016/j.ejor.2011.07.012

Zeinebou, Z., & Abdellatif, B. (2013). Development of a Model of Decision Support for Optimization of Physical Flows in a Container Terminal. *Proceedings of the International Conference Advanced Logistics and Transport (ICALT)* (pp. 421-426). Academic Press. 10.1109/ICAdLT.2013.6568496

Zeinebou, Z., & Abdellatif, B. (2014). Comparing the Effectiveness of Different Metaheuristics for the Optimization Problem of Allocation of Berths in a Containers Terminal. *Proceedings of the Sixth International Conference on Information, Process, and Knowledge Management Eknow*. Academic Press.

Zhang, C., Liu, J., Wan, Y.-W., Murty, K. G., & Linn, R. J. (2003). Storage space allocation in container terminals. *Transportation Research*, *37*(10), 883–903. doi:10.1016/S0191-2615(02)00089-9

Zoubeir, Z., & Benabdelhafid, A. (2014, April). The Development of a Decision Support Model for the Problem of Berths Allocation in Containers Terminal Using a Hybrid of Genetic Algorithm and Simulated Annealing. *Proceedings of the Asian Conference on Intelligent Information and Database Systems* (pp. 454-463). Cham: Springer.

Chapter 8
Improving Interhospital Medical Patient Transportation in Morocco:
A Forecasting Collaborative Approach

Youness Frichi
https://orcid.org/0000-0002-3061-7699
High School of Technology, Sidi Mohamed Ben Abdellah University, Morocco

Fouad Jawab
https://orcid.org/0000-0002-0508-7278
High School of Technology, Sidi Mohamed Ben Abdellah University, Morocco

Abderrahmane Ben Kacem
University Abdelmalek Essaadi, Tangier, Morocco

Oualid Kamach
University Abdelmalek Essaadi, Tangier, Morocco

Samir Chafik
Moroccan School of Engineering Sciences, Morocco

ABSTRACT

Healthcare facilities are nowadays facing several challenges in terms of quality of care, costs, and performance. Collaboration with stakeholders is a promising way to overcome these challenges. In Morocco, healthcare access and continuity of care remain difficult due, among others, to the various stakeholders involved and the lack of ambulances for extra-hospital and interhospital medical patient transportation (MPT). In this chapter, the aim was to explore collaboration in healthcare supply chain to improve the availability of ambulances for interhospital MPT (transfers). For this purpose, an overview of the MPT system in Morocco was presented while

DOI: 10.4018/978-1-7998-0268-6.ch008

highlighting its main issues. Then, a case study of three hospitals in Casablanca City was analyzed employing a collaborative approach. It consisted in forecasting transfer requests for next periods based on past data, and redistributing the ambulances of the three hospitals according to the forecasts. Findings attest to the variability in demand in the three hospitals and therefore the need for a dynamic allocation of ambulances.

INTRODUCTION

In Morocco, healthcare infrastructure, including the number of healthcare facilities and physicians, has undergone significant changes over the years, enabling the health system to make significant progress. According to statistics from the Ministry of Health, life expectancy increased from 64.6 in 1990 to 75.8 years in 2015, infant and child mortality fell from 76‰ in 1990 to 27.6‰ in 2011, and maternal mortality declined from 317 per 100,000 live births in 1990 to 72.6 in 2015 (Ministry of health, 2016). However, access to healthcare remains difficult due to many deficiencies, including distance to healthcare facilities, unbalanced distribution of healthcare provision, insufficient number of health professionals, cost of care, and inadequacy of the medical transportation system, (Yaakoubd, 2010). All these difficulties have been highlighted in several scientific publications that have mentioned the shortcomings of the health system in terms of governance (Dehbi, 2017), medical coverage, resource allocation (Alami, 2017; Legros & Chaoui, 2012), etc. However, medical transportation issues have not been the subject of any specific research work. Little is known about its organization and functioning as well as solutions for its improvement.

The interest in medical transportation is derived from its crucial role in achieving the Sustainable Development Goals (SDG), which the United Nations member states have committed to achieve by 2030, in particular SDG 3 on improving health and well-being that aims to promote access to healthcare (United Nations, 2015).

Organizations, including healthcare facilities, can rely on collaboration to effectively manage their activities and enhance their performance (Singh, Garg, & Sachdeva, 2018). It is recognized that collaboration among health system stakeholders leads to improved health outcomes (Morley & Cashell, 2017). The current study objective is to discuss collaboration between healthcare facilities to face medical transportation challenges. Among the existing collaborative approaches, the one considered for the purpose of this chapter is collaborative forecasting. The basic idea is that hospitals can forecast transportation demands based on past performed transportation, and then redistribute their ambulances according to the established forecasts.

The remainder of this chapter is organized as follow. The second section presents backgrounds about medical patient transportation, healthcare supply chain collaboration and demand forecasting methods. Third section takes stock of the current situation of the medical patient transportation in Morocco, while highlighting its main difficulties and challenges. Fourth section details time series forecasting models. Fifth section develops ARIMA forecasting model to predict interhospital transportation demand for three hospitals in Casablanca city. Sixth section discusses results and provides insights into options for improving medical transportation.

BACKGROUND

Medical Patient Transportation (MPT)

Medical patient transportation (MPT) is a hospital logistics activity that refers to operations of patients' movement within and outside hospitals using appropriate means. It has a vital role in providing patients with the care they need (Jawab, Frichi, & Boutahari, 2018; Naesens & Gelders, 2009). As shown in Figure 1, the MPT facilitates and promotes patients' access to healthcare by acting on distance and time components. It plays an important role in assuring the first contact between patients and healthcare facilities. Thus, makes it a vital activity in saving patients' lives and reducing mortality rates (Swalehe & Aktas, 2016; Tlili, Abidi, & Krichen, 2018).

The MPT can be performed in different modes: land (road and rail), air and water (Kulshrestha & Singh, 2016). The choice of the transportation mode is determined according to patient's health requirements, availability of transportation means, weather, distance, geography, etc. (Kulshrestha & Singh, 2016; Lemaître et al., 2010). There is a distinction between three types of MPT:

- Extra-hospital MPT, or primary transportation: is the movement of patients from home or the accident site to a hospital (Davies & Chesters, 2015).
- Interhospital MPT, or secondary transportation: is the transfer of patients from one health facility to another for advanced diagnostics and specialized care (Chen et al., 2013).
- Intra-hospital MPT: is the movement of patients between care units within the same building for diagnostic or therapeutic reasons. Patients are pushed on stretchers, beds or wheelchairs or transported by ambulances in campus-based hospital (Hanne et al., 2009).

Figure 1. Horned beast diagram of MPT

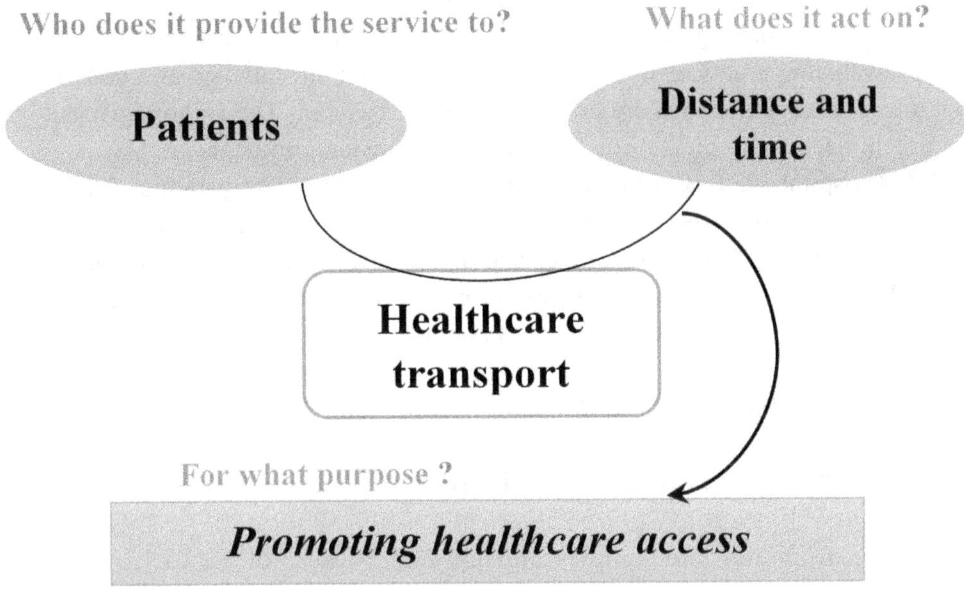

Improving patient access to healthcare is largely dependent on effective management of extra-hospital MPT. The optimization of this type of transportation, for urgent and non-urgent cases, have been widely discussed in the literature. The objective of most researches was to reduce response times and the associated costs, in particular through effective ambulances redeployment (Bélanger, Ruiz, & Soriano, 2012; Benabdouallah, Bojji, & El Yaakoubi, 2016; Coppi, Detti, & Raffaelli, 2013; Fogue et al., 2016). In this regard, Zhang et al. (2015) proposed a mathematical model to respond to a greater number of non-urgent requests with available resources and to minimize the travelling cost. Tlili et al. (2018) developed a model for enhancing the response-time of emergency medical services (EMS) by resolving ambulance routing problems. They developed a genetic based algorithm and tested it with real data. Swalehe & Aktas (2016) employed system status management (SSM) technique to reduce ambulance response times. Enayati et al. (2018) developed a real-time approach for redeployment of available ambulances in order to compensate for the loss in coverage due to busy ambulances.

Interhospital MPT (transfers) is important for the continuity of healthcare. Any delay or poor organization of transfers can contribute significantly to mortality (Kulshrestha & Singh, 2016). Decision for transfers must be made after taking into account the associated benefits and risks. A study by Venema et al. (2019) showed that transfers can have a positive or negative impact on patients' conditions depending, among others, on the transfer time. Hunt (2018) provided an overview of the different types of transfers in the UK, the associated hazards, human factors around decision-making, communication, equipment and organization. Verma et al. (2013) evaluated practices of injured patients transfers in Jamaica and concluded that the performed transfers are not adequately carried out. The authors insisted on the urgent need for implementing standardized transfers protocols.

Intra-hospital MPT is not of little importance. In fact, late patients' deliveries to a care unit such as the operating room or medical imaging unit results in the underutilization of valuable resources and disrupt the department initially planned schedule. Consequently, following appointments are often delayed, making waiting times inevitable (Beaudry et al., 2010). Patients handling should be carried out in accordance with standards and recommendations, not only for the patient well-being but also for the handler's health (Malet & Benchekroun, 2012).

Healthcare Supply Chain Collaboration

Healthcare institutions are complex organizations because of the variety and the diversity of their medical and logistical activities, which are managed by several internal and external stakeholders from different disciplines (Frichi, Jawab, & Boutahari, 2019). Collaboration between these stakeholders is of utmost importance to achieve health systems' objectives such as improving quality of care, reducing costs and uncertainties, increasing innovation, etc. (Morley & Cashell, 2017). Studies have proven that when healthcare facilities work in collaboration with stakeholders, they gain valuable advantages (Morley & Cashell, 2017). One area in which collaborative practices have been widely applied and proven their relevance is the supply chain. In commercial supply chain, collaboration has enabled achieving common goals between organizations by sharing information, risks, investments, resources and benefits (Singh et al., 2018). This also applies to collaboration in healthcare supply chain, which has been recognized as a powerful initiative leading to improved efficiency and responsiveness (Matopoulos & Michailidou, 2013). Healthcare supply chain collaborative practices include Vendor Management Inventory (VMI), Collaborative Planning, Forecasting and Replenishment (CPFR), etc.

The VMI is an inventory management tool based on collaboration between a vendor and a customer. The vendor is responsible for maintaining the customer's inventory level (Kwon, Kim, & Martin, 2016). This collaborative approach tends to improve service level and costs through better plan inventories and deliveries. However, the implementation of VMI in the healthcare supply chain remains poor, preventing health facilities from taking full advantage of its potential benefits (Machado Guimarães et al., 2013).

The CPFR aims to improve the supply chain through increased collaboration between trading partners, in particular by sharing information related to sales forecasting and planning (Jawab, Talbi, & Bouami, 2006). Its implementation leads to improved replenishment efficiency, reduced inventory shortage cost, decreased order variability, etc. (Hollmann, Scavarda, & Thomé, 2015). The application of such practices in healthcare settings has proven difficult, notably because of the diversity of stakeholders and complex technological requirements (Moons, Waeyenbergh, & Pintelon, 2019).

Undoubtedly the adoption of collaborative practices produces tangibles results. It leads to cost reduction, improved quality of care and healthcare delivery performance. However, healthcare supply chain collaboration is often limited to procurement agreements and sharing administrative functions between nearby institutions (Motiwala et al., 2008). Despite the fact that transportation costs represent major proportion of the overall healthcare supply chain cost, it still not being the subject of collaboration among healthcare sittings (Kwon et al., 2016).

Demand Forecasting

Demand forecasting consists of estimating the future consumption of a good or service. Forecasting methods are classified into qualitative and quantitative methods. The qualitative methods include market researches, expert opinions (Delphi method, nominal group, etc.), customer surveys, etc. They are intuitive methods based on subjective assessments, and are appropriate for medium- and long-term forecasts. Usually these methods are useful when little historical data is available or when quantitative methods are not relevant (Chopra et Peter, 2013; pp:180). Quantitative methods are based on mathematical or statistical models that are either deterministic or probabilistic. In a deterministic model the relationship between the explained variable Y and the explanatory variables $X_1, \ldots, X_n$ is formulated as $Y = f(X_1, \ldots, X_n; A_1, \ldots, A_m)$. The function f and the coefficients $A_1, \ldots, A_m$ are known with certainty. Examples of deterministic models are mathematical laws in the physical sciences. In social sciences models are rather probabilistic and can be expressed as $Y = f(X_1, \ldots, X_n; A_1, \ldots, A_m) + \xi$, with ξ is a noise or error component. The function f and the coefficients $A_1, \ldots, A_m$ are unknown and have to be determined from previous values or data (Abraham et Ledolter, 2009).

Forecasting techniques have known a wide application in the health sector. Matteson *et al.* (2011) used forecasting to estimate the hourly volume of EMS call arrivals rates. Their approach took into consideration the variation in the number of calls per day of the week and per week of the year. On the same issue, Channouf et al. (2007) studied and compared models for making daily and hourly predictions of EMS call arrivals. Kadri et al. (2014) and Carvalho-Silva et al. (2018) proposed forecasting models to predict patients' arrivals in emergency departments. Zhu et al. (2017) used different techniques to predict the number of hospital daily discharged inpatients in order to plan new admissions, they also compared the quality of obtained results. Jones et al. (2002) developed a forecasting model to predict the daily number of occupied beds due to emergency admissions.

Most researches have focused on developing forecasting models to deal with admissions or discharges. None of the reviewed works have considered predicting MPT demand especially Interhospital MPT.

MPT IN MOROCCO

Health System Organization

The Moroccan health system is structured around two sectors:

- Public sector is mainly composed of healthcare resources of the Ministry of Health, Defense department and communities.
- Private sector is made up of two sub-sectors: for-profit sub-sector, that includes hospital clinics, pharmacists, laboratories, etc. and not-for-profit sub-sector, which groups healthcare resources of National Fund for Social Security, the National Fund of Social Welfare Bodies, the Moroccan Red Crescent, and NGOs.

The national health system is characterized by a predominance of the public sector, mainly the healthcare provision of the Ministry of Health, which has four layers. The first is primary healthcare, that is provided in Basic Healthcare Centers. The second corresponds to provincial or prefectural hospitals. The third refers to regional hospitals, and the fourth is designated by university hospitals. This hierarchical organization leads to patient transfers from lower-level to higher-level institutions for specialized care.

MPT Issues

Although considerable efforts have been made to improve healthcare service coverage, a significant part of the population remains poorly served due to the distance from healthcare facilities. In 2012, the average distance travelled by the population for a medical consultation is 43.4 km (ONDH, 2015). Also, in 2014, 47.8% of the rural population is more than 20 km from the nearest consultation point (HCP, 2018). Given these figures, the distance is considered as one of the most challenging barriers for seeking care. It is responsible for 6.2% of non-use of healthcare in the event of illness, this rate rises to 9.9% in rural areas against 3.3% in urban areas (ONDH, 2015). Further, it accounts for 21% of women's reasons for non-use of childbirth services (Ministry of health, 2012). Long distances between residence and healthcare sittings accentuate the critical aspect of the MPT and put it at the top of priorities.

Despite its importance, the MPT is suffering from several problems, namely the lack of coordination between stakeholders and the quantitative deficit of the ambulance fleet:

- The MPT system is characterized by the diversity of actors involved in its management without the existence of a real coordination between them (Figure 2). For example, Civil Protection has no formal link with the Ministry of Health or municipalities. Similarly, ambulances belonging to associations (not-for-profit private sub-sector) are managed autonomously and independently of the public health system (ONDH, 2012). This compartmentalization does not facilitate the coordination of MPT activities to ensure timely and effective interventions (Wilson et al., 2015).
- The ambulance fleet counts nearly 1062 ambulances under the responsibility of the Ministry of Health, 423 belonging to the private sector, and 944 acquired within the framework of the National Initiative for Human Development, which are managed by the municipalities. As for the Civil Protection, there is no official data on its fleet size. Nevertheless, the inadequacy of the ambulance fleet has been mentioned in some national reports (CESE, 2013) and studies (Derdar, 2015), which have highlighted the unavailability of ambulances or even their absence in some healthcare centers.

Figure 2. Main actors of the MPT system in Morocco

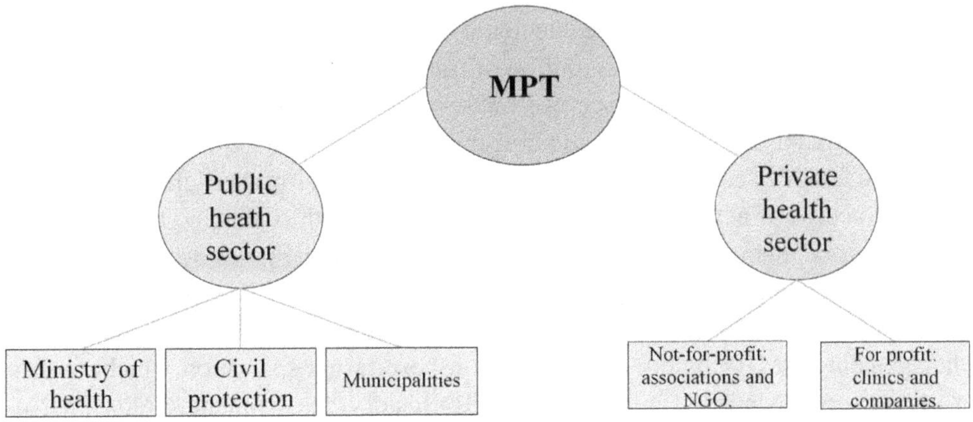

Patients' access to healthcare services is ensured, first and foremost, by extra-hospital MPT, which in emergency situations such as road accidents, fires, etc., is carried out by the Civil Protection services, whose scope of intervention is limited to their geographical territories. In fact, Civil Protection services transport patients (road accident victims, burn victims, etc.) from the scene of the accident or home to the most appropriate healthcare facility in their territory. They shouldn't evacuate patients to hospitals outside their perimeter (ONDH, 2012). When patients are transported to inappropriate hospitals, it is up to the host hospital to transfer them to the appropriate one. The transfer is provided by hospital's ambulances.

In order to better manage hospital emergencies, the Ministry of Health adopted in 2018 the Acceleration Plan of Upgrading Medical Emergencies 2019-2021, which aims to develop and upgrade Emergency Medical Assistance Services (EMAS), and Mobile Emergency and Resuscitation Services (MERS) attached to EMAS. The new strategy attempts to provide medical transportation with new equipment specific to each specialty and to renew the ambulance fleet by acquiring new ambulances.

Transfers or interhospital MPT is necessary in the case of incorrect patient transportation by the Civil Protection services, but also in the following situations: patients health require specialized care, medical tests unavailable on-site, patients requiring hemodialysis sessions that take place in separate centers, unavailability of physicians or hospital beds, etc.

Research Problem

The inadequacy of the ambulance fleet, mentioned above, requires an optimal use of ambulances. Nevertheless, it is reported, in some hospitals, that ambulances are only active for few hours and are discharged during the rest of the day, while requests for transfers in other hospitals are unsatisfied or delayed due to ambulance unavailability, which can lead to patient health complications. This mismatch could be explained by a low number of transportation requests at the first hospital and a high number at the second one, but also it may be due to the static allocation of ambulances, which does not take into account the evolution of transfers requests over time.

The discrepancy in ambulance use between hospitals should be corrected in a manner that maximizes the satisfied number of transportation requests. By doing so, healthcare facilities could achieve operational effectiveness and efficiency, resulting in timely access to healthcare. To this end, it is proposed to proceed by a dynamic reallocation of ambulances according to transfers needs (Figure 3). This involves implementing a predictive approach to sizing the ambulance fleet of each hospital, based on its transfers history. The idea is close to the principle of the System Status Management (SSM) technique applied for extra-hospital transportation, which consists of a dynamic reallocation of ambulances based on history data (Swalehe & Aktas, 2016).

Figure 3. Description of the current and improved situation of ambulance allocation

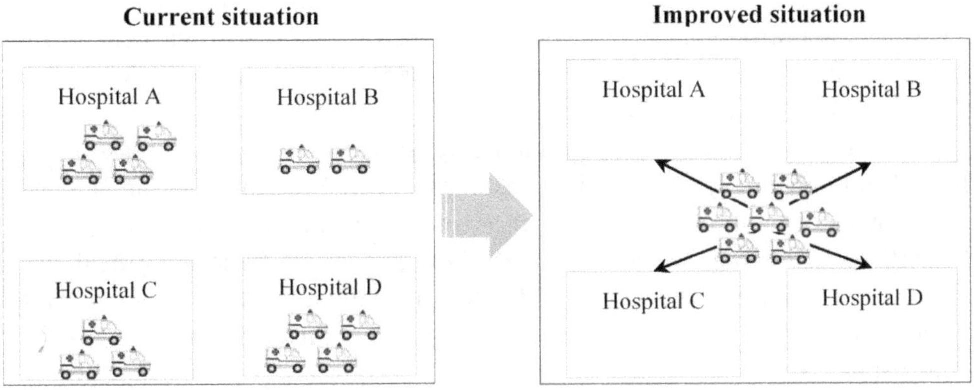

It is worth mentioning that transportation demands (*D*) for each hospital should not be expressed in number of requests but in transportation time. This because the travel distance may vary significantly from one request to another, so an ambulance is likely to be busy for a period ranging from few minutes to many hours. Ambulance busyness does not depend on the number of requests but rather on the travel time.

To the best of authors' knowledge, the forecast of interhospital MPT demand has not been the subject of specific studies and more precisely in the Moroccan context. Forecasting studies have more concerned emergency services (call volumes, patient arrivals, etc.), which is quite logical given its uncertain and urgent character. Nevertheless, in the Moroccan context, interhospital MPT has the same uncertain and urgent character, because patients are evacuated by the Civil Protection services to hospitals that are in most cases inadequate. Then, patients' transfers to the appropriate hospitals is performed by the host hospital using its own resources (i.e. ambulances and crew).

METHOD

Time Series Modelling

Qualitative methods, as mentioned above, are used for medium- and long-term forecasts, and are adapted to new situations for which there is little information. This does not correspond exactly to the case of interhospital MPT presented here. Moreover, qualitative forecasting methods do not make use of past data, that should be analyzed to generate deeper knowledge about the phenomenon under study. A study by Ong et al. (2009) showed that requests for healthcare are not random, but rather a health problem that occurs according to time patterns and trends that can be observed historically. For instance, it was found that patient arrivals in emergency department is a chronological sequence with a trend and other seasonal components (Ong et al., 2009). Hence, it would be useful to deploy time series to forecast future requests in the healthcare context.

Hospitals often record transportation data, so it is interesting to make use of these data in order to provide reliable estimates of future transportation demands by deploying quantitative methods, such as time series (Figure 4). For this purpose, the ARIMA (*AutoRegressive Integrated Moving Average*) forecasting method is used for its advantages, which are highlighted in the literature such as: accessibility in terms of methodological constraints, less complex mathematical models, etc. (Kadri et al., 2014).

ARIMA Modeling

The forecast variable (*D*) corresponds to the monthly travel time of interhospital MPT. Considering that past data constitute a time series $\{D_1, D_2, \ldots, D_{t-1}\}$, so it can be examined mathematically for analytical purposes and predict future behavior. One of the most advanced techniques for modeling time series is ARMA (*p,q*). This technique uses stochastic mathematical models (Kadri et al., 2014), and allows to express the time series in the form of the following equation:

$$D_t = \alpha_1 D_{t-1} + \alpha_2 D_{t-2} + \ldots \alpha_p D_{t-p} + \varepsilon_t + \beta_1 \varepsilon_{t-1} + \beta_2 \varepsilon_{t-2} + \ldots \beta_q \varepsilon_{t-q} \text{ with } \{\varepsilon_t\} \sim N(0,\sigma^2) \quad (1)$$

$$D_t = \sum_{i=1}^{i=p} \pm_i D_{t-i} + \varepsilon_t + \sum_{j=1}^{j=q} {}^2{}_j \varepsilon_{t-j} \quad (2)$$

Figure 4. Time series modeling

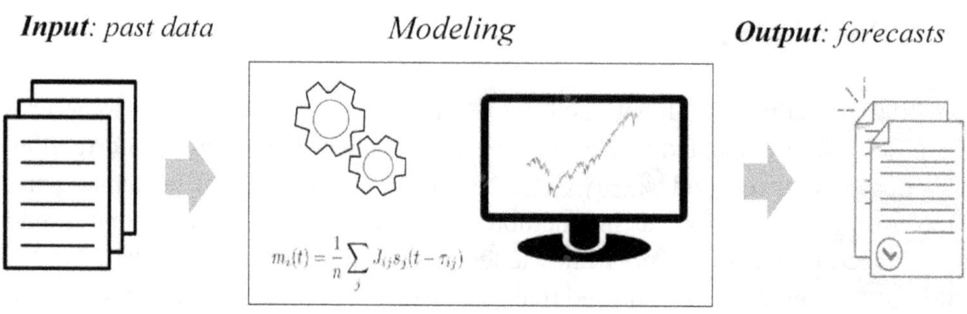

The coefficients α_i and β_j are respectively the parameters of the autoregressive and moving average part of the model. The ε_t are error terms assumed to be independent and identically distributed, sampled from a normal distribution with a zero mean and σ standard deviation $N(0,\sigma^2)$. The $\sum_{i=1}^{i=p}\alpha_i D_{t-i}$ are the autoregressive (AR) processes that describe how an observation is influenced by the p previous observations. The second part $\varepsilon_t + \sum_{j=1}^{j=q}\beta_j \varepsilon_{t-j}$ presents the moving average (MA) processes, which assumes that each observation depends upon the current white noise term ε_t as well as q previous errors ε_{t-j} (Jones et al., 2002). p and q orders are obtained by analyzing the autocorrelation and partial autocorrelation function: p corresponds to the number of significant peaks of the partial autocorrelation function (PACF) and q to the number of significant peaks of the autocorrelation function (ACF). The p and q are selected in a manner that minimizes the following criteria: AIC (Akaike's Information Criterion), AICc (Akaike's Information Criterion corrected) and BIC (Bayesian Information Criterion). In particular, Hyndman & Athanasopoulos (2018) recommended to select p and q based on the smallest AICc.

In time series analysis, it is useful to use the backshift operator B (Hyndman & Athanasopoulos, 2018) defined as:

$$B^k D_t = D_{t-k} \tag{3}$$

Using the backshift operator in equation (1):

$$D_t - \alpha_1 B D_t - \alpha_2 B^2 D_t - \ldots - \alpha_p B^p D_t p = \varepsilon_t + \beta_1 B\varepsilon_t + \beta_2 B^2\varepsilon_t + \ldots + \beta_q B^q \varepsilon_t \ \{\varepsilon_t\} \sim N(0,\sigma^2) \tag{4}$$

$$(1 - \alpha_1 B - \alpha_2 B^2 - \ldots - \alpha_p B^p) D_t = (1 + \beta_1 B + \beta_2 B^2 + \ldots + \beta_q B^q)\varepsilon t \tag{5}$$

$$\Phi\,(B)\, D_t = \ (B)\, \varepsilon_t \tag{6}$$

where:

$$\Phi\,(B) = 1 - \alpha_1 B - \alpha_2\, B^2 - \ldots - \alpha_p\, B^p \tag{7}$$

$$(B) = 1 + \beta_1 B + \beta_2 B^2 + \ldots + \beta_q B^q \tag{8}$$

The ARMA model only applies to stationary series. If the process is not stationary, it is recommended first to make it stationary, by simple or logarithmic differencing.

In this case, it is an ARIMA model (*p*,*d*,*q*), where *d* is the degree of integration of the series, which means the number of differences needed for stationarity. The differentiated series D'_t is:

$$D'_t = D_t - D_{t-1} \tag{9}$$

Or by using the backshift operator:

$$D'_t = (1 - B) \times D_t \tag{10}$$

For d-order differencing:

$$D^{(d)}_t = (1 - B)^d \times D_t \tag{11}$$

The ARIMA(*p*,*1*,*q*) model can be expressed as follows:

$$D'_t - \alpha_1 D'_{t-1} - \alpha_2 D'_{t-2} - \dots \alpha_p D'_{t-p} = \varepsilon_t + \beta_1 \varepsilon_{t-1} + \beta_2 \varepsilon_{t-2} + \dots \beta_q \varepsilon_{t-q} \ \{\varepsilon_t\} \sim N(0,\sigma^2) \tag{12}$$

$$\Phi\ (B)D'_t = \ (B)\ \varepsilon_t \tag{13}$$

Replacing D'_t using equation (10):

$$\Phi\ (B)\ (1 - B)\ D_t = \ (B)\ \varepsilon_t \tag{14}$$

The ARIMA(*p*,*d*,*q*) can be written in backshift notation as:

$$\Phi\ (B)\ (1 - B)^d\ D_t = \ (B)\ \varepsilon_t \tag{15}$$

Time series of some phenomena may show seasonal fluctuations during specific times (winter, summer, weekend, etc.). In this case, it is useful to exploit the correlation between data at successive periods of time by deploying SARIMA model, which measures the seasonal effect (Kadri et al., 2014).

To validate an ARIMA model, time series data could be divided into two groups. The first group is used to develop the model (training data), while the second is used to test the predictive ability of the model (test data) (Hyndman & Athanasopoulos, 2018). Another very powerful way to validate the model is through residual analysis, which is examined by the evaluation of various residual properties: normality, independence, etc. (Kadri et al., 2014).

FORECASTING INTERHOSPITAL MPT DEMANDS: CASE STUDY

Data Analysis

Data related to interhospital MPT from three hospitals A, B and C of Casablanca city are analyzed to forecast future demands. These data contain the monthly number of performed transfers from January 2016 to December 2018, but do not include travel times. Given the unavailability of details on transportation times, it was decided to base the analysis on the number of transfers.

Descriptive statistics for the three hospitals data are presented in the Table 1. A preliminary analysis of the figures shows that between 90% and 93% of the performed transfers are from the emergency department (ED). This proves that the majority of patients arriving to the ED are misdirected and should have been transported or referred directly to the appropriate hospital. The highest monthly number of transfers 282 is recorded at the hospital B, and the lowest number 76 at the hospital A.

Let's note S_A, S_B and S_C time series corresponding to the number of transfers performed by hospitals A, B and C respectively. These time series are analyzed using *RStudio* software (Figure 5). The volumes of transfers of hospitals A and B are high and fluctuate significantly comparing to hospital C, whose evolution is smooth and almost stable over time. For hospitals A and B, the curves are characterized by unusual peaks and troughs whose values are sometimes shocking.

Figure 6 provides the boxplot diagram of mean monthly volume of transfers performed by A, B and C. It shows the median, first and third quartiles, interquartile interval and outliers. The number of transfers vary widely from month to month and between the three hospitals. Data from hospital A show that September is the month with the highest number of transfers, while July and February are the least

Table 1. Descriptive statistics of the monthly number of transfers in the three hospitals

Statistics	Hospital A	Hospital B	Hospital C
Min	76	133	91
Max	199	282	110
Mean	131.7	211,6	99.62
Median	137	212	100
1st Q	97.5	184.8	94
3rd Q	155.5.2	231.8	104.25
Total number of transfers from the ED	10866 (≈ 90%)	7085 (93%)	4352 (91%)
Total number of transfers during hospitalization	1216 (10%)	533 (7%)	430 (9%)

Figure 5. The evolution of the number of transfers performed by hospitals A, B and C

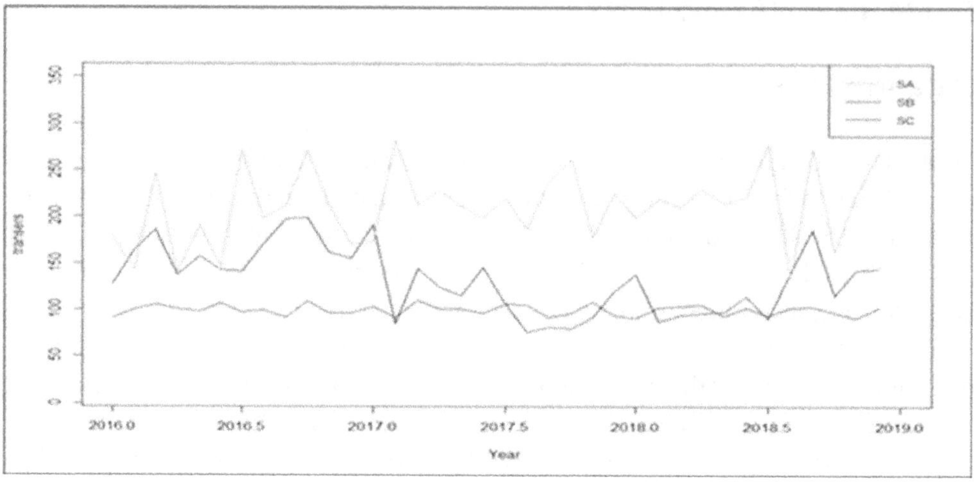

busy months. The volume of transfers at the hospital B is at its highest-level during July and October, and lowest level in January and August. For the hospital C, the busiest periods are March and June, and the least busy are January and September.

From this comparison, it can be seen that some months of the year correspond to periods of overload for one hospital and relief for another. For example, the number of transfers performed during September at the hospital A is highest, while it is the lowest for the hospital C. Similarly, July appears to be the busiest month for the hospital B and the least busy for the hospital A. It is clear that the consumption of resources related to patient transfer operations is not regular throughout the year. It would therefore be appropriate to make a dynamic and flexible adaptation in the allocation of the material and human resources required for interhospital transportation.

Generated ARIMA Models

The first step in determining ARIMA models for S_A, S_B and S_C is to verify their stationarity. Several tests exist to check the time series stationarity: Dickey-Fuller test (Dickey & Fuller, 1979), Phillips-Perron test (Phillips & Perron, 1988), Kwiatkowski-Phillips-Schmidt-Shin test (Kwiatkowski, Phillips, Schmidt, & Shin, 1992), etc. The stationarity of S_A, S_B and S_C is examined by applying the Dickey-Fuller test, which tests the null hypothesis that the time series is non-stationary. Results revealed that S_A is non-stationary (*p-value* $S_A = 0{,}585 > 0{,}05$) while S_B and S_C are stationary (*p-value* S_B = *p-value* $S_C = 0.04 < 0{,}05$). S_A was differentiated ($d=1$) to become stationary (*p-value* $S'_A = 0{,}04 < 0{,}05$).

Figure 6. Box-plot of mean monthly transfers volumes

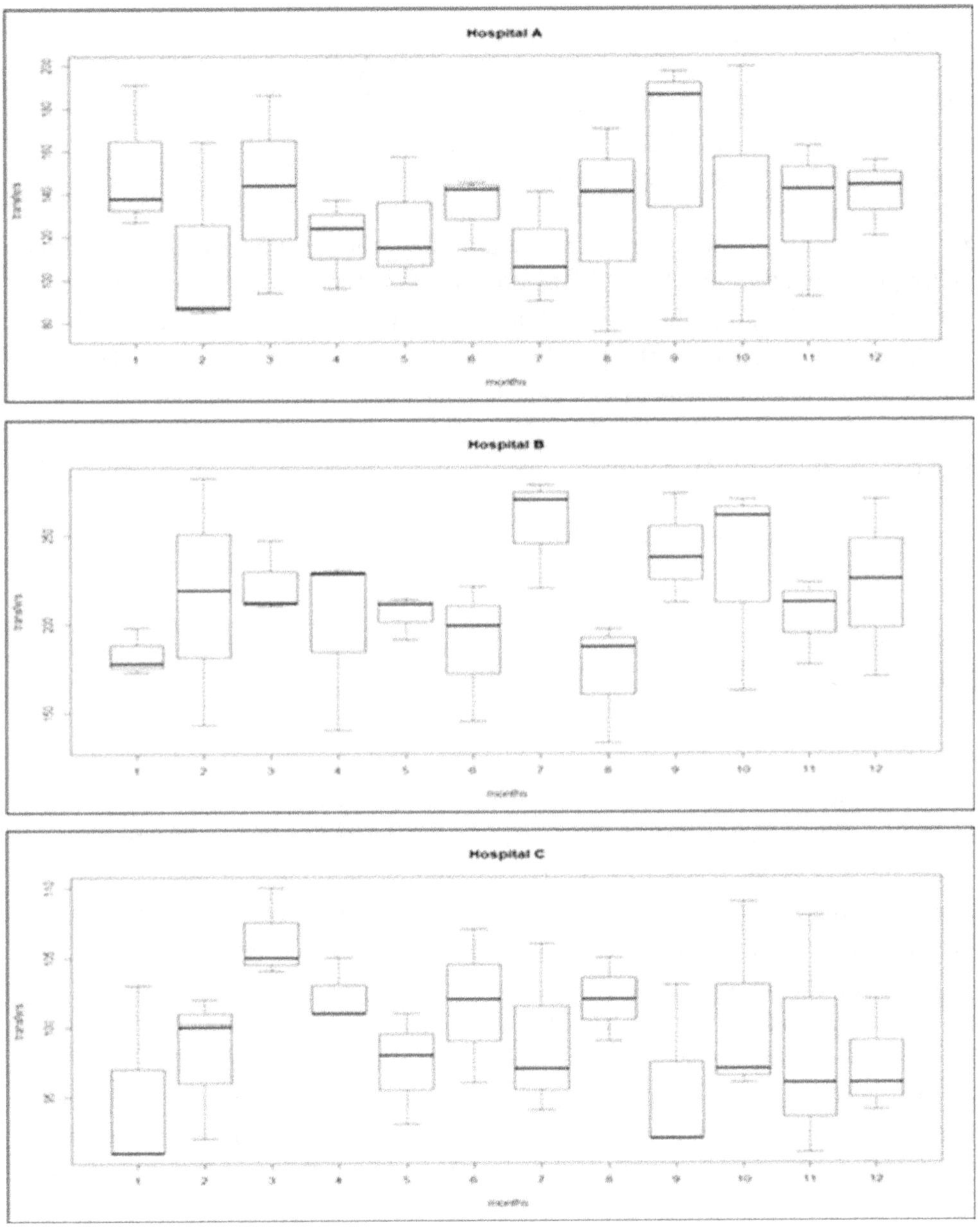

The p and q parameters were defined by plotting on the *RStudio* software the ACF and PACF functions. They were chosen based on the minimum Akaike Information Criterion corrected (AICc). The best-fit ARIMA models for S_A, S_B and S_C are ARIMA(0,1,1), ARIMA(1,0,0) and ARIMA(0,0,1) respectively. Models' coefficients

Table 2. Coefficients of the three models

Coefficients	S_A ARIMA(0,1,1)	S_B ARIMA(1,0,0)	S_C ARIMA(0,0,1)
α_1	-	$-0,3589 \pm 0,1592$	-
β_1	$-0,5844 \pm 0,1432$	-	$-0,6488 \pm 0.1726$

α_i and β_j were estimated using the maximum likelihood estimation (Table2). It is a technique that determines the models' coefficients in a manner that maximizes the probability of obtaining the observed data (Hyndman & Athanasopoulos, 2018).

Mathematical equations of the ARIMA models for the monthly number of transfers at hospital A, B and C, using the form of equation (15), are as follow:

$$S_A\text{: } (1\text{-}B)\ D_t = \mu + (1 - 0{,}5844)\ \varepsilon_t \quad (16)$$

$$S_B\text{: } (1 + 0.3589B)\ D_t = \mu + \varepsilon_t \quad (17)$$

$$S_C\text{: } D_t = \mu + (1 - 0{,}6488B)\ \varepsilon_t \quad (18)$$

Residual Analysis

To validate the obtained models, a residual analysis is required. Residuals of a good model should be independent and follow a gaussian distribution (Kadri et al., 2014). Therefore, it is necessary to check how is the shape of the residuals' distributions of the three developed ARIMA models as well as their autocorrelation. Figure 7 shows that the residuals of the three models are randomly distributed around zero and their autocorrelation functions (ACF) do not reveal any significant pikes (ACF are not large for any non-zero lag).

The observations resulting from the graphs were confirmed by statistical tests. Residuals normality is checked using the Shapiro–Wilk test (Shapiro & Wilk, 1965), which tests the null hypothesis that data come from a normally distributed population. The p-value corresponding to the Shapiro–Wilk test applied to the residuals from the three models are not significant, over 0.05 (*p-value* $S_A = 0{,}3729$, *P-value* $S_B = 0{,}4889$, *P-value* $S_C = 0{,}7745$) indicating that the residuals are normally distributed. Residuals independency is examined by applying the Ljung–Box test (Ljung & Box, 1978), which verifies the null hypothesis that data are randomly distributed. The three p-value resulting from Ljung–Box test are not significant (*p-value* $S_A = 0{,}7371$, *p-value* $S_B = 0{,}7111$, *p-value* $S_B = 0{,}3098$), meaning that residuals are uncorrelated.

As the residuals from the three models are white noise (normally distributed and non-autocorrelated), it can be concluded that the models fit data well.

Figure 7. Residual diagnostic

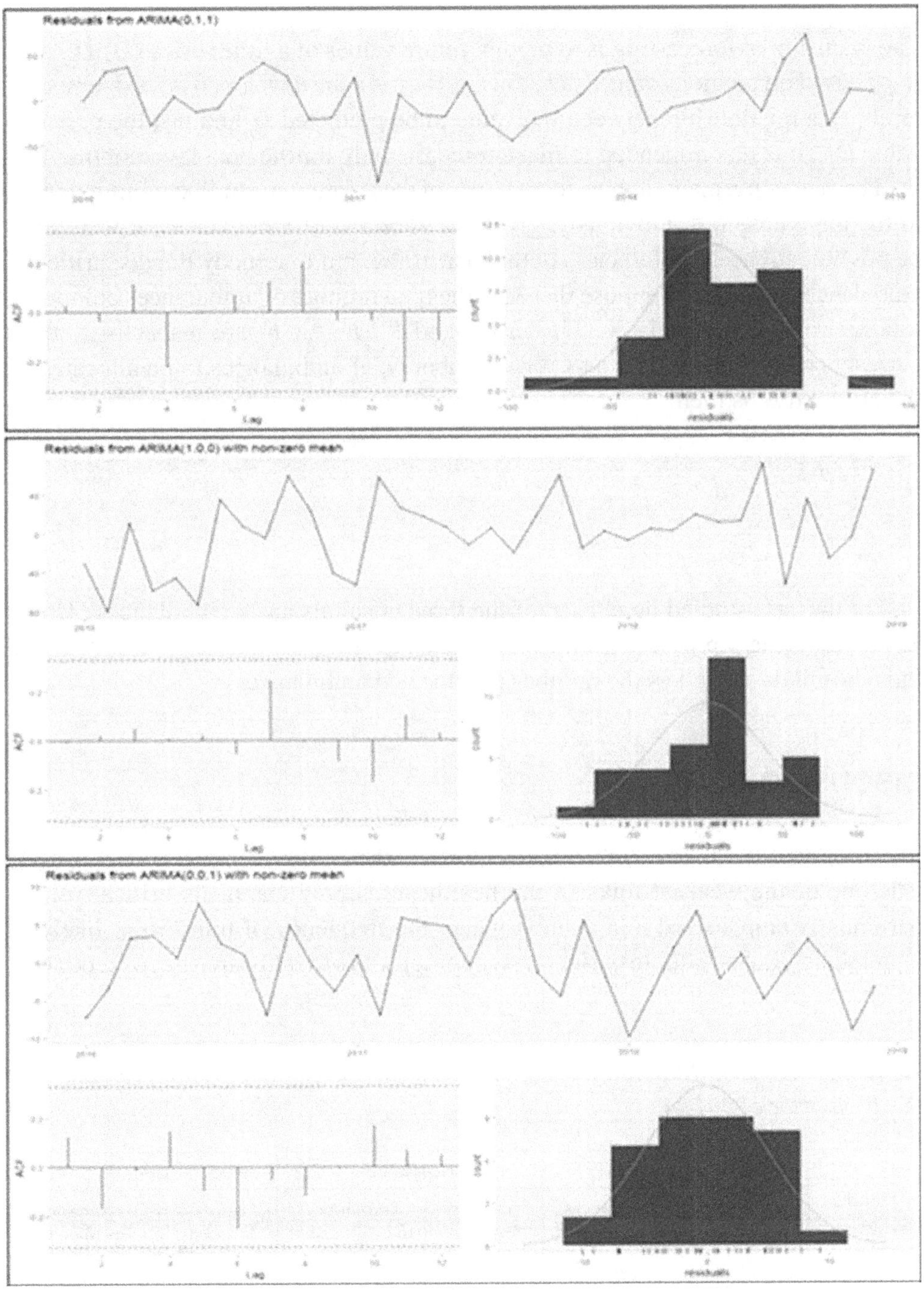

Forecasting

The main aim of forecasting is to predict future values of a time series $\{D_t, D_{t+1}, ..., D_{t+h}\}$ based on previous values $\{D_1, D_2, ..., D_{t-1}\}$. As the developed ARIMA models establish a relationship between the value to be predicted D_t and just the previous value D_{t-1}, it is recommended to make forecasts only for the next few months.

The question remains as how to make use of these forecasts to allocate ambulances to the three hospitals. Obviously, given the shortage of ambulances, it would not be possible to meet the forecasts demand at 100%, but to remedy the disparities in ambulance allocation. Suppose that M is the total number of ambulances belonging to a network of hospitals $H_1, H_2, ..., H_n$, and $F_1, F_2, ..., F_n$ are respectively their corresponding transfer forecasts. The number N_i of ambulances to be allocated to the Hospital H_i is then:

$$N_{\mathrm{i}} = \frac{Fi}{\sum_{i=1}^{i=n} Fi} \times M.$$

For the case studied here, each of the three hospitals has 4 ambulances ($M = 4 + 4 + 4$). Table 3 provides monthly forecasts, for the first quarter of 2019, of the three hospitals as well as the number of allocated ambulances.

DISCUSSION

Interhospital MPT is a crucial component of healthcare service provision. However, it is one of the weakest links in the healthcare supply chain. Its critical role is particularly emphasized in a context where the frequency of transfers is likely to increase significantly due to the increasing complexity of healthcare, the concentration

Table 3. Forecasts of the number of transfers and ambulances to be allocated for the 1st quarter of 2019

Months	Hospital A		Hospital B		Hospital C	
	Transfers forecasts	Ambulances to be allocated	Transfers forecasts	Ambulances to be allocated	Transfers forecasts	Ambulances to be allocated
Jan - 2019	175	4	230	5	108	3
Feb - 2019	182	4	280	6	101	2
Ma - 2019	210	5	250	5	109	2

of skills in specialized centers and the lack of available intensive care beds (Terry, 2001). In Morocco one of the major challenges faced by interhospital MPT is the lack of ambulances in some hospitals, which causes delays in patient transfers and consequently compromises their safety. To cope with this challenge, healthcare facilities have to find effective and sustainable solutions without increasing the hospital's financial burden. Collaboration among healthcare supply chain stakeholders is known to be a powerful way to enhance hospitals' effectiveness. While most existing studies have examined collaboration in inventory management, few have provided empirical evidence on collaboration in transportation activities. In this chapter, the aim was to introduce MPT system in Morocco and examine how collaboration could improve ambulances availability. For that purpose, a case study of three hospitals in Casablanca city was discussed. Data related to the number of monthly performed transfers during the last three years were analyzed. It turned out that some periods of overload for one hospital coincide with periods of relief for another. Considering this, it was interesting to find a way to balance the load by sharing ambulances to adapt the capacity of each hospital. By applying ARIMA modelling, it becomes possible to forecast future transfer requests and to make a monthly allocation of ambulances in accordance with the predicted number of transfers. The proposed solution allows adapting hospital's transport capacity according to demand forecasts. The redistributing of ambulances does not require new investment, which makes it affordable for hospitals to implement, especially in a context of increasing budgetary constraints. The proposed collaborative solution could be generalized to other hospitals in Morocco or other countries suffering from the same problem, namely ambulances shortage.

The allocation of ambulances according to demand forecasts, not only benefits patients by providing a timely access to healthcare, but also healthcare professionals by reducing the workload associated with peak periods. It is recognized that equitable distribution of workload has an influence on health personnel satisfaction, and therefore on the quality of care (Frichi, Jawab, & Boutahari, 2018).

Certainly, forecasting techniques are powerful tools for predicting the future, and have proven to be successful in various research fields including the health sector, however their applicability and the quality of the results they generate depend greatly on the veracity of the recorded data. These techniques require, in particular, detailed data on past performance. Unfortunately, this is not the case of interhospital MPT in Morocco, where hospitals only record the number of performed transfers. They indicate neither the ambulance travel times nor the transfer causes. The unavailability of detailed data about transfers is the main limitation of this study. On that point, an effective and user-friendly registration system would enable recording information related to transfers, that could serve as a basis to forecast future transfers.

It is noteworthy that the forecast of interhospital MPT demand can be modeled as a regression forecasting, by making assumptions about the existence of a relationship between the number of transfers and the number of patient admissions, available physicians and nurses, hospital beds, as well as the available medical specialties and facilities, etc. Nevertheless, these likely relationships should be verified by statistical methods to prove the existence of correlations.

Furthermore, to improve transfer operations, the Ministry of Health should consider reorganizing interhospital MPT activities through its centralization. Thus, ambulance allocation could be carried out by specialized regional units whose role would be to ensure ambulance deployment and redeployment in real time. Then, the interhospital MPT could benefit in its practices from scientific advances made in the field of extra-hospital transportation. Another option is to move to subcontracted interhospital MPT activities. In this case, transfers will be managed and performed by private companies with skilled staff and appropriate material. Subcontracting experiences have already been set up for intra-hospital MPT, and other logistics activities such as: catering, cleaning, waste management, gardening, etc. (Jawab et al., 2018).

CONCLUSION

This chapter contributes to the current knowledge on MPT in Morocco, which still little addressed in the literature, in spite of its important role in facilitating healthcare access and continuity. The objective of this study was to examine the effect of collaboration to cope with MPT challenges. Understanding how the MPT system is organized and its issues is the first step toward improvement. Accordingly, the chapter initially introduces the MPT in Morocco and its difficulties. Then, it provided empirical application in the area of collaboration in interhospital MPT. As expected, collaboration improved the availability of ambulances based on each hospital forecasts.

Collaborative practices are the key to improving interhospital MPT effectiveness and efficiency. Nevertheless, collaboration among hospitals can be challenging because of several barriers, which are cultural (e.g. lack of trust), technical (e.g. lack of supply chain skills and knowledge, underuse of information and communication technologies) and systemic (e.g. regulations and policies). MPT stakeholders need to remove these barriers and work together to reap the full potential benefits of collaboration and be able to identify opportunities for improving performance. Therefore, building a collaboration culture that promotes information and resources sharing is of greatest value. By doing so, hospitals can reduce waiting times, arise the number of fulfilled requests, and improve patient care.

REFERENCES

Abraham, B., & Ledolter, J. (2009). *Statistical Methods for Forecasting*. John Wiley & Sons.

Alami, R. (2017). Health Financing Systems, Health Equity and Universal Health Coverage in Arab Countries. *Development and Change*, *48*(1), 146–179. doi:10.1111/dech.12290

Beaudry, A., Laporte, G., Melo, T., & Nickel, S. (2010). Dynamic transportation of patients in hospitals. *OR-Spektrum*, *32*(1), 77–107. doi:10.100700291-008-0135-6

Bélanger, V., Ruiz, A., & Soriano, P. (2012). Déploiement et Redéploiement des Véhicules Ambulanciers dans la Gestion d'un Service Préhospitalier d'Urgence. *INFOR*, *50*(1), 1–30. doi:10.3138/infor.50.1.001

Benabdouallah, M., Bojji, C., & El Yaakoubi, O. (2016). Deployment and redeployment of ambulances using a heuristic method and an Ant Colony Optimization - Case study. *Proceedings of the 2016 Third International Conference on Systems of Collaboration (SysCo)* (pp. 1–4). Academic Press. 10.1109/SYSCO.2016.7831330

Carvalho-Silva, M., Monteiro, M. T. T., de Sá-Soares, F., & Dória-Nóbrega, S. (2018). Assessment of forecasting models for patients arrival at Emergency Department. *Operations Research for Health Care*, *18*, 112–118. doi:10.1016/j.orhc.2017.05.001

CESE. (2013). Les soins de santé de base Vers un accès équitable et généralisé.

Channouf, N., L'Ecuyer, P., Ingolfsson, A., & Avramidis, A. N. (2007). The application of forecasting techniques to modeling emergency medical system calls in Calgary, Alberta. *Health Care Management Science*, *10*(1), 25–45. doi:10.100710729-006-9006-3 PMID:17323653

Chen, J., Awasthi, A., Shechter, S., Atkins, D., Lemke, L., Fisher, L., & Dodek, P. (2013). Using operations research to plan improvement of the transport of critically ill patients. *Prehospital Emergency Care*, *17*(4), 466–474. doi:10.3109/10903127.2013.811561 PMID:23992200

Chopra, S., & Peter, M. (2013). Supply Chain Management : Strategy, Planning, and Operation (Fifth edit).

Coppi, A., Detti, P., & Raffaelli, J. (2013). A planning and routing model for patient transportation in health care. *Electronic Notes in Discrete Mathematics*, *41*, 125–132. doi:10.1016/j.endm.2013.05.084

Davies, G., & Chesters, A. (2015). Transport of the trauma patient. *British Journal of Anaesthesia*, *115*(1), 33–37. doi:10.1093/bja/aev159 PMID:26089445

Dehbi, B. (2017). La problématique de gouvernance sanitaire au nord de l'Afrique: Cas du Maroc, de l'Algérie et de la Tunisie. *Africa Development. Afrique et Developpement*, *42*(1), 121–145.

Derdar, M. (2015). Traditional Delivery among Rural Women in Morocco: A Case Study of Sidi Smail Area. *Asian Journal of Multidisciplinary Studies*, *3*(8), 148–155.

Dickey, D. A., & Fuller, W. A. (1979). Distribution of the Estimators for Autoregressive Time Series with a Unit Root. *Journal of the American Statistical Association*, *74*(366a), 427–431.

Enayati, S., Mayorga, M. E., Rajagopalan, H. K., & Saydam, C. (2018). Real-time Ambulance Redeployment Approach to Improve Service Coverage with Fair and Restricted Workload for EMS Providers. *Omega*, *79*, 67–80. doi:10.1016/j.omega.2017.08.001

Fogue, M., Sanguesa, J. A., Naranjo, F., Gallardo, J., Garrido, P., & Martinez, F. J. (2016). Non-emergency patient transport services planning through genetic algorithms. *Expert Systems with Applications*, *61*, 262–271. doi:10.1016/j.eswa.2016.05.028

Frichi, Y., Jawab, F., & Boutahari, S. (2018). Elaboration of an association matrix of satisfaction factors in healthcare facilities and hospital logistics activities. *Proceedings of the 2018 International Colloquium on Logistics and Supply Chain Management (LOGISTIQUA)* (pp. 32–37). Tangier: IEEE. 10.1109/LOGISTIQUA.2018.8428259

Frichi, Y., Jawab, F., & Boutahari, S. (2019). Identification of health system stakeholders in Morocco. *Proceedings of the International Conference on Industrial Engineering and Operations Management* (pp. 1193–1199). Bangkok, Thailand: IEOM Society.

Hanne, T., Melo, T., Nickel, S., Melo, T., & Nickel, S. (2009). Bringing Robustness to Patient Flow Management Through Optimized Patient Transports in Hospitals. *Interfaces*, *39*(3), 241–255. doi:10.1287/inte.1080.0379

HCP. (2018). *Les indicateurs sociaux du Maroc* (Edition 2018). Rabat.

Hollmann, R. L., Scavarda, L. F., & Thomé, A. M. T. (2015). Collaborative planning, forecasting and replenishment: A literature review. *International Journal of Productivity and Performance Management*, *64*(7), 971–993. doi:10.1108/IJPPM-03-2014-0039

Hunt, D. (2018). Transfer of the critically ill adult patient. *Surgery (United Kingdom), 36*(4), 166–170.

Hyndman, R. J., & Athanasopoulos, G. (2018). Forecasting: principles and practice. OTexts.

Jawab, F., Frichi, Y., & Boutahari, S. (2018). Hospital Logistics Activities. In *Proceedings of the International Conference on Industrial Engineering and Operations Management* (pp. 3228–3237). Bandung: IEOM Society.

Jawab, F., Talbi, A., & Bouami, D. (2006). Le réapprovisionnement continu dans les réseaux industriels, vers une meilleure gestion des interfaces de la "supply chain." La Revue Des Sciences de Gestion, (2), 123-137.

Jones, S. A., Joy, M. P., & Pearson, J. (2002). Forecasting demand of emergency care. *Health Care Management Science, 5*(4), 297–305. doi:10.1023/A:1020390425029 PMID:12437279

Kadri, F., Harrou, F., Chaabane, S., & Tahon, C. (2014). Time series modelling and forecasting of emergency department overcrowding. *Journal of Medical Systems, 38*(9), 107. doi:10.100710916-014-0107-0 PMID:25053208

Kulshrestha, A., & Singh, J. (2016). Inter-hospital and intra-hospital patient transfer: Recent concepts. *Indian Journal of Anaesthesia, 60*(7), 451–457. doi:10.4103/0019-5049.186012 PMID:27512159

Kwiatkowski, D., Phillips, P. C., Schmidt, P., & Shin, Y. (1992). Testing the null hypothesis of stationarity against the alternative of a unit root: How sure are we that economic time series have a unit root? *Journal of Econometrics, 54*(1–3), 159–178. doi:10.1016/0304-4076(92)90104-Y

Kwon, I. W. G., Kim, S. H., & Martin, D. G. (2016). Healthcare supply chain management; strategic areas for quality and financial improvement. *Technological Forecasting and Social Change, 113*, 422–428. doi:10.1016/j.techfore.2016.07.014

Legros, M., & Chaoui, F. (2012). *Les systèmes de santé en Algérie, Maroc et Tunisie : Défis nationaux et enjeux partagés. Les Notes IPEMED, Etudes et Analyses 13.* Paris.

Lemaître, P., Venditti, J., Guérin, A., Gueugniaud, P., Dubien, P., Bagou, G., & Gallon, M. (2010). Les transferts héliportés (hors pédiatriques). Proceedings of the Conférence congrès urgences (pp. 975–984). Academic Press.

Ljung, G. M., & Box, G. E. (1978). On a measure of lack of fit in time series models. *Biometrika, 65*(2), 297–303. doi:10.1093/biomet/65.2.297

Machado Guimarães, C., Crespo de Carvalho, J., & Maia, A. (2013). Vendor managed inventory (VMI): Evidences from lean deployment in healthcare. *Strategic Outsourcing*, *6*(1), 8–24. doi:10.1108/17538291311316045

Malet, D., & Benchekroun, T. (2012). Comprendre la manutention de patient pour la valoriser: une voie de construction de la santé des soignants. Perspectives Interdisciplinaires Sur Le Travail et La Santé, 14(1).

Matopoulos, A., & Michailidou, L. (2013). Implementing collaborative practices in the healthcare supply chain : Insights into hospital-vendor operations. *Int. J. Logistics Systems and Management*, *15*(2/3), 288–303. doi:10.1504/IJLSM.2013.053773

Matteson, D. S., McLean, M. W., Woodard, D. B., & Henderson, S. G. (2011). Forecasting emergency medical service call arrival rates. Annals of Applied Statistics, 5(2 B), 1379-1406.

Ministry of health. (2012). Enquête Nationale sur la Population et la Santé Familiale (ENPSF-2011). Rabat.

Ministry of health. (2016). Santé en Chiffres 2015.

Moons, K., Waeyenbergh, G., & Pintelon, L. (2019). Measuring the logistics performance of internal hospital supply chains – a literature study. *Omega (United Kingdom)*, *82*, 205–217.

Morley, L., & Cashell, A. (2017). Collaboration in Health Care. *Journal of Medical Imaging and Radiation Sciences*, *48*(2), 207–216. doi:10.1016/j.jmir.2017.02.071 PMID:31047370

Motiwala, S. S., McLaughlin, J. E., King, J., Hodgson, B., & Hamilton, M. (2008). Advancing the health care supply chain and promoting leadership through strategic partnerships with industry. *Healthcare Management Forum*, *21*(2), 23–28. doi:10.1016/S0840-4704(10)60542-X PMID:18795555

Naesens, K., & Gelders, L. (2009). Reorganising a service department : Central Patient Transportation. *Production Planning and Control*, *20*(6), 478–483. doi:10.1080/09537280902938621

ONDH. (2012). Les disparités dans l'accès aux soins au Maroc - Etude de cas.

ONDH. (2015). Enquête Panel de ménages 2012 - rapport des premiers résultats. Rabat.

Ong, M. E. H., Ho, K. K., Tan, T. P., Koh, S. K., Almuthar, Z., Overton, J., & Lim, S. H. (2009). Using demand analysis and system status management for predicting ED attendances and rostering. *The American Journal of Emergency Medicine*, *27*(1), 16–22. doi:10.1016/j.ajem.2008.01.032 PMID:19041529

Phillips, P. C. B., & Perron, P. (1988). Testing for a Unit Root in Time Series Regression. *Biometrika*, *75*(2), 335–346. doi:10.1093/biomet/75.2.335

Shapiro, S. S., & Wilk, M. B. (1965). An Analysis of Variance Test for Normality (Complete Samples). *Biometrika*, *52*(3–4), 591–611.

Shumway, R. H., & Stoffer, D. S. (2017). *Time Series Analysis and Its Applications with R Examples* (4th ed.). Springer.

Singh, H., Garg, R. K., & Sachdeva, A. (2018). Supply chain collaboration: A state-of-the-art literature review. *Uncertain Supply Chain Management*, *6*, 149–180. doi:10.5267/j.uscm.2017.8.002

Swalehe, M., & Aktas, S. G. (2016). Dynamic Ambulance Deployment to Reduce Ambulance Response Times Using Geographic Information Systems: A Case Study of Odunpazari District of Eskisehir Province, Turkey. *Procedia Environmental Sciences*, *36*, 199–206. doi:10.1016/j.proenv.2016.09.033

Terry, M. (2001). *Handbook of Patient Transportation*. London: Cambridge University Press.

Tlili, T., Abidi, S., & Krichen, S. (2018). A mathematical model for efficient emergency transportation in a disaster situation. *The American Journal of Emergency Medicine*, *36*(9), 1585–1590. doi:10.1016/j.ajem.2018.01.039 PMID:29395774

United Nations. (2015). Health - United Nations Sustainable Development. Retrieved from https://www.un.org/sustainabledevelopment/health/

Venema, E., Groot, A. E., Lingsma, H. F., Hinsenveld, W., Treurniet, K. M., Chalos, V., ... Roozenbeek, B. (2019). Effect of Interhospital Transfer on Endovascular Treatment for Acute Ischemic Stroke. *Stroke*, *50*(4), 923–930. doi:10.1161/STROKEAHA.118.024091 PMID:30862265

Verma, V., Singh, G. K., Calvello, E. J. B., Kumar, S., Singh, C. M., & Harjai, M. (2013). Inter-hospital transfer of trauma patients in a developing country: A prospective descriptive study. *Indian Journal of Community Health*, *25*(3), 309–315.

Wilson, M. H., Habig, K., Wright, C., Hughes, A., Davies, G., & Imray, C. H. E. (2015). Pre-hospital emergency medicine. *Lancet*, *386*(10012), 2526–2534. doi:10.1016/S0140-6736(15)00985-X PMID:26738719

Yaakoubd, A.-I. (2010). La dimension sociale de la santé au Maroc. In A. Aboussad, M. Cherkaoui, & P. Vimard (Eds.), Santé et vulnérabilité au Maroc (p. 43). Academic Press.

Zhang, Z., Liu, M., & Lim, A. (2015). A memetic algorithm for the patient transportation problem. *Omega*, *54*, 60–71. doi:10.1016/j.omega.2015.01.011

Zhu, T., Luo, L., Zhang, X., Shi, Y., & Shen, W. (2017). Time-Series Approaches for Forecasting the Number of Hospital Daily Discharged Inpatients. *IEEE Journal of Biomedical and Health Informatics*, *21*(2), 515–526. doi:10.1109/JBHI.2015.2511820 PMID:28055928

Related Readings

To continue IGI Global's long-standing tradition of advancing innovation through emerging research, please find below a compiled list of recommended IGI Global book chapters and journal articles in the areas of global supply chains, logistics systems, and quality management. These related readings will provide additional information and guidance to further enrich your knowledge and assist you with your own research.

Aital, P., & Vijai, P. (2016). 'Green' Supply Chain Management: Resource Allocation Strategies for Sustainable Operations. In R. Dubey & A. Gunasekaran (Eds.), *Strategic Management of Sustainable Manufacturing Operations* (pp. 1–23). Hershey, PA: IGI Global. doi:10.4018/978-1-5225-0350-7.ch001

Auvray, T., Dallery, T., & Rigot, S. (2017). The Need for News Forms of Financial Intermediation. In L. Saglietto & C. Cezanne (Eds.), *Global Intermediation and Logistics Service Providers* (pp. 143–161). Hershey, PA: IGI Global. doi:10.4018/978-1-5225-2133-4.ch008

Bag, S. (2016). Identifying Green Supply Chain Management Enablers in South African Mining Industry using Ecological Modernization Theory Approach. In R. Dubey & A. Gunasekaran (Eds.), *Strategic Management of Sustainable Manufacturing Operations* (pp. 95–119). Hershey, PA: IGI Global. doi:10.4018/978-1-5225-0350-7.ch005

Bag, S. (2016). Modeling the Soft Skills of Green Procurement Professionals using Interpretive Structural Modeling Approach. In R. Dubey & A. Gunasekaran (Eds.), *Strategic Management of Sustainable Manufacturing Operations* (pp. 120–131). Hershey, PA: IGI Global. doi:10.4018/978-1-5225-0350-7.ch006

Bag, S., Anand, N., & Pandey, K. K. (2017). Green Supply Chain Management Model for Sustainable Manufacturing Practices. In M. Khan, M. Hussain, & M. Ajmal (Eds.), *Green Supply Chain Management for Sustainable Business Practice* (pp. 153–189). Hershey, PA: IGI Global. doi:10.4018/978-1-5225-0635-5.ch006

Balasubramanian, S., & Sundarakani, B. (2017). Assessing the Green Supply Chain Management for the United Arab Emirates Construction Industry. In M. Khan, M. Hussain, & M. Ajmal (Eds.), *Green Supply Chain Management for Sustainable Business Practice* (pp. 83–110). Hershey, PA: IGI Global. doi:10.4018/978-1-5225-0635-5.ch004

Barlatier, P., Giannopoulou, E., & Pénin, J. (2017). Exploring the Role of Open Innovation Intermediaries: The Case of Public Research Valorization. In L. Saglietto & C. Cezanne (Eds.), *Global Intermediation and Logistics Service Providers* (pp. 87–103). Hershey, PA: IGI Global. doi:10.4018/978-1-5225-2133-4.ch005

Bazan, E., & Jaber, M. Y. (2017). The Development and Analysis of Environmentally Responsible Supply Chain Models. In M. Khan, M. Hussain, & M. Ajmal (Eds.), *Green Supply Chain Management for Sustainable Business Practice* (pp. 52–82). Hershey, PA: IGI Global. doi:10.4018/978-1-5225-0635-5.ch003

Bernardes, S., Leite, P., Pesenti, G. S., Viana, E. A., Ladeira, V., Castro, C., ... Renato de Sousa, P. (2017). Information Management Applied to the Development of the Management Process and Improving Energy Efficiency in Transport. In G. Jamil, A. Soares, & C. Pessoa (Eds.), *Handbook of Research on Information Management for Effective Logistics and Supply Chains* (pp. 166–179). Hershey, PA: IGI Global. doi:10.4018/978-1-5225-0973-8.ch009

Bharti, A., & Mittal, A. (2018). Perishable Goods Supply Cold Chain Management in India. In A. Kumar & S. Saurav (Eds.), *Supply Chain Management Strategies and Risk Assessment in Retail Environments* (pp. 232–246). Hershey, PA: IGI Global. doi:10.4018/978-1-5225-3056-5.ch013

Boyonas, M. I., Olavarria, L., & Saenz, M. J. (2016). Scenario Planning: Preparing the Future of Global Supply Chains. In S. Joshi & R. Joshi (Eds.), *Designing and Implementing Global Supply Chain Management* (pp. 51–91). Hershey, PA: IGI Global. doi:10.4018/978-1-4666-9720-1.ch004

Brown, J. R., Bushuev, M. A., Kretinin, A. A., & Guiffrida, A. L. (2017). Recent Developments in Green Supply Chain Management: Sourcing and Logistics. In M. Khan, M. Hussain, & M. Ajmal (Eds.), *Green Supply Chain Management for Sustainable Business Practice* (pp. 191–217). Hershey, PA: IGI Global. doi:10.4018/978-1-5225-0635-5.ch007

Bruno, G. (2017). Identification of Potential Clients, Providers, and Competitors in Supply Chain Networks. In G. Jamil, A. Soares, & C. Pessoa (Eds.), *Handbook of Research on Information Management for Effective Logistics and Supply Chains* (pp. 89–106). Hershey, PA: IGI Global. doi:10.4018/978-1-5225-0973-8.ch005

Cassière, F., & Noireaux, V. (2017). International Distribution: A Cross-Cultural Reading of Intermediation. In L. Saglietto & C. Cezanne (Eds.), *Global Intermediation and Logistics Service Providers* (pp. 243–264). Hershey, PA: IGI Global. doi:10.4018/978-1-5225-2133-4.ch013

Chen, Y. (2018). An Interactive Platform for Sustainable Supply Chains. *International Journal of Interactive Communication Systems and Technologies*, *8*(2), 56–73. doi:10.4018/IJICST.2018070104

Costa, E., Soares, A. L., Pinho de Sousa, J., & Jamil, G. L. (2017). Information Management for Network Transformation in Industrial Enterprises Associations: The Case of the Internationalization Process. In G. Jamil, A. Soares, & C. Pessoa (Eds.), *Handbook of Research on Information Management for Effective Logistics and Supply Chains* (pp. 415–436). Hershey, PA: IGI Global. doi:10.4018/978-1-5225-0973-8.ch022

Das, R. (2018). Developing Sustainable Retail Food Value Chain for India: A Challenge for the Next Century. In A. Kumar & S. Saurav (Eds.), *Supply Chain Management Strategies and Risk Assessment in Retail Environments* (pp. 285–300). Hershey, PA: IGI Global. doi:10.4018/978-1-5225-3056-5.ch016

Das, R. (2018). Technologies Enabling Omni-Channel: Understanding Key Success Factors for IT Framework. In A. Kumar & S. Saurav (Eds.), *Supply Chain Management Strategies and Risk Assessment in Retail Environments* (pp. 78–96). Hershey, PA: IGI Global. doi:10.4018/978-1-5225-3056-5.ch005

Edwards, J. S. (2016). Systems for Knowledge Management along the Supply Chain. In S. Joshi & R. Joshi (Eds.), *Designing and Implementing Global Supply Chain Management* (pp. 92–104). Hershey, PA: IGI Global. doi:10.4018/978-1-4666-9720-1.ch005

El Meladi, Y., Glavee-Geo, R., & Buvik, A. (2017). Textile and Clothing Exporting Firms' Evaluation of LSPs' Capabilities and Logistics Outsourcing Performance. In L. Saglietto & C. Cezanne (Eds.), *Global Intermediation and Logistics Service Providers* (pp. 185–207). Hershey, PA: IGI Global. doi:10.4018/978-1-5225-2133-4.ch010

Fattam, N., & Paché, G. (2017). 4PL Intermediation: Exploring Dimensions of Social Capital. In L. Saglietto & C. Cezanne (Eds.), *Global Intermediation and Logistics Service Providers* (pp. 64–85). Hershey, PA: IGI Global. doi:10.4018/978-1-5225-2133-4.ch004

Fernandes da Anunciação, P., Garcia, B., & Fonseca, G. (2017). Importance of Stakeholders Identification in Information Distribution Chain Management for Public Value Detection in Public Initiatives. In G. Jamil, A. Soares, & C. Pessoa (Eds.), *Handbook of Research on Information Management for Effective Logistics and Supply Chains* (pp. 131–146). Hershey, PA: IGI Global. doi:10.4018/978-1-5225-0973-8.ch007

Fernandes da Anunciação, P., Lobo, M., Pereira, O., & Mateus, G. (2017). The Importance of Perception and Appreciation of the Information Management for Effective Logistics and Supply Chain in Transport Sector. In G. Jamil, A. Soares, & C. Pessoa (Eds.), *Handbook of Research on Information Management for Effective Logistics and Supply Chains* (pp. 453–468). Hershey, PA: IGI Global. doi:10.4018/978-1-5225-0973-8.ch024

Fernandes da Anunciação, P., Zambon, A. C., Andrade, F. D., & Sanches de Sousa, C. S. (2017). Competitive Intelligence Competitive Intelligence: A Proposal for Value Creation through Information and Knowledge – The Limeira Gross Domestic Product Sector: Brazil. In G. Jamil, A. Soares, & C. Pessoa (Eds.), *Handbook of Research on Information Management for Effective Logistics and Supply Chains* (pp. 273–286). Hershey, PA: IGI Global. doi:10.4018/978-1-5225-0973-8.ch015

Folinas, D. (2019). Containers in Ports can be Tracked Smartly: Lessons Learned From a Case Study. *International Journal of Applied Logistics*, *9*(1), 39–52. doi:10.4018/IJAL.2019010103

Fonseca, G. L., Rodello, I. A., & Fernandes da Anunciação, P. (2017). Information Management and Enterprise Resource Planning: An Analysis of the Medical Products Distribution Chain. In G. Jamil, A. Soares, & C. Pessoa (Eds.), *Handbook of Research on Information Management for Effective Logistics and Supply Chains* (pp. 334–349). Hershey, PA: IGI Global. doi:10.4018/978-1-5225-0973-8.ch019

Ganguly, A., Chatterjee, D., & Rao, H. V. (2017). Evaluating the Risks Associated with Supply Chain Agility of an Enterprise. *International Journal of Business Analytics*, *4*(3), 15–34. doi:10.4018/IJBAN.2017070102

Ganguly, A., Chatterjee, D., & Talukdar, A. (2019). Knowledge Sharing Barriers Affecting Pharmaceutical Supply Chain Performance. In H. Nozari & A. Szmelter (Eds.), *Global Supply Chains in the Pharmaceutical Industry* (pp. 269–291). Hershey, PA: IGI Global. doi:10.4018/978-1-5225-5921-4.ch012

Giridhar, V., Joshi, R., & Sadarangani, P. H. (2016). Purchase Intentions of Consumer towards Foreign Brand Apparel: Evidences from India. In S. Joshi & R. Joshi (Eds.), *Designing and Implementing Global Supply Chain Management* (pp. 185–209). Hershey, PA: IGI Global. doi:10.4018/978-1-4666-9720-1.ch010

Girisaballa, S., & Bhattacharya, S. (2016). Sustainable Supply Chain: An Institutional Perspective. In R. Dubey & A. Gunasekaran (Eds.), *Strategic Management of Sustainable Manufacturing Operations* (pp. 272–302). Hershey, PA: IGI Global. doi:10.4018/978-1-5225-0350-7.ch012

Golpîra, H. (2017). Supply Chain Network Design Optimization with Risk-Averse Retailer. *International Journal of Information Systems and Supply Chain Management, 10*(1), 16–28. doi:10.4018/IJISSCM.2017010102

Gunasundari, E. (2019). Best Practices in the Pharmaceutical Supply Chain Management. In H. Nozari & A. Szmelter (Eds.), *Global Supply Chains in the Pharmaceutical Industry* (pp. 228–247). Hershey, PA: IGI Global. doi:10.4018/978-1-5225-5921-4.ch010

Gurtu, A., Searcy, C., & Jaber, M. Y. (2017). Sustainable Supply Chains. In M. Khan, M. Hussain, & M. Ajmal (Eds.), *Green Supply Chain Management for Sustainable Business Practice* (pp. 1–26). Hershey, PA: IGI Global. doi:10.4018/978-1-5225-0635-5.ch001

Herrera, J. E., Argüello, L. V., Gonzalez-Feliu, J., & Jaimes, W. A. (2017). Decision Support System Design Requirements, Information Management, and Urban Logistics Efficiency: Case Study of Bogotá, Colombia. In G. Jamil, A. Soares, & C. Pessoa (Eds.), *Handbook of Research on Information Management for Effective Logistics and Supply Chains* (pp. 223–238). Hershey, PA: IGI Global. doi:10.4018/978-1-5225-0973-8.ch012

Hietajärvi, A., & Karvonen, I. (2016). Management of Risks in Export Networks: The Role of Collaboration. *International Journal of Applied Logistics, 6*(1), 47–63. doi:10.4018/IJAL.2016010104

Hingley, M., & Vilalta-Perdomo, E. L. (2017). Roles of Intermediaries in Developing Resilient Systems: A Community Approach to Food Micro-Producers. In L. Saglietto & C. Cezanne (Eds.), *Global Intermediation and Logistics Service Providers* (pp. 43–63). Hershey, PA: IGI Global. doi:10.4018/978-1-5225-2133-4.ch003

Hu, J., & Haddud, A. (2017). Exploring the Impact of Globalization and Technology on Supply Chain Management: A Case of International E-Commerce Business. *International Journal of Operations Research and Information Systems, 8*(4), 1–22. doi:10.4018/IJORIS.2017100101

Iltchev, P., Palczewska, A., Pilichowska, K., Kozlowski, R., & Marczak, M. (2017). Benefits of the Transics Fleet Management System. In G. Jamil, A. Soares, & C. Pessoa (Eds.), *Handbook of Research on Information Management for Effective Logistics and Supply Chains* (pp. 287–302). Hershey, PA: IGI Global. doi:10.4018/978-1-5225-0973-8.ch016

Jamil, G. L. (2017). Numbers Can Restrict Results?: Qualitative Research Methods as Information and Knowledge Management Support in Supply Chain and Logistics Sectors. In G. Jamil, A. Soares, & C. Pessoa (Eds.), *Handbook of Research on Information Management for Effective Logistics and Supply Chains* (pp. 1–22). Hershey, PA: IGI Global. doi:10.4018/978-1-5225-0973-8.ch001

Jamil, G. L., & Jamil, C. C. (2017). Information and Knowledge Management Perspective Contributions for Fashion Studies: Observing Logistics and Supply Chain Management Processes. In G. Jamil, A. Soares, & C. Pessoa (Eds.), *Handbook of Research on Information Management for Effective Logistics and Supply Chains* (pp. 199–221). Hershey, PA: IGI Global. doi:10.4018/978-1-5225-0973-8.ch011

Janawade, V. (2017). Perceived Quality of an Intermediary and Its Relations with Image and Perceived Value: An Insight from the Case of Airline Alliances. In L. Saglietto & C. Cezanne (Eds.), *Global Intermediation and Logistics Service Providers* (pp. 286–316). Hershey, PA: IGI Global. doi:10.4018/978-1-5225-2133-4.ch015

Jeble, S. C. (2016). Sustainable Supply Chain Management: Literature Review. In R. Dubey & A. Gunasekaran (Eds.), *Strategic Management of Sustainable Manufacturing Operations* (pp. 303–330). Hershey, PA: IGI Global. doi:10.4018/978-1-5225-0350-7.ch013

Joshi, B. P., & Kumar, S. (2016). Intuitionistic Fuzzy Sets-Based Method for Multi-Criteria Decision-Making. In S. Joshi & R. Joshi (Eds.), *Designing and Implementing Global Supply Chain Management* (pp. 22–35). Hershey, PA: IGI Global. doi:10.4018/978-1-4666-9720-1.ch002

Joshi, R., & Joshi, S. (2016). Assessing the Readiness of Farmers towards Cold Chain Management: Evidences from India. In S. Joshi & R. Joshi (Eds.), *Designing and Implementing Global Supply Chain Management* (pp. 219–235). Hershey, PA: IGI Global. doi:10.4018/978-1-4666-9720-1.ch012

Jridi, K., Jaziri-Bouagina, D., & Triki, A. (2017). The SCM, CRM Information System, and KM – An Integrating Theoretical View: The Case of Sales Force Automation. In G. Jamil, A. Soares, & C. Pessoa (Eds.), *Handbook of Research on Information Management for Effective Logistics and Supply Chains* (pp. 239–254). Hershey, PA: IGI Global. doi:10.4018/978-1-5225-0973-8.ch013

Kaiwartya, O., Tiwari, P. K., Kumar, S., & Prasad, M. (2016). Dynamic Vehicle Routing Solution in the Framework of Nature-Inspired Algorithms. In S. Joshi & R. Joshi (Eds.), *Designing and Implementing Global Supply Chain Management* (pp. 36–50). Hershey, PA: IGI Global. doi:10.4018/978-1-4666-9720-1.ch003

Kasemsap, K. (2016). The Role of Sustainable Performance Measurement System in Global Supply Chain. In R. Dubey & A. Gunasekaran (Eds.), *Strategic Management of Sustainable Manufacturing Operations* (pp. 331–348). Hershey, PA: IGI Global. doi:10.4018/978-1-5225-0350-7.ch014

Kasemsap, K. (2016). The Roles of Lean and Green Supply Chain Management Strategies in the Global Business Environments. In S. Joshi & R. Joshi (Eds.), *Designing and Implementing Global Supply Chain Management* (pp. 152–173). Hershey, PA: IGI Global. doi:10.4018/978-1-4666-9720-1.ch008

Kasemsap, K. (2017). Advocating Information System, Information Integration, and Information Sharing in Global Supply Chain. In G. Jamil, A. Soares, & C. Pessoa (Eds.), *Handbook of Research on Information Management for Effective Logistics and Supply Chains* (pp. 107–130). Hershey, PA: IGI Global. doi:10.4018/978-1-5225-0973-8.ch006

Kasemsap, K. (2017). Advocating Sustainable Supply Chain Management and Sustainability in Global Supply Chain. In M. Khan, M. Hussain, & M. Ajmal (Eds.), *Green Supply Chain Management for Sustainable Business Practice* (pp. 234–271). Hershey, PA: IGI Global. doi:10.4018/978-1-5225-0635-5.ch009

Kasemsap, K. (2017). The Roles of Logistics Service Providers and Supply Chain Integration in Global Supply Chain. In L. Saglietto & C. Cezanne (Eds.), *Global Intermediation and Logistics Service Providers* (pp. 265–285). Hershey, PA: IGI Global. doi:10.4018/978-1-5225-2133-4.ch014

Kasemsap, K. (2018). Enhancing Closed-Loop Supply Chain in Global Supply Chain. In A. Kumar & S. Saurav (Eds.), *Supply Chain Management Strategies and Risk Assessment in Retail Environments* (pp. 159–180). Hershey, PA: IGI Global. doi:10.4018/978-1-5225-3056-5.ch009

Kasemsap, K. (2018). Retail Management and Electronic Retailing. In A. Kumar & S. Saurav (Eds.), *Supply Chain Management Strategies and Risk Assessment in Retail Environments* (pp. 139–158). Hershey, PA: IGI Global. doi:10.4018/978-1-5225-3056-5.ch008

Kozlowski, R., Iltchev, P., Palczewska, A., Pilichowska, K., & Marczak, M. (2017). Analysis of the Possibility to Implement the Transics System and GBOX Assist Systems in a Selected Company. In G. Jamil, A. Soares, & C. Pessoa (Eds.), *Handbook of Research on Information Management for Effective Logistics and Supply Chains* (pp. 303–315). Hershey, PA: IGI Global. doi:10.4018/978-1-5225-0973-8.ch017

Kros, J. F., Liao, Y., Kirchoff, J. F., & Zemanek, J. E. Jr. (2019). Traceability in the Supply Chain. *International Journal of Applied Logistics*, *9*(1), 1–22. doi:10.4018/IJAL.2019010101

Kwon, I. G., Hong, S., & Kim, S. (2017). Do Collaborative Relationships in Supply Chain Pay-Off? *International Journal of Organizational and Collective Intelligence*, *7*(1), 36–46. doi:10.4018/IJOCI.2017010103

Lahmar, A., Chabchoub, H., Galasso, F., & Lamothe, J. (2018). The VESP Model: A Conceptual Model of Supply Chain Vulnerability. *International Journal of Risk and Contingency Management*, *7*(2), 42–66. doi:10.4018/IJRCM.2018040103

Lahmar, A., Galasso, F., Lamothe, J., & Chabchoub, H. (2018). Classification Essay of SCRM Research. In A. Kumar & S. Saurav (Eds.), *Supply Chain Management Strategies and Risk Assessment in Retail Environments* (pp. 213–230). Hershey, PA: IGI Global. doi:10.4018/978-1-5225-3056-5.ch012

Lambourdière, E., Verny, J., & Corbin, E. (2017). Exploring the Sources of the Competitive Advantage of Logistics Service Providers. In L. Saglietto & C. Cezanne (Eds.), *Global Intermediation and Logistics Service Providers* (pp. 163–184). Hershey, PA: IGI Global. doi:10.4018/978-1-5225-2133-4.ch009

Lazzareschi, V. H., & Brito, M. S. (2017). Strategic Information Management: Proposal of Business Project Model. In G. Jamil, A. Soares, & C. Pessoa (Eds.), *Handbook of Research on Information Management for Effective Logistics and Supply Chains* (pp. 59–88). Hershey, PA: IGI Global. doi:10.4018/978-1-5225-0973-8.ch004

Leu, J., Lee, L. J., & Krischke, A. (2016). Value Engineering-Based Method for Implementing the ISO14001 System in the Green Supply Chains. *International Journal of Strategic Decision Sciences*, *7*(4), 1–20. doi:10.4018/IJSDS.2016100101

Lima de Magalhães, J., & Moreira, A. (2017). Information Systems Management in the Supply Chain in an Official Pharmaceutical Laboratory. In G. Jamil, A. Soares, & C. Pessoa (Eds.), *Handbook of Research on Information Management for Effective Logistics and Supply Chains* (pp. 350–373). Hershey, PA: IGI Global. doi:10.4018/978-1-5225-0973-8.ch020

Liotard, I., & Revest, V. (2017). Intermediation and Innovation Contests on the Internet: Lessons from the Study of Two Platforms. In L. Saglietto & C. Cezanne (Eds.), *Global Intermediation and Logistics Service Providers* (pp. 104–122). Hershey, PA: IGI Global. doi:10.4018/978-1-5225-2133-4.ch006

Lopes, B., Falcão, L., & Canellas, T. (2017). Supply-Side: Mapping High Capacity Suppliers of Goods and Services. In G. Jamil, A. Soares, & C. Pessoa (Eds.), *Handbook of Research on Information Management for Effective Logistics and Supply Chains* (pp. 147–165). Hershey, PA: IGI Global. doi:10.4018/978-1-5225-0973-8.ch008

Loya, V. M., Alcaraz, J. L., Reza, J. R., & Gayosso, D. G. (2017). The Impact of ICT on Supply Chain Agility and Human Performance. In G. Jamil, A. Soares, & C. Pessoa (Eds.), *Handbook of Research on Information Management for Effective Logistics and Supply Chains* (pp. 180–198). Hershey, PA: IGI Global. doi:10.4018/978-1-5225-0973-8.ch010

Mani, V., Agrawal, R., Sharma, V., & Kavitha, T. N. (2016). Supply Chain Social Sustainability and Manufacturing. In R. Dubey & A. Gunasekaran (Eds.), *Strategic Management of Sustainable Manufacturing Operations* (pp. 149–175). Hershey, PA: IGI Global. doi:10.4018/978-1-5225-0350-7.ch008

Messina, D., Santos, C., Soares, A. L., & Barros, A. C. (2017). Risk and Visibility in Supply Chains: An Information Management Perspective. In G. Jamil, A. Soares, & C. Pessoa (Eds.), *Handbook of Research on Information Management for Effective Logistics and Supply Chains* (pp. 34–57). Hershey, PA: IGI Global. doi:10.4018/978-1-5225-0973-8.ch003

Mohammadi, M., & Mukhtar, M. (2017). A Service-oriented Methodology for Supporting Business Process Architecture Layers in Supply Chain Management. *International Journal of Information Systems and Supply Chain Management, 10*(4), 18–43. doi:10.4018/IJISSCM.2017100102

Moradeyo, A. A. (2018). Understanding Supply Chain Collaboration and Risk Management. *International Journal of Risk and Contingency Management, 7*(3), 42–52. doi:10.4018/IJRCM.2018070102

Mostafa, S., & Dumrak, J. (2017). A Waste Elimination Process: An Approach for Lean and Sustainable Manufacturing Systems. In M. Khan, M. Hussain, & M. Ajmal (Eds.), *Green Supply Chain Management for Sustainable Business Practice* (pp. 111–152). Hershey, PA: IGI Global. doi:10.4018/978-1-5225-0635-5.ch005

Mukherjee, S., & Mukerjee, A. (2016). Sustainable Business Development by Responding to Climate Change: A Case of the Tata Group. In R. Dubey & A. Gunasekaran (Eds.), *Strategic Management of Sustainable Manufacturing Operations* (pp. 176–191). Hershey, PA: IGI Global. doi:10.4018/978-1-5225-0350-7.ch009

Nageswar, A. K., & Yellampalli, S. (2019). Distributed Trust Using Blockchain for Efficient Pharmaceutical Supply Chain. In H. Nozari & A. Szmelter (Eds.), *Global Supply Chains in the Pharmaceutical Industry* (pp. 248–268). Hershey, PA: IGI Global. doi:10.4018/978-1-5225-5921-4.ch011

Najar, T., & Amami, M. (2019). Supply Chain and Inter-Organizational Information Systems Role. In H. Nozari & A. Szmelter (Eds.), *Global Supply Chains in the Pharmaceutical Industry* (pp. 27–55). Hershey, PA: IGI Global. doi:10.4018/978-1-5225-5921-4.ch002

Negi, S., & Anand, N. (2018). Wastage and Cold Chain Infrastructure Relationship in Indian Food Supply Chain: A Study From Farm to Retail. In A. Kumar & S. Saurav (Eds.), *Supply Chain Management Strategies and Risk Assessment in Retail Environments* (pp. 247–266). Hershey, PA: IGI Global. doi:10.4018/978-1-5225-3056-5.ch014

Nikabadi, M. S., & Hajihoseinali, A. (2018). E-Waste Recycling System in Closed Loop Supply Chain. *International Journal of System Dynamics Applications*, *7*(2), 55–80. doi:10.4018/IJSDA.2018040104

Ogonowska, M. (2017). Convention and Visitors Bureau: A Key Intermediary in the Events Industry. In L. Saglietto & C. Cezanne (Eds.), *Global Intermediation and Logistics Service Providers* (pp. 226–241). Hershey, PA: IGI Global. doi:10.4018/978-1-5225-2133-4.ch012

Osiecka-Brzeska, K. (2019). Sustainable Supply Chain as a Part of CSR Strategy: The Example of Polpharma, Poland. In H. Nozari & A. Szmelter (Eds.), *Global Supply Chains in the Pharmaceutical Industry* (pp. 293–315). Hershey, PA: IGI Global. doi:10.4018/978-1-5225-5921-4.ch013

Özdemir, E., & Yılmaz, M. (2018). Omni-Channel Retailing: The Risks, Challenges, and Opportunities. In A. Kumar & S. Saurav (Eds.), *Supply Chain Management Strategies and Risk Assessment in Retail Environments* (pp. 97–118). Hershey, PA: IGI Global. doi:10.4018/978-1-5225-3056-5.ch006

Pal, K. (2018). Building High Quality Big Data-Based Applications in Supply Chains. In A. Kumar & S. Saurav (Eds.), *Supply Chain Management Strategies and Risk Assessment in Retail Environments* (pp. 1–24). Hershey, PA: IGI Global. doi:10.4018/978-1-5225-3056-5.ch001

Panwar, N., Uniyal, D., & Rautela, K. S. (2016). Mapping Sustainable Tourism into Emergency Management Structure to Enhance Humanitarian Networks and Disaster Risk Reduction using Public-Private Partnerships (PPP) Initiatives in Himalayan States: The Global Supply Chain Issues and Strategies. In S. Joshi & R. Joshi (Eds.), *Designing and Implementing Global Supply Chain Management* (pp. 129–151). Hershey, PA: IGI Global. doi:10.4018/978-1-4666-9720-1.ch007

Pessoa, C. R., & Júnior, M. D. (2017). A Telecommunications Approach in Systems for Effective Logistics and Supply Chains. In G. Jamil, A. Soares, & C. Pessoa (Eds.), *Handbook of Research on Information Management for Effective Logistics and Supply Chains* (pp. 437–452). Hershey, PA: IGI Global. doi:10.4018/978-1-5225-0973-8.ch023

Pessoa, C. R., & Marques, M. E. (2017). Information Technology and Communication Management in Supply Chain Management. In G. Jamil, A. Soares, & C. Pessoa (Eds.), *Handbook of Research on Information Management for Effective Logistics and Supply Chains* (pp. 23–33). Hershey, PA: IGI Global. doi:10.4018/978-1-5225-0973-8.ch002

Petrisor, I., & Cozmiuc, D. (2017). Global Supply Chain Management Organization at Siemens in the Advent of Industry 4.0. In L. Saglietto & C. Cezanne (Eds.), *Global Intermediation and Logistics Service Providers* (pp. 123–142). Hershey, PA: IGI Global. doi:10.4018/978-1-5225-2133-4.ch007

Poças Rascão, J. (2017). Information System for Logistics and Distribution Management. In G. Jamil, A. Soares, & C. Pessoa (Eds.), *Handbook of Research on Information Management for Effective Logistics and Supply Chains* (pp. 374–414). Hershey, PA: IGI Global. doi:10.4018/978-1-5225-0973-8.ch021

Polat, O. (2017). An Overview of Feeder Services in the Era of Mega Containerships. In L. Saglietto & C. Cezanne (Eds.), *Global Intermediation and Logistics Service Providers* (pp. 317–339). Hershey, PA: IGI Global. doi:10.4018/978-1-5225-2133-4.ch016

Ponnusamy, S. K., & Christopher, F. C. (2019). Production Process in the Pharmaceutical Industry. In H. Nozari & A. Szmelter (Eds.), *Global Supply Chains in the Pharmaceutical Industry* (pp. 158–179). Hershey, PA: IGI Global. doi:10.4018/978-1-5225-5921-4.ch007

Ponnusamy, S. K., & Ragini, Y. P. (2019). Product Lifecycle in the Pharmaceutical Industry. In H. Nozari & A. Szmelter (Eds.), *Global Supply Chains in the Pharmaceutical Industry* (pp. 112–132). Hershey, PA: IGI Global. doi:10.4018/978-1-5225-5921-4.ch005

Ponnusamy, S. K., & Saravanan, A. (2019). Characteristics of Pharmaceutical Supply Chains. In H. Nozari & A. Szmelter (Eds.), *Global Supply Chains in the Pharmaceutical Industry* (pp. 181–205). Hershey, PA: IGI Global. doi:10.4018/978-1-5225-5921-4.ch008

Quillaud, A. (2017). A Framework for Thinking Intermediation in Logistics Management. In L. Saglietto & C. Cezanne (Eds.), *Global Intermediation and Logistics Service Providers* (pp. 19–42). Hershey, PA: IGI Global. doi:10.4018/978-1-5225-2133-4.ch002

Ragini, Y. P. (2019). Pharmaceutical Development Process. In H. Nozari & A. Szmelter (Eds.), *Global Supply Chains in the Pharmaceutical Industry* (pp. 133–157). Hershey, PA: IGI Global. doi:10.4018/978-1-5225-5921-4.ch006

Rana, P., & Pandey, D. (2016). Challenges and Issues in E-Banking Services and Operations in Developing Countries. In S. Joshi & R. Joshi (Eds.), *Designing and Implementing Global Supply Chain Management* (pp. 237–281). Hershey, PA: IGI Global. doi:10.4018/978-1-4666-9720-1.ch013

Saglietto, L. (2017). Intermediary and Intermediation: Which Logistics Services? In L. Saglietto & C. Cezanne (Eds.), *Global Intermediation and Logistics Service Providers* (pp. 1–18). Hershey, PA: IGI Global. doi:10.4018/978-1-5225-2133-4.ch001

Saha, S. K., & Jha, A. (2018). Role of Information Technology on Supply Chain Management of Pharmaceutical Industry. *International Journal of Applied Logistics*, *8*(2), 39–68. doi:10.4018/IJAL.2018070103

Saravanan, A. (2019). Pharmaceutical and Life Sciences Supply Chain Management. In H. Nozari & A. Szmelter (Eds.), *Global Supply Chains in the Pharmaceutical Industry* (pp. 206–227). Hershey, PA: IGI Global. doi:10.4018/978-1-5225-5921-4.ch009

Saththasivam, G., & Fernando, Y. (2017). Integrated Sustainable Supply Chain Management: Current Practices and Future Direction. In M. Khan, M. Hussain, & M. Ajmal (Eds.), *Green Supply Chain Management for Sustainable Business Practice* (pp. 218–233). Hershey, PA: IGI Global. doi:10.4018/978-1-5225-0635-5.ch008

Satolo, E. G., Simon, A. T., & Braga, S. S. Jr. (2016). Sustainable Development and the Integration of Normative Standards. In R. Dubey & A. Gunasekaran (Eds.), *Strategic Management of Sustainable Manufacturing Operations* (pp. 192–226). Hershey, PA: IGI Global. doi:10.4018/978-1-5225-0350-7.ch010

Saurav, S. (2018). Realizing the Potential of Retail Analytics. In A. Kumar & S. Saurav (Eds.), *Supply Chain Management Strategies and Risk Assessment in Retail Environments* (pp. 60–76). Hershey, PA: IGI Global. doi:10.4018/978-1-5225-3056-5.ch004

Saurav, S. (2018). Supply Chain Management in Pharmaceutical Industry: Opportunities and Challenges for Retailers. In A. Kumar & S. Saurav (Eds.), *Supply Chain Management Strategies and Risk Assessment in Retail Environments* (pp. 267–284). Hershey, PA: IGI Global. doi:10.4018/978-1-5225-3056-5.ch015

Shafiu, I., Wang, W. Y., & Singh, H. (2016). Information Security Compliance Behaviour of Supply Chain Stakeholders: Influences and Differences. *International Journal of Information Systems and Supply Chain Management, 9*(1), 1–16. doi:10.4018/IJISSCM.2016010101

Sharma, M., & Kumar, J. (2016). Operational Efficacy of 3PL in Reverse Logistics and Closed Loop Supply Chain: Service Quality Challenges in Emerging Markets. In S. Joshi & R. Joshi (Eds.), *Designing and Implementing Global Supply Chain Management* (pp. 106–128). Hershey, PA: IGI Global. doi:10.4018/978-1-4666-9720-1.ch006

Shibin, K. T. (2016). Enablers of Sustainable Manufacturing Overview, Framework and Further Research Directions. In R. Dubey & A. Gunasekaran (Eds.), *Strategic Management of Sustainable Manufacturing Operations* (pp. 52–73). Hershey, PA: IGI Global. doi:10.4018/978-1-5225-0350-7.ch003

Simão, J. C., & Fernandes da Anunciação, P. (2017). Port Single Window and Logistics Single Window: Two Competitiveness Proposals in the Port Value Chain. In G. Jamil, A. Soares, & C. Pessoa (Eds.), *Handbook of Research on Information Management for Effective Logistics and Supply Chains* (pp. 316–333). Hershey, PA: IGI Global. doi:10.4018/978-1-5225-0973-8.ch018

Singh, A., Panackal, N., & Venkataramani, B. (2016). Environmental Accounting for Industrial Growth and Sustainable Development in India: An Overview and Theoretical Framework. In R. Dubey & A. Gunasekaran (Eds.), *Strategic Management of Sustainable Manufacturing Operations* (pp. 74–94). Hershey, PA: IGI Global. doi:10.4018/978-1-5225-0350-7.ch004

Singh, H. (2018). Applications of Intelligent Video Analytics in the Field of Retail Management: A Study. In A. Kumar & S. Saurav (Eds.), *Supply Chain Management Strategies and Risk Assessment in Retail Environments* (pp. 42–59). Hershey, PA: IGI Global. doi:10.4018/978-1-5225-3056-5.ch003

Singh, N. K. (2018). Designing Distribution Centres for Omni-Channel Fulfilment: In Indian Context. In A. Kumar & S. Saurav (Eds.), *Supply Chain Management Strategies and Risk Assessment in Retail Environments* (pp. 119–137). Hershey, PA: IGI Global. doi:10.4018/978-1-5225-3056-5.ch007

Singh, R., & Sankhi, A. (2016). An Empirical Study on Factors Leading to Employee Retention for Manufacturing Industry in India. In R. Dubey & A. Gunasekaran (Eds.), *Strategic Management of Sustainable Manufacturing Operations* (pp. 24–51). Hershey, PA: IGI Global. doi:10.4018/978-1-5225-0350-7.ch002

Singh, S., Olugu, E. U., & Musa, S. N. (2016). Development of Key Performance Measures for Sustainable Manufacturing in Global SMEs. In S. Joshi & R. Joshi (Eds.), *Designing and Implementing Global Supply Chain Management* (pp. 210–218). Hershey, PA: IGI Global. doi:10.4018/978-1-4666-9720-1.ch011

Smriti, K. (2018). Building an Effective Customer Loyalty Program. In A. Kumar & S. Saurav (Eds.), *Supply Chain Management Strategies and Risk Assessment in Retail Environments* (pp. 195–212). Hershey, PA: IGI Global. doi:10.4018/978-1-5225-3056-5.ch011

Smriti, K. (2018). Predicting Online Returns. In A. Kumar & S. Saurav (Eds.), *Supply Chain Management Strategies and Risk Assessment in Retail Environments* (pp. 181–194). Hershey, PA: IGI Global. doi:10.4018/978-1-5225-3056-5.ch010

Soares, E. R., & Zaidan, F. H. (2017). Composition of the Financial Logistic Costs of the IT Organizations Linked to the Financial Market: Financial Indicators of the Software Development Project. In G. Jamil, A. Soares, & C. Pessoa (Eds.), *Handbook of Research on Information Management for Effective Logistics and Supply Chains* (pp. 255–272). Hershey, PA: IGI Global. doi:10.4018/978-1-5225-0973-8.ch014

Sousa, M. J., Cruz, R., Dias, I., & Caracol, C. (2017). Information Management Systems in the Supply Chain. In G. Jamil, A. Soares, & C. Pessoa (Eds.), *Handbook of Research on Information Management for Effective Logistics and Supply Chains* (pp. 469–485). Hershey, PA: IGI Global. doi:10.4018/978-1-5225-0973-8.ch025

Srivastav, G., & Rawat, P. S. (2016). Indian Handicraft and Globalization: The Export Context. In S. Joshi & R. Joshi (Eds.), *Designing and Implementing Global Supply Chain Management* (pp. 175–184). Hershey, PA: IGI Global. doi:10.4018/978-1-4666-9720-1.ch009

Strang, K. D., & Vajjhala, N. R. (2017). Student Resistance to a Mandatory Learning Management System in Online Supply Chain Courses. *Journal of Organizational and End User Computing*, *29*(3), 49–67. doi:10.4018/JOEUC.2017070103

Subramanian, K., Joshi, K. P., & Deshmukh, S. (2018). Improving Forecasting for Customer Service Supply Chain Using Big Data Analytics. In A. Kumar & S. Saurav (Eds.), *Supply Chain Management Strategies and Risk Assessment in Retail Environments* (pp. 25–41). Hershey, PA: IGI Global. doi:10.4018/978-1-5225-3056-5.ch002

Suganya, S. (2019). Global Macrotrends in Pharmaceutical Industry. In H. Nozari & A. Szmelter (Eds.), *Global Supply Chains in the Pharmaceutical Industry* (pp. 86–110). Hershey, PA: IGI Global. doi:10.4018/978-1-5225-5921-4.ch004

Szmelter, A. (2019). Global Pharmaceutical Industry: Characteristics and Trends. In H. Nozari & A. Szmelter (Eds.), *Global Supply Chains in the Pharmaceutical Industry* (pp. 57–85). Hershey, PA: IGI Global. doi:10.4018/978-1-5225-5921-4.ch003

Szmelter, A. (2019). Logistics Thinking: The Basics of Logistics. In H. Nozari & A. Szmelter (Eds.), *Global Supply Chains in the Pharmaceutical Industry* (pp. 1–26). Hershey, PA: IGI Global. doi:10.4018/978-1-5225-5921-4.ch001

Tambo, T., & Mikkelsen, O. E. (2016). Fashion Supply Chain Optimization: Linking Make-to-Order Purchasing and B2B E-Commerce. In S. Joshi & R. Joshi (Eds.), *Designing and Implementing Global Supply Chain Management* (pp. 1–21). Hershey, PA: IGI Global. doi:10.4018/978-1-4666-9720-1.ch001

Tiwari, A., Kumar, K., & Roy, S. (2016). Sustainable Non Traditional Manufacturing Processes: A Case with Electrochemical Machining (ECM). In R. Dubey & A. Gunasekaran (Eds.), *Strategic Management of Sustainable Manufacturing Operations* (pp. 227–271). Hershey, PA: IGI Global. doi:10.4018/978-1-5225-0350-7.ch011

Vanany, I., & Syamil, A. (2016). Teaching Supply Chain Management Using an Innovative Practical Game. *International Journal of Information Systems and Supply Chain Management*, *9*(4), 82–99. doi:10.4018/IJISSCM.2016100105

Vargas-Hernández, J. G., & Hernández, A. I. (2019). Collaboration in the Mexican Pharmaceutical Industry: An Analysis Within the Institutional Framework. In H. Nozari & A. Szmelter (Eds.), *Global Supply Chains in the Pharmaceutical Industry* (pp. 316–333). Hershey, PA: IGI Global. doi:10.4018/978-1-5225-5921-4.ch014

Venkatesh, V., & Luthra, S. (2016). Role of Sustainable Procurement in Sustainable Manufacturing Operations: An Indian Insight. In R. Dubey & A. Gunasekaran (Eds.), *Strategic Management of Sustainable Manufacturing Operations* (pp. 132–148). Hershey, PA: IGI Global. doi:10.4018/978-1-5225-0350-7.ch007

Vijayan, G., & Kamarulzaman, N. H. (2017). An Introduction to Sustainable Supply Chain Management and Business Implications. In M. Khan, M. Hussain, & M. Ajmal (Eds.), *Green Supply Chain Management for Sustainable Business Practice* (pp. 27–50). Hershey, PA: IGI Global. doi:10.4018/978-1-5225-0635-5.ch002

Vlachos, I. P., & Gutnik, S. (2016). Together We E-Export: Horizontal Cooperation Among Austrian Food Companies in Global Supply Chains and the Role of Electronic Business Tools. *International Journal of Information Systems and Supply Chain Management*, *9*(1), 17–40. doi:10.4018/IJISSCM.2016010102

Yavuz, M., & Deligönül, B. (2017). The Importance of Logistics Information Technologies and Knowledge Management Capabilities on Intermediaries' Performance. In L. Saglietto & C. Cezanne (Eds.), *Global Intermediation and Logistics Service Providers* (pp. 208–225). Hershey, PA: IGI Global. doi:10.4018/978-1-5225-2133-4.ch011

About the Contributors

Jalel Euchi is faculty member at the department of Management Information Systems, CBE, Qassim University, KSA and Gafsa University, Tunisia. He received his Ph.D. in 2011 in computer science, in the field of optimization and Transportation problems from Sfax University in Tunisia and LeHavre University in France. His M. Sc. in 2007 in Operational Research and Production Management from the University of Sfax in Tunisia. It is an associate researcher in research unit (LOGIQ), Sfax university, Tunisia also in (LMAH), LeHavre university, France. He has published extensively in the reputed journals like International Journal of Operational research, Swarm and evolutionary Computation, Management Decision, Journal of operational research society, Vehicular Communications. He is the referee of many journals published by Springer, and Elsevier publishers. He is life member of Operational Research Society of Tunisia. His primary research interests include complex vehicle routing problems, heuristics and meta-heuristics algorithms to solve the NP-Hard problems, computational operations research, decision-making, and logistics research and supply chains.

***

Abderrahmane Benkacem is a PhD candidate in logistics, his resaerch intersts focus on hospital logistics. He received the logistics engineering master's degree from Hassan 2 University of Casablanca in 2015.

Dalel Bouzidi is a Ph.D. student in Quantitatives Methods in Sfax University. He is an associate researcher in Laboratoire de recherche "LOgistique, Gestion Industrielle et Qualite" (LOGIQ), Sfax University, Tunisia. He is life member of Operational Research Society of Tunisia. His primary research interests include mathematical management, computational operations research, decision making, structural analysis and supply chains.

Samir Chafik received his engineering degree in industrial computer science from EMSI of Casablanca, Morocco, in 1993. He received the DEA (M.S.) and Ph.D in automatic control from INSA of Lyon in 1996 and 2000 respectively. Since 2000, he has been a teacher in the Industrial Engineering Department and a member of the AMPERE laboratory of the INSA of Lyon. He joined EMSI of Casablanca in 2013, where he is currently an assistant Professor.

Arzu Eren Şenaras is an Associate Professor at Department of Econometrics in Bursa Uludağ University.

Carlos Hernán Fajardo-Toro received a PhD degree in Computer Science (Tools for developing intelligent software) and the degree of MSc in Management and Logistics and Supply Chain of the University of Vigo (Spain). He serves currently as a full-time teacher at the School of Business Administration - EAN (Bogota, Colombia).

Youness Frichi is a PhD candidate in hospital logistics at Sidi Mohamed Ben Abdellah University of Fez. His main research interest centres on how hospital logistics could improve the quality of care. He received the engineering degree in industrial engineering from the National School of Applied Sciences of Fez in 2013.

Şahin İnanç is a Lecturer at Bursa Uludağ University.

Fouad Jawab is a professor at the Higher School of Technology of Fez (EST) in Morocco. He is Director of the Research Laboratory in International Management, Decision Techniques and Logistics (MIDLOG), a member of the Research Laboratory, in energy production and sustainable development (LPE2D) and he directs the Professional License "LOGISTICS". He headed the Department of Management Science and Technology (STG), as well as the University Diploma of Technology (DUT) "Logistics and Transport Management" (GLT). Hospital logistics is one of his main areas of research.

Marwa Mallek is a PhD student in Operations Research at the Faculty of Economics and Management of Sfax in Tunisia. He is a member of the research unit LOGIQ (Logistics, Industrial and Quality Management). He obtained his Master of Science in Transport and Logistic in 2013 at the Higher Institute of Industrial Management of Sfax in Tunisia (ISGI). Her research interests include multi-criteria decision making, multi-objective optimization, mathematical programming, energy optimization, and hybrid energy systems.

Juan Carlos Rivera received his B.S. (2005) in industrial engineering and a M:S. in computer sciences (2008) from National University of Colombia; and he receives his PhD. (2014) in systems optimization and dependability from Troyes University of Technology. His research interests include logistic, production and finance applications of optimization and simulation models, and metaheuristic methods. Currently he is faculty member of Mathematical science department of Universidad EAFIT.

Paloma Martínez Sánchez PhD. in Logistic and Supply Chain; MSc. in Quality and Productivity; Postgraduate studies on strategic and competitive management; Engineer on Agroindustrial Production

Paola Sanchez-Sanchez received a BS degree in industrial engineering in 2001, the MS degree in Systems Engineering in 2006, and the PhD degree in Engineering in 2012, all of them from the Universidad Nacional de Colombia, Medellin, Colombia. Since 2005, she has worked in education as a teacher in different universities. At present, she is associate professor of the engineering faculty in the Simón Bolívar University, Barranquilla, Colombia. Her current interests are in developing and understanding the methods of computational intelligence in the modeling and forecasting of time series; quantitative optimization; the application of knowledge extraction techniques in databases using computational intelligence; and the development of intelligent systems with learning machines.

Index

N

P

S

T

V

W

www.ingramcontent.com/pod-product-compliance
Lightning Source LLC
LaVergne TN
LVHW081321300926
849161LV00008B/1838